From *The Private Life of Marie Antoinette*

It was thus, with libels and ill-natured ballads, that the enemies of Marie Antoinette hailed the first days of her reign. They exerted themselves every way to render her unpopular. Their aim was, beyond all doubt, to have her sent back to Germany; and there was not a moment to be lost in its accomplishment. That the indifference of the King towards his amiable and beautiful wife had lasted so long, was already a matter of wonder; day after day it was to be expected that the seductive charms of Marie Antoinette would undo all the machinations.

THE PRIVATE LIFE OF
MARIE ANTOINETTE

New York, NY

Cover Art: Réunion des Musées Nationaux / Art Resource, NY
Marie-Antoinette, Queen of France, with a rose by Louise Elizabeth Vigee-LeBrun

Designed by Jillian Harris
Art Direction by Bruce Hall

Printed in Canada

THE PRIVATE LIFE OF
MARIE
ANTOINETTE

MADAME JEANNE-LOUISE-
HENRIETTE CAMPAN

New York, NY

CONTENTS

CHAPTER X

CHAPTER XI

CHAPTER XII

CHAPTER XIII

CHAPTER XIV

CHAPTER XV

CHAPTER XVI

CHAPTER XVII

CHAPTER XVIII

CHAPTER XIX

CHAPTER XX

CHAPTER XXI

CHAPTER XXII

CHAPTER XXIII

NOTE

The following titles have the signification given below during the period covered by this work:

MONSEIGNEUR	*The Dauphin.*
MONSIEUR	*The eldest brother of the King, Comte de Provence, afterwards Louis XVIII.*
MONSIEUR LE PRINCE	*The Prince de Condé, head of the House of Condé.*
MONSIEUR LE DUC	*The Duc de Bourbon, the eldest son of the Prince de Condé (and the father of the Duc d'Enghien shot by Napoleon).*
MONSIEUR LE GRAND	*The Grand Equerry under the ancien régime.*
MONSIEUR LE PREMIER	*The First Equerry under the ancien régime.*
ENFANS DE FRANCE	*The royal children.*
MADAME MESDAMES	*Sisters or daughters of the King, or Princesses near the Throne (sometimes used also for the wife of Monsieur, the eldest brother of the King, the Princesses Adélaïde, Victoire, Sophie, Louise, daughters of Louis XV, and aunts of Louis XVI).*
MADAME ELISABETH	*The Princesse Elisabeth, sister of Louis XVI.*
MADAME ROYALE	*The Princesse Marie Thérèse, daughter of Louis XVI, afterwards Duchesse d'Angoulême.*
MADEMOISELLE	*The daughter of Monsieur, brother of the King.*

Introduction

Louis XVI meant to write his own Memoirs; the manner in which his private papers were arranged indicated this design. The Queen also had this intention; she long preserved a large correspondence, and a great number of minute reports, made in the spirit and upon the event of the moment. But after the 20th day of June, 1792, she was obliged to burn a large portion of what she had collected, and the remainder were conveyed out of France.

Considering the rank and situation of persons capable of elucidating by their writings the history of our political storms, it will not be imagined that I aim at placing myself on a level with them; but I have spent half my life either with the daughters of Louis XV or with Marie Antoinette. I knew the character of those Princesses; I became privy to some extraordinary facts, the publication of which may be interesting, and the truth of the details will form the merit of my work.

Twenty years before the Revolution I often heard it remarked that the imposing character of the power of Louis XIV was no longer to be found in the Palace of Versailles; that the institutions of the ancient monarchy were rapidly sinking; and that the people, crushed beneath the weight of taxes, were miserable, though silent; but that they began to give ear to the bold speeches of the philosophers, who loudly proclaimed their sufferings and their rights; and, in short, that the age would not pass away without the occurrence of some great outburst, which would unsettle France, and change the course of its progress.

Destiny having formerly placed me near crowned heads, I now amuse my solitude when in retirement with collecting a variety of facts which may prove interesting to my family when I shall be no more. I have put together all that concerned the domestic life of an unfortunate princess, whose reputation is not yet cleared of the stains it received from the attacks of calumny, and who justly merited a different lot in life, a different place in the opinion of mankind after her fall.

Madame Jeanne-Louise-Henriette Campan

I

The Private Life of Marie Antoinette

I WAS fifteen years of age when I was appointed reader to Mesdames. I will begin by describing the Court at that period.

Maria Leczinska was just dead; the death of the Dauphin had preceded hers by three years; the Jesuits were suppressed, and piety was to be found at Court only in the apartments of Mesdames. The Duc de Choiseul ruled.

Etiquette still existed at Court with all the forms it had acquired under Louis XIV; dignity alone was wanting. As to gaiety, there was none. Versailles was not the place at which to seek for assemblies where French spirit and grace were displayed. The focus of wit and intelligence was Paris.

The King thought of nothing but the pleasures of the chase: it might have been imagined that the courtiers indulged themselves in making epigrams by hearing them say seriously, on those days when the King did not hunt, "The King does nothing to-day."

The arrangement beforehand of his movements was also a matter of great importance with Louis XV. On the first day of the year he noted down in his almanac the clays of departure for Compiègne, Fontainebleau, Choisy, etc. The weightiest matters, the most serious events, never deranged this distribution of his time.

Since the death of the Marquise de Pompadour, the King had no titled mistress; he contented himself with his *seraglio* in the Parc-aux-Cerfs. It is well known that the monarch found the separation of Louis de Bourbon from the King of France the most animating feature of his royal existence. "They would have it so; they thought it for the best," was his way of expressing himself when the measures of his ministers were unsuccessful. The King delighted to manage the most disgraceful points of his private expenses himself; he one day sold to a head clerk in the War Department a house in which one of his mistresses had lodged; the contract ran in the name of Louis de Bourbon, and the purchaser himself took in a bag the price of the house in gold to the King in his private closet.

Louis XV saw very little of his family. He came every morning by a private staircase into the apartment of Madame Adélaïde. He often brought, and drank there coffee that he had made himself. Madame Adélaïde pulled a bell which apprised Madame Victoire of the King's visit; Madame Victoire, on rising to go to her sister's apartment, rang for Madame Sophie, who in her turn rang for Madame Louise. The apartments of Mesdames were of very large dimensions. Madame Louise occupied the farthest room. This latter lady was deformed and very short; the poor Princess used to run with all her might to join the daily meeting, but, having a number of rooms to cross, she frequently, in spite of her haste, had only just time to embrace her father before he set out for the chase.

Every evening, at six, Mesdames interrupted my reading to them to accompany the Princes to Louis XV; this visit was called the King's *débotter*, and was marked by a kind of etiquette. Mesdames put on an enormous hoop, which set out a petticoat ornamented with gold or embroidery; they fastened a long train round their waists, and concealed the undress of the rest of their clothing by a long cloak of black taffety which enveloped them up to the chin. The *chevaliers d'honneur*, the ladies in waiting, the pages, the equerries, and the ushers bearing large flambeaux, accompanied them to the King. In a moment the whole palace, generally so still, was in motion; the King kissed each Princess on the forehead, and the visit was so short that the reading which it interrupted was frequently resumed at the end of a quarter of an hour; Mesdames returned to their apartments, and untied the strings of their petticoats and trains; they resumed their tapestry, and I my book.

During the summer season the King sometimes came to the residence of Mesdames before the hour of his *débotter*. One day he found me alone in Madame Victoire's closet, and asked me where *Coche* was; I started, and he repeated his question, but without being at all the more understood. When the King was gone I asked Madame of whom he spoke. She told me that it was herself, and very coolly explained to me, that, being the fattest of his daughters, the King had given her the familiar name of *Coche*; that he called Madame Adélaïde, *Loque*, Madame Sophie, *Graille*, and Madame Louise, *Chiffe*. The people of the King's household observed that he knew a great number of such words; possibly he had amused himself with picking them out from dictionaries. If this style of speaking betrayed the habits and tastes of the King, his manner savoured nothing of such vulgarity; his walk was easy and noble, he had a dignified carriage of the head, and his aspect, without being severe, was imposing; he combined great politeness with a truly regal demeanour, and gracefully saluted the humblest woman whom curiosity led into his path.

He was very expert in a number of trifling matters which never occupy attention but when there is a lack of something better to employ it; for instance, he would knock off the top of an egg-shell at a single stroke of his fork; he therefore always ate eggs when he dined in public, and the Parisians who came on Sundays to see the King dine, returned home less struck with his fine figure than with the dexterity with which he broke his eggs.

Repartees of Louis XV, which marked the keenness of his wit and the elevation of his sentiments, were quoted with pleasure in the assemblies of Versailles.

This Prince was still beloved; it was wished that a style of life suitable to his age and dignity should at length supersede the errors of the past, and justify the love of his subjects. It was painful to judge him harshly. If he had established avowed mistresses at Court, the uniform devotion of the Queen was blamed for it. Mesdames were reproached for not seeking to prevent the King's forming an intimacy with some new favourite. Madame Henriette, twin sister of the Duchess of Parma, was much regretted, for she had considerable influence over the King's mind, and it was remarked that if she had lived she would have been assiduous in finding him amusements in the bosom of his family, would have followed him in his short excursions, and would have done the honours of the *petits soupers* which he was so fond of giving in his private apartments.

Mesdames too much neglected the means of pleasing the King, but the cause of that was obvious in the little attention he had paid them in their youth.

In order to console the people under their sufferings, and to shut their eyes to the real depredations on the treasury, the ministers occasionally pressed the most extravagant measures of reform in the King's household, and even in his personal expenses.

Cardinal Fleury, who in truth had the merit of reëstablishing the finances, carried this system of economy so far as to obtain from the King the suppression of the household of the four younger Princesses. They were brought up as mere boarders in a convent eighty leagues distant from the Court. Saint Cyr would have been more suitable for the reception of the King's daughters; but probably the Cardinal shared some of those prejudices which will always attach to even the most useful institutions, and which, since the death of Louis XIV, had been raised against the noble establishment of Madame de Maintenon. Madame Louise often assured me that at twelve years of age she was not mistress of the whole alphabet, and never learnt to read fluently until after her return to Versailles.

Madame Victoire attributed certain paroxysms of terror, which she was never able to conquer, to the violent alarms she experienced at the Abbéy of Fontevrault, whenever she was sent, by way of penance, to pray alone in the vault where the sisters were interred.

A gardener belonging to the abbéy died raving mad. His habitation, without the walls, was near a chapel of the abbéy, where Mesdames were taken to repeat the prayers for those in the agonies of death. Their prayers were more than once interrupted by the shrieks of the dying man.

When Mesdames, still very young, returned to Court, they enjoyed the friendship of Monseigneur the Dauphin, and profited by his advice. They devoted themselves ardently to study, and gave up almost the whole of their time to it; they enabled themselves to write French correctly, and acquired a good knowledge of history. Italian, English, the higher branches of mathematics, turning and dialling, filled up in succession their leisure moments. Madame Adélaïde, in particular, had a most insatiable desire to learn; she was taught to play upon all instruments, from the horn (will it be believed!) to the Jew's-harp.

Madame Adélaïde was graced for a short time with a charming figure; but never did beauty so quickly vanish. Madame Victoire was handsome and very graceful; her address, mien, and smile were in perfect accordance with the goodness of her heart. Madame Sophie was remarkably ugly; never did I behold a person with so unprepossessing an appearance; she walked with the greatest rapidity; and, in order to recognise the people who placed themselves along her path without looking at them, she acquired the habit of leering on one side, like a hare. This Princess was so exceedingly diffident that a person might be with her daily for years together without hearing her utter a single word. It was asserted, however, that she displayed talent, and even amiability, in the society of some favourite ladies. She taught herself a great deal, but she studied alone;

the presence of a reader would have disconcerted her very much. There were, however, occasions on which the Princess, generally so intractable, became all at once affable and condescending, and manifested the most communicative good-nature; this would happen during a storm; so great was her alarm on such an occasion that she then approached the most humble, and would ask them a thousand obliging questions; a flash of lightning made her squeeze their hands; a peal of thunder would drive her to embrace them, but with the return of the calm, the Princess resumed her stiffness, her reserve, and her repellent air, and passed all by without taking the slightest notice of any one, until a fresh storm restored to her at once her dread and her affability.

Mesdames found in a beloved brother, whose rare attainments are known to all Frenchmen, a guide in everything wanting to their education. In their august mother, Maria Leczinska, they possessed the noblest example of every pious and social virtue; that Princess, by her eminent qualities and her modest dignity, veiled the failings of the King, and while she lived she preserved in the Court of Louis XV that decorous and dignified tone which alone secures the respect due to power. The Princesses, her daughters, were worthy of her; and if a few degraded beings did aim the shafts of calumny at them, these shafts dropped harmless, warded off by the elevation of their sentiments and the purity of their conduct.

If Mesdames had not tasked themselves with numerous occupations, they would have been much to be pitied. They loved walking, but could enjoy nothing beyond the public gardens of Versailles; they would have cultivated flowers, but could have no others than those in their windows.

The Marquise de Durfort, since Duchesse de Civrac[1], afforded to Madame Victoire agreeable society. The Princess spent almost all her evenings with that lady, and ended by fancying herself domiciled with her.

Madame de Narbonne had, in a similar way, taken pains to make her intimate acquaintance pleasant to Madame Adélaïde.

Madame Louise had for many years lived in great seclusion; I read to her five hours a day. My voice frequently betrayed the exhaustion of my lungs; the Princess would then prepare sugared water for me, place it by me, and apologise for making me read so long, on the score of having prescribed a course of reading for herself.

One evening, while I was reading, she was informed that M. Bertin, *ministre des parties casuelles*, desired to speak with her; she went out abruptly, returned, resumed her silks and embroidery, and made me resume my book; when I retired she commanded me to be in her closet the next morning at eleven o'clock. When I got there the Princess was gone out ; I learnt that she had gone at seven in the morning to the Convent of the Carmelites of St. Denis, where she was desirous of taking the veil. I went to Madame Victoire; there I heard that the King alone had been acquainted with Madame Louise's project; that he had kept it faithfully secret, and that, having long previously opposed her wish, he had only on the preceding evening sent her his consent; that she had gone alone into the convent, where she was expected; and that a few minutes

1. The Duchesse de Civrac, grandmother of two heroes of La Vendée, Lescure and La Roche-Jaquelin, by the marriage of her eldest daughter with M. d'Onissan; and of the unfortunate Labedoyere by the marriage of her second daughter with M. de Chastellux.

afterwards she had made her appearance at the grating, to show to the Princesse de Guistel, who had accompanied her to the convent gate, and to her equerry, the King's order to leave her in the monastery.

Upon receiving the intelligence of her sister's departure, Madame Adélaïde gave way to violent paroxysms of rage, and reproached the King bitterly for the secret, which he had thought it his duty to preserve. Madame Victoire missed the society of her favourite sister, but she shed tears in silence only. The first time I saw this excellent Princess after Madame Louise's departure, I threw myself at her feet, kissed her hand, and asked her, with all the confidence of youth, whether she would quit us as Madame Louise had done. She raised me, embraced me, and said, pointing to the lounge upon which she was extended, "Make yourself easy, my dear; I shall never have Louise's courage. I love the conveniences of life too well; this lounge is my destruction." As soon as I obtained permission to do so, I went to St. Denis to see my late mistress; she deigned to receive me with her face uncovered, in her private parlour; she told me she had just left the wash-house, and that it was her turn that day to attend to the linen. "I much abused your youthful lungs for two years before the execution of my project," added she. "I knew that here I could read none but books tending to our salvation, and I wished to review all the historians that had interested me."

She informed me that the King's consent for her to go to St. Denis had been brought to her while I was reading; she prided herself, and with reason, upon having returned to her closet without the slightest mark of agitation, though she said she felt so keenly that she could scarcely regain her chair. She added that moralists were right when they said that happiness does not dwell in palaces; that she had proved it; and that, if I desired to be happy, she advised me to come and enjoy a retreat in which the liveliest imagination might find full exercise in the contemplation of a better world. I had no palace, no earthly grandeur to sacrifice to God; nothing but the bosom of a united family; and it is precisely there that the moralists whom she cited have placed true happiness. I replied that, in private life, the absence of a beloved and cherished daughter would be too cruelly felt by her family. The Princess said no more on the subject.

The seclusion of Madame Louise was attributed to various motives; some were unkind enough to suppose it to have been occasioned by her mortification at being, in point of rank, the last of the Princesses. I think I penetrated the true cause. Her aspirations were lofty; she loved everything sublime; often while I was reading she would interrupt me to exclaim, "That is beautiful; that is noble!" There was but one brilliant action that she could perform,—to quit a palace for a cell, and rich garments for a stuff gown. She achieved it!

I saw Madame Louise two or three times more at the grating. I was informed of her death by Louis XVI. "My Aunt Louise," said he to me, "your old mistress, is just dead at St. Denis. I have this moment received intelligence of it. Her piety and resignation were admirable, and yet the delirium of my good aunt recalled to her recollection that she was a princess, for her last words were, 'To paradise, haste, haste, full speed.' No doubt she thought she was again giving orders to her equerry."

Madame Victoire, good, sweet-tempered, and affable, lived with the most amiable simplicity in a society wherein she was much caressed; she was adored by her household. Without quitting Versailles, without sacrificing her easy chair, she fulfilled the duties of religion with punctuality, gave to the poor all she possessed, and strictly observed Lent and the fasts. The table of Mesdames acquired a reputation for dishes of abstinence, spread abroad by the assiduous parasites at that of their *maître d'hôtel*. Madame Victoire was not indifferent to good living, but she had the most religious scruples respecting dishes of which it was allowable to partake at penitential times. I saw her one day exceedingly tormented by her doubts about a water-fowl, which was often served up to her during Lent. The question to be determined was, whether it was *maigre or gras*. She consulted a bishop, who happened to be of the party: the prelate immediately assumed the grave attitude of a judge who is about to pronounce sentence. He answered the Princess that, in a similar case of doubt, it had been resolved that after dressing the bird it should be pricked over a very cold silver dish; if the gravy of the animal congealed within a quarter of an hour, the creature was to be accounted flesh; but if the gravy remained in an oily state, it might be eaten without scruple. Madame Victoire immediately made the experiment: the gravy did not congeal; and this was a source of great joy to the Princess, who was very partial to that sort of game. The abstinence which so much occupied the attention of Madame Victoire was so disagreeable to her, that she listened with impatience for the midnight hour of Holy Saturday; and then she was immediately supplied with a good dish of fowl and rice, and sundry other succulent viands. She confessed with such amiable candour her taste for good cheer and the comforts of life, that it would have been necessary to

be as severe in principle as insensible to the excellent qualities of the Princess, to consider it a crime in her.

Madame Adélaïde had more mind than Madame
Victoire; but she was altogether deficient in that kindness
which alone creates affection for the great,— abrupt manners, a harsh voice, and a short way of speaking, rendering
her more than imposing. She carried the idea of the prerogative of rank to a high pitch. One of her chaplains was
unlucky enough to say *Dominus vobiscum* with rather too
easy an air; the Princess rated him soundly for it after mass,
and told him to remember that he was not a bishop, and not
again to think of officiating in the style of a prelate.

Mesdames lived quite separate from the King. Since
the death of Madame de Pompadour he had lived alone.
The enemies of the Duc de Choiseul did not know in what
department, nor through what channel, they could prepare and bring about the downfall of the man who stood in
their way. The King was connected only with women of so
low a class that they could not be made use of for any delicate intrigue; moreover, the Parc-aux-Cerfs was a seraglio,
the beauties of which were often replaced; it was desirable
to give the King a mistress who could form a circle, and in
whose drawing-room the long-standing attachment of the
King for the Duc de Choiseul might be overcome. It is true
that Madame du Barry was selected from a class sufficiently
low. Her origin, her education, her habits, and everything
about her bore a character of vulgarity and shamelessness;
but by marrying her to a man whose pedigree dated from
1400, it was thought scandal would be avoided. The con-
queror of Mahon conducted this coarse intrigue. Such a
mistress was judiciously selected for the diversion of the latter

years of a man weary of grandeur, fatigued with pleasure, and cloyed with voluptuousness. Neither the wit, the talents, the graces of the Marquise de Pompadour, her beauty, nor even her love for the King, would have had any further influence over that worn-out being.

He wanted a Roxalana of familiar gaiety, without any respect for the dignity of the sovereign. Madame du Barry one day so far forgot propriety as to desire to be present at a Council of State. The King was weak enough to consent to it. There she remained ridiculously perched upon the arm of his chair, playing all sorts of childish monkey tricks, calculated to please an old sultan.

Another time she snatched a packet of sealed letters from the King's hand. Among them she had observed one from Comte de Broglie. She told the King that she knew that rascal Broglie spoke ill of her to him, and that for once, at least, she would make sure he should read nothing respecting her. The King wanted to get the packet again; she resisted, and made him run two or three times round the table, which was in the middle of the council-chamber, and then, on passing the fireplace, she threw the letters into the grate, where they were consumed. The King became furious; he seized his audacious mistress by the arm, and put her out of the door without speaking to her. Madame du Barry thought herself utterly disgraced; she returned home, and remained two hours, alone, abandoned to the utmost distress. The King went to her; she threw herself at his feet, in tears, and he pardoned her.

Madame la Maréchale de Beauvau, the Duchesse de Choiseul, and the Duchesse de Grammont had renounced the honour of the King's intimate acquaintance rather than share it with Madame du Barry. But a few years after the death of Louis XV, Madame la Maréchale being alone at the Val, a house belonging to M. de Beauvau, Mademoiselle de Dillon saw the Countess's calash take shelter in the forest of St. Germain during a violent storm. She invited her in, and the Countess herself related these particulars, which I had from Madame de Beauvau.

The Comte du Barry, surnamed *le roué* (the profligate), and Mademoiselle du Barry advised, or rather prompted, Madame du Barry in furtherance of the plans of the party of the Maréchal de Richelieu and the Duc d'Aiguillon. Sometimes they even set her to act in such a way as to have a useful influence upon great political measures. Under pretence that the page who accompanied Charles I in his flight was a Du Barry or Barrymore, they persuaded the Comtesse du Barry to buy in London that fine portrait which we now have in the Museum. She had the picture placed in her drawing-room, and when she saw the King hesitating upon the violent measure of breaking up his Parliament, and forming that which was called the Maupeou Parliament, she desired him to look at the portrait of a king who had given way to his Parliament.

The men of ambition who were labouring to overthrow the Duc de Choiseul strengthened themselves by their concentration at the house of the favourite, and succeeded in their project. The bigots, who never forgave that minister the suppression of the Jesuits, and who had always been hostile to a treaty of alliance with Austria, influenced the minds of Mesdames. The Duc de La Vauguyon, the young Dauphin's governor, infected them with the same prejudices.

Such was the state of the public mind when the young Archduchess Marie Antoinette arrived at the Court of Versailles, just at the moment when the party which brought her there was about to be overthrown.

Madame Adélaïde openly avowed her dislike to a princess of the House of Austria; and when M. Campan, my father-in-law, went to receive his orders, at the moment of setting off with the household of the Dauphiness, to go and receive the Archduchess upon the frontiers, she said she disapproved of the marriage of her nephew with an archduchess; and that, if she had the direction of the matter, she would not send for an Austrian.

II

M ARIE Antoinette Josephe Jeanne de Lorraine, Archduchess of Austria, daughter of François de Lorraine and of Maria Theresa, was born on the 2nd of November, 1755, the day of the earthquake at Lisbon; and this catastrophe, which appeared to stamp the era of her birth with a fatal mark, without forming a motive for superstitious fear with the Princess, nevertheless made an impression upon her mind. As the Empress already had a great number of daughters, she ardently desired to have another son, and playfully wagered against her wish with the Duc de Tarouka, who had insisted that she would give birth to an archduke. He lost by the birth of the Princess, and had executed in porcelain a figure with one knee bent on the earth, and presenting tablets, upon which the following lines by Metastasio were engraved:

I lose by your fair daughter's birth
Who prophesied a son ;

But if she share her mother's worth,
Why, all the world has won !

The Queen was fond of talking of the first years of her youth. Her father, the Emperor Francis, had made a deep impression upon her heart; she lost him when she was scarcely seven years old. One of those circumstances which fix themselves strongly in the memories of children frequently recalled his last caresses to her. The Emperor was setting out for Innspruck; he had already left his palace, when he ordered a gentleman to fetch the Archduchess Marie Antoinette, and bring her to his carriage. When she came, he stretched out his arms to receive her, and said, after having pressed her to his bosom, "I wanted to embrace this child once more." The Emperor died suddenly during the journey, and never saw his beloved daughter again.

The Queen often spoke of her mother, and with profound respect, but she based all her schemes for the education of her children on the essentials which had been neglected in her own. Maria Theresa, who inspired awe by her great qualities, taught the Archduchesses to fear and respect rather than to love her; at least I observed this in the Queen's feelings towards her august mother. She therefore never desired to place between her own children and herself that distance which had existed in the imperial family. She cited a fatal consequence of it, which had made such a powerful impression upon her that time had never been able to efface it.

The wife of the Emperor Joseph II was taken from him in a few days by an attack of smallpox of the most virulent kind. Her coffin had recently been deposited in the vault of the imperial family. The Archduchess Josepha, who had been betrothed to the King of Naples, at the instant she was quitting Vienna received an order from the Empress not to set off without having offered up a prayer in the vault of her forefathers. The Archduchess, persuaded that she should take the disorder to which her sister-in-law had just fallen a victim, looked upon this order as her death-warrant. She loved the young Archduchess Marie Antoinette tenderly; she took her upon her knees, embraced her with tears, and told her she was about to leave her, not for Naples, but never to see her again; that she was going down then to the tomb of her ancestors, and that she should shortly go again there to remain. Her anticipation was realised; confluent small-pox carried her off in a very few days, and her youngest sister ascended the throne of Naples in her place.

The Empress was too much taken up with high po-litical interests to have it in her power to devote herself to maternal attentions. The celebrated Wansvietten, her physi-cian, went daily to visit the young imperial family, and after-wards to Maria Theresa, and gave the most minute details respecting the health of the Archdukes and Archduchesses, whom she herself sometimes did not see for eight or ten days at a time. As soon as the arrival of a stranger of rank at Vienna was made known, the Empress brought her family about her, admitted them to her table, and by this concerted meeting induced a belief that she herself presided over the education of her children.

The chief governesses, being under no fear of inspec-tion from Maria Theresa, aimed at making themselves be-loved by their pupils by the common and blamable practice of indulgence, so fatal to the future progress and happiness of children. Marie Antoinette was the cause of her governess being dismissed, through a confession that all her copies and all her letters were invariably first traced out with pencil; the Comtesse de Brandès was appointed to succeed her, and fulfilled her duties with great exactness and talent. The Queen looked upon having been confided to her care so late as a misfortune, and always continued upon terms of friendship with that lady. The education of Marie Antoinette was certainly very much neglected. With the exception of the Italian language, all that related to *belles lettres*, and particularly to history, even that of her own country, was almost entirely unknown to her. This was soon found out at the Court of France, and thence arose the generally received opinion that she was deficient in sense. It will be seen in the course of these "Memoirs" whether that opinion was well or ill-founded. The public prints, however, teemed with assertions of the superior talents of Maria Theresa's children. They often noticed the answers which the young Princesses gave in Latin to the harangues addressed to them; they uttered them, it is true, but without understanding them; they knew not a single word of that language.

Mention was one day made to the Queen of a drawing made by her, and presented by the Empress to M. Gérard, chief clerk of Foreign Affairs, on the occasion of his going to Vienna to draw up the articles for her marriage-contract. "I should blush," said she, "if that proof of the quackery of my education were shown to me. I do not believe that I ever put a pencil to that drawing." However, what had been taught her she knew perfectly well. Her facility of learning was inconceivable, and if all her teachers had been as well informed and as faithful to their duty as the Abbé Metastasio, who taught her Italian, she would have attained as great a superiority in the other branches of her education. The Queen spoke that language with grace and ease, and translated the most difficult poets. She did not write French correctly, but she spoke it with the greatest fluency, and even affected to say that she had lost German. In fact she attempted in 1787 to learn her mother-tongue, and took lessons assiduously for six weeks; she was obliged to relinquish them, finding all the difficulties which a Frenchwoman, who should take up the study too late, would have to encounter. In the same manner she gave up English, which I had taught her for some time, and in which she had made rapid progress. Music was the accomplishment in which the Queen most delighted. She did not play well on any instrument, but she had become able to read at sight like a first-rate professor. She attained this degree of perfection in France, this branch of her education having been neglected at Vienna as much as the rest. A few days after her arrival at Versailles, she was introduced to her singing-master, La Garde, author of the opera of "Eglé." She made a distant appointment with him, needing, as she said, rest after the fatigues of the journey and the numerous fêtes which had taken place at Versailles; but her motive was her desire to conceal how ignorant she was of the rudiments of music. She asked M. Campan whether his son, who was a good musician, could give her lessons secretly for three months. "The Dauphiness," added she, smiling, "must be careful of the reputation of the Archduchess." The lessons were given privately, and at the end of three months of constant application she sent for M. la Garde, and surprised him by her skill.

The desire to perfect Marie Antoinette in the study of the French language was probably the motive which determined Maria Theresa to provide for her as teachers two

French actors: Aufresne, for pronunciation and declamation, and Sainville, for taste in French singing; the latter had been an officer in France, and bore a bad character. The choice gave just umbrage to our Court. The Marquis de Durfort, at that time ambassador at Vienna, was ordered to make a representation to the Empress upon her selection. The two actors were dismissed, and the Princess required that an ecclesiastic should be sent to her. Several eminent ecclesiastics declined taking upon themselves so delicate an office; others who were pointed out by Maria Theresa (among the rest the Abbé Grisel) belonged to parties which sufficed to exclude them.

The Archbishop of Toulouse one day went to the Duc de Choiseul at the moment when he was much embarrassed upon the subject of this nomination; he proposed to him the Abbé de Vermond, librarian of the Collège des Quatre Nations. The eulogistic manner in which he spoke of his *protégé* procured the appointment for the latter on that very day; and the gratitude of the Abbé de Vermond towards the prelate was very fatal to France, inasmuch as after seventeen years of persevering attempts to bring him into the ministry, he succeeded at last in getting him named Comptroller-General and President of the Council.

This Abbé de Vermond directed almost all the Queen's actions. He established his influence over her at an age when impressions are most durable; and it was easy to see that he had taken pains only to render himself beloved by his pupil, and had troubled himself very little with the care of instructing her. He might have even been accused of having, by a sharp-sighted though culpable policy, purposely left her in ignorance. Marie Antoinette spoke the French language with much grace, but wrote it less perfectly. The Abbé de Vermond revised all the letters which she sent to Vienna. The insupportable folly with which he boasted of it displayed the character of a man more flattered at being admitted into her intimate secrets than anxious to fulfil worthily the high office of her preceptor.

His pride received its birth at Vienna, where Maria Theresa, as much to give him authority with the Archduchess as to make herself acquainted with his character, permitted him to mix every evening with the private circle of her family, into which the future Dauphiness had been admitted for some time. Joseph II, the elder Archduchess, and a few noblemen honoured by the confidence of Maria Theresa, composed the party; and reflections on the world, on courts, and the duties of princes were the usual topics of conversation. The Abbé de Vermond, in relating these particulars, confessed the means which he had made use of to gain admission into this private circle. The Empress, meeting him at the Archduchess's, asked him if he had formed any connections in Vienna. "None, Madame," replied he; "the apartment of the Archduchess and the hôtel of the ambassador of France are the only places which the man honoured with the care of the Princess's education should frequent." A month afterwards Maria Theresa, through a habit common enough among sovereigns, asked him the same question, and received precisely the same answer. The next day he received an order to join the imperial family every evening.

It is extremely probable, from the constant and well-known intercourse between this man and Comte de Mercy, ambassador of the Empire during the whole reign of Louis

XVI, that he was useful to the Court of Vienna,[1] and that he often caused the Queen to decide on measures, the consequences of which she did not consider. Not of high birth,[2] imbued with all the principles of the modern philosophy, and yet holding to the hierarchy of the Church more tenaciously than any other ecclesiastic; vain, talkative, and at the same time cunning and abrupt; very ugly and affecting singularity; treating the most exalted persons as his equals, sometimes even as his inferiors, the Abbé de Vermond received ministers and bishops when in his bath; but said at the same time that Cardinal Dubois was a fool; that a man such as he, having obtained power, ought to make cardinals, and refuse to be one himself.

Intoxicated with the reception he had met with at the Court of Vienna, and having till then seen nothing of high life, the Abbé de Vermond admired no other customs than those of the imperial family; he ridiculed the etiquette of the House of Bourbon incessantly; the young Dauphiness was constantly incited by his sarcasms to get rid of it, and it was he who first induced her to suppress an infinity of practices of which he could discern neither the prudence nor the political aim. Such is the faithful portrait of that man whom the evil star of Marie Antoinette had reserved to guide her first steps upon a stage so conspicuous and so full of danger as that of the Court of Versailles.

1. A person who had dined with the abbé one day at the Comte de Mercy's said to that ambassador, "How can you bear that tiresome proser?" "How can you ask it?" replied M. de Mercy; "you could answer the question yourself: it is because I want him."

2. The Abbé de Vermond was the son of a village surgeon, and brother of an *accoucheur*, who had acted in that capacity for the Queen: when he was with her Majesty, in speaking to his brother, he never addressed him otherwise than as Monsieur l'Accoucheur.

It will be thought, perhaps, that I draw the character of the Abbé de Vermond too unfavourably; but how can I view with any complacency one who, after having arrogated to himself the office of confidant and sole counsellor of the Queen, guided her with so little prudence, and gave us the mortification of seeing that Princess blend, with qualities which charmed all that surrounded her, errors alike injurious to her glory and her happiness?

While M. de Choiseul, satisfied with the person whom M. de Brienne had presented, despatched him to Vienna with every eulogium calculated to inspire unbounded confidence, the Marquis de Durfort sent off a hairdresser and a few French fashions; and then it was thought sufficient pains had been taken to form the character of a princess destined to share the throne of France.

The marriage of Monseigneur the Dauphin with the Archduchess was determined upon during the administration of the Duc de Choiseul. The Marquis de Durfort, who was to succeed the Baron de Breteuil in the embassy to Vienna, was appointed proxy for the marriage ceremony; but six months after the Dauphin's marriage the Duc de Choiseul was disgraced, and Madame de Marsan and Madame de Guéménée, who grew more powerful through the Duke's disgrace, conferred that embassy upon Prince Louis de Rohan, afterwards cardinal and grand almoner.

Hence it will be seen that the *Gazette de France* is a sufficient answer to those libellers who dared to assert that the young Archduchess was acquainted with the Cardinal de Rohan before the period of her marriage. A worse selection in itself, or one more disagreeable to Maria Theresa, than that which sent to her, in quality of ambassador, a man so frivolous and so immoral as Prince Louis de Rohan, could not have been made. He possessed but superficial knowledge upon any subject, and was totally ignorant of diplomatic affairs. His reputation had gone before him to Vienna, and his mission opened under the most unfavourable auspices. In want of money, and the House of Rohan being unable to make him any considerable advances, he obtained from his Court a patent which authorised him to borrow the sum of 600,000 livres upon his benefices, ran in debt above a million, and thought to dazzle the city and Court of Vienna by the most indecent and ill-judged extravagance. He formed a suite of eight or ten gentlemen, of names sufficiently high-sounding; twelve pages equally well born, a crowd of officers and servants, a company of chamber musicians, etc. But this idle pomp did not last; embarrassment and distress soon showed themselves; his people, no longer receiving pay, in order to make money, abused the privileges of ambassadors, and smuggled [1] with so much effrontery that Maria Theresa, to put a stop to it without offending the Court of France, was compelled to suppres the privileges in this respect of all the diplomatic bodies,—a step which rendered the person and conduct of Prince Louis odious in every foreign Court He seldom obtained private audiences from the Empress, who did not esteem him, and who expressed herself without reserve upon his conduct both as; bishop and as an ambassador. He thought to obtain favour by assisting to effect the marriage of the Archduchess Elizabeth, the elder sister

---

1. I have often heard the Queen say, that in the office of the secretary of the Prince de Rohan, there were sold in one year at Vienna, more silk stockings than at Lyons and Paris together.

of Marie Antoinette, with Louis XV, an affair which was awkwardly undertaken, and of which Madame du Barry had no difficulty in causing the failure. I have deemed it my duty to omit no particular of the moral and political character of a man whose existence was subsequently so injurious to the reputation of Marie Antoinette.

III

A SUPERB pavilion had been prepared upon the frontier near Kehl. It consisted of a vast *salon*, connected with two apartments, one of which was assigned to the lords and ladies of the Court of Vienna, and the other to the suite of the Dauphiness, composed of the Comtesse de Noailles, her lady of honour; the Duchesse de Cossé, her *dame d'atours*; four ladies of the palace; the Comte de Saulx-Tavennes, *chevalier d'honneur*; the Comte de Tessé, first equerry; the Bishop of Chartres, first almoner; the officers of the Body Guard, and the equerries.

When the Dauphiness had been entirely undressed, in order that she might retain nothing belonging to a foreign Court (an etiquette always observed on such an occasion), the doors were opened; the young Princess came forward, looking round for the Comtesse de Noailles; then, rushing into her arms, she implored her, with tears in her eyes, and with heartfelt sincerity, to be her guide and support.

While doing justice to the virtues of the Comtesse de Noailles, those sincerely attached to the Queen have always considered it as one of her earliest misfortunes not to have found, in the person of her adviser, a woman indulgent, enlightened, and administering good advice with that amiability which disposes young persons to follow it. The Comtesse de Noailles had nothing agreeable in her appearance; her demeanour was stiff and her mien severe. She was perfect mistress of etiquette; but she wearied the young Princess with it, without making her sensible of its importance. It would have been sufficient to represent to the Dauphiness that in France her dignity depended much upon customs not necessary at Vienna to secure the respect and love of the good and submissive Austrians for the imperial family; but the Dauphiness was perpetually tormented by the remonstrances of the Comtesse de Noailles, and at the same time was led by the Abbé de Vermond to ridicule both the lessons upon etiquette and her who gave them. She preferred raillery to argument, and nicknamed the Comtesse de Noailles *Madame L'Etiquette*.

The fêtes which were given at Versailles on the marriage of the Dauphin were very splendid. The Dauphiness arrived there at the hour for her toilet, having slept at La Muette, where Louis XV had been to receive her; and where that Prince, blinded by a feeling unworthy of a sovereign and the father of a family, caused the young Princess, the royal family, and the ladies of the Court, to sit down to supper with Madame du Barry.

The Dauphiness was hurt at this conduct; she spoke of it openly enough to those with whom she was intimate, but she knew how to conceal her dissatisfaction in public, and her behaviour showed no signs of it.

She was received at Versailles in an apartment on the ground floor, under that of the late Queen, which was not ready for her until six months after her marriage.

The Dauphiness, then fifteen years of age, beaming with freshness, appeared to all eyes more than beautiful. Her walk partook at once of the dignity of the Princesses of her house, and of the grace of the French; her eyes were mild, her smile amiable. When she went to chapel, as soon as she had taken the first few steps in the long gallery, she discerned, all the way to its extremity, those persons whom she ought to salute with the consideration due to their rank; those on whom she should bestow an inclination of the head; and lastly, those who were to be satisfied with a smile, calculated to console them for not being entitled to greater honours.

Louis XV was enchanted with the young Dauphiness; all his conversation was about her graces, her vivacity, and the aptness of her repartees. She was yet more successful with the royal family when they beheld her shorn of the splendour of the diamonds with which she had been adorned during the first days of her marriage. When clothed in a light dress of gauze or taffety she was compared to the Venus dei Medici, and the Atalanta of the Marly Gardens. Poets sang her charms; painters attempted to copy her features. One artist's fancy led him to place the portrait of Marie Antoinette in the heart of a fullblown rose. His ingenious idea was rewarded by Louis XV.

The King continued to talk only of the Dauphiness; and Madame du Barry ill-naturedly endeavoured to damp his enthusiasm. Whenever Marie Antoinette was the topic, she pointed out the irregularity of her features, criticised the *bons mots* quoted as hers, and rallied the King upon his prepossession in her favour. Madame du Barry was affronted at not receiving from the Dauphiness those attentions to which she thought herself entitled; she did not conceal her vexation from the King; she was afraid that the grace and cheerfulness of the young Princess would make the domestic circle of the royal family more agreeable to the old sovereign, and that he would escape her chains; at the same time, hatred to the Choiseul party contributed powerfully to excite the enmity of the favourite.

The fall of that minister took place in November, 1770, six months after his long influence in the Council had brought about the alliance with the House of Austria and the arrival of Marie Antoinette at the Court of France. The Princess, young, frank, volatile, and inexperienced, found herself without any other guide than the Abbé de Vermond, in a Court ruled by the enemy of the minister who had brought her there, and in the midst of people who hated Austria, and detested any alliance with the imperial house.

The Duc d'Aiguillon, the Duc de La Vauguyon, the Maréchal de Richelieu, the Rohans, and other considerable families, who had made use of Madame du Barry to overthrow the Duke, could not flatter themselves, notwithstanding their powerful intrigues, with a hope of being able to break off an alliance solemnly announced, and involving such high political interests. They therefore changed their mode of attack, and it will be seen how the conduct of the Dauphin served as a basis for their hopes.

The Dauphiness continually gave proofs of both sense and feeling. Sometimes she even suffered herself to be carried away by those transports of compassionate kindness which are not to be controlled by the customs which rank establishes.

In consequence of the fire in the Place Louis XV, which occurred at the time of the nuptial entertainments, the Dauphin and Dauphiness sent their whole income for the year to the relief of the unfortunate families who lost their relatives on that disastrous day.

This was one of those ostentatious acts of generosity which are dictated by the policy of princes, at least as much as by their compassion; but the grief of Marie Antoinette was profound, and lasted several days; nothing could console her for the loss of so many innocent victims; she spoke of it, weeping, to her ladies, one of whom, thinking, no doubt, to divert her mind, told her that a great number of thieves had been found among the bodies, and that their pockets were filled with watches and other valuables. "They have at least been well punished," added the person who related these particulars. "Oh, no, no, madame!" replied the Dauphiness; "they died by the side of honest people."

The Dauphiness had brought from Vienna a considerable number of white diamonds; the King added to them the gift of the diamonds and pearls of the late Dauphiness, and also put into her hands a collar of pearls, of a single row, the smallest of which was as large as a filbert, and which had been brought into France by Anne of Austria, and appropriated by that Princess to the use of the Queens and Dauphinesses of France. [1]

The three Princesses, daughters of Louis XV, joined in making her magnificent presents. Madame Adélaïde at the

---

1. I mention this collar thus particularly because the Queen thought it her duty, notwithstanding this appropriation, to give it up to the commissaries of the National Assembly, when they came to strip the King and Queen of the crown diamonds.

same time gave the young Princess a key to the private cor-ridors of the Château, by means of which, without any suite, and without being perceived, she could get to the apart-ments of her aunts, and see them in private. The Dauphi-ness, on receiving the key, told them, with infinite grace, that if they had meant to make her appreciate the superb pres-ents they were kind enough to bestow upon her, they should not at the same time have offered her one of such inestima-ble value; since to that key she should be indebted for an in-timacy and advice unspeakably precious at her age. She did, indeed, make use of it very frequently; but Madame Victoire alone permitted her, so long as she continued Dauphiness, to visit her familiarly. Madame Adélaïde could not overcome her prejudices against Austrian princesses, and was wearied with the somewhat petulant gaiety of the Dauphiness. Ma-dame Victoire was concerned at this, feeling that their so-ciety and counsel would have been highly useful to a young person otherwise likely to meet with none but sycophants. She endeavoured, therefore, to induce her to take pleasure in the society of the Marquise de Durfort, her lady of hon-our and favourite. Several agreeable entertainments took place at the house of this lady, but the Comtesse de Noailles and the Abbé de Vermond soon opposed these meetings.

A circumstance which happened in hunting, near the village of Acheres, in the forest of Fontainebleau, afforded the young Princess an opportunity of displaying her respect for old age, and her compassion for misfortune. An aged peasant was wounded by the stag; the Dauphiness jumped out of her calash, placed the peasant, with his wife and chil-dren, in it, had the family taken back to their cottage, and bestowed upon them every attention and every necessary assistance. Her heart was always open to the feelings of compassion, and the recollection of her rank never restrained her sensibility. Several persons in her service entered her room one evening, expecting to find nobody there but the officer in waiting; [1] they perceived the young Princess seated by the side of this man, who was advanced in years; she had placed near him a bowl full of water, was stanching the blood which issued from a wound he had received in his hand with her handkerchief, which she had torn up to bind it, and was fulfilling towards him all the duties of a pious sister of charity. The old man, affected even to tears, out of respect allowed his august mistress to act as she thought proper. He had hurt himself in endeavouring to move a rather heavy piece of furniture at the Princess's request.

In the month of July, 1770, an unfortunate occurrence that took place in a family which the Dauphiness honoured with her favour contributed again to show not only her sensibility but also the benevolence of her disposition. One of her women in waiting had a son who was an officer in the *gens d'armes* of the guard; this young man thought himself affronted by a clerk in the War Department, and imprudently sent him a challenge; he killed his adversary in the forest of Compiègne. The family of the young man who was killed, being in possession of the challenge, demanded justice. The King, distressed on account of several duels which had recently taken place, had unfortunately declared that he would show no mercy on the first event of that kind which could be proved; the culprit was therefore arrested. His mother,

---

1. Ushers and grooms of the chamber were known at that time as officers of the interior.

in the deepest grief, hastened to throw, herself at the feet of the Dauphiness, the Dauphin, and the young Princesses. After an hour's supplication they obtained from the King the favour so much desired. On the next day a lady of rank; while congratulating the Dauphiness, had the malice to add that the mother had neglected no means of success on the occasion, having solicited not only the royal family, but even Madame du Barry. The Dauphiness replied that the fact justified the favourable opinion she had formed of the worthy woman; that the heart of a mother should hesitate at nothing for the salvation of her son; and that in her place, if she had thought it would be serviceable, she would have thrown herself at the feet of Zamora.[1]

Some time after the marriage entertainments the Dauphiness made her entry into Paris, and was received with transports of joy. After dining in the King's apartment at the Tuileries, she was forced, by the reiterated shouts of the multitude, with whom the garden was filled, to present herself upon the balcony fronting the principal walk. On seeing such a crowd of heads with their eyes fixed upon her, she exclaimed, "*Grand Dieu*! what a concourse !" "Madame," said the old Duc de Brissac, the Governor of Paris, "I may tell you, without fear of offending the Dauphin, that they are so many lovers." The Dauphin took no umbrage at either acclamations or marks of homage of which the Dauphiness was the object. The most mortifying indifference, a coldness which frequently degenerated into rudeness, were

1. A little Indian, who carried Comtesse du Barry's train. Louis XV often amused himself with the little marmoset; having facetiously made him governor of Louveciennes, he received an annual income of 3000 francs.

the sole feelings which the young Prince then manifested towards her. Not all her charms could gain even upon his senses. This estrangement, which lasted a long time, was said to be the work of the Duc de La Vauguyon. The Dauphiness, in fact, had no sincere friends at Court except the Duc de Choiseul and his party. Will it be credited that the plans laid against Marie Antoinette went so far as divorce? I have been assured of it by persons holding high situations at Court, and many circumstances tend to confirm the opinion. On the journey to Fontainebleau, in the year of the marriage, the inspectors of public buildings were gained over to manage so that the apartment intended for the Dauphin, communicating with that of the Dauphiness, should not be finished, and a room at the extremity of the building was temporarily assigned to him. The Dauphiness, aware that this was the result of intrigue, had the courage to complain of it to Louis XV, who, after severe reprimands, gave orders so positive that within the week the apartment was ready. Every method was tried to continue or augment the indifference which the Dauphin long manifested towards his youthful spouse. She was deeply hurt at it, but she never suffered herself to utter the slightest complaint on the subject. Inattention to, even contempt for, the charms which she heard extolled on all sides, nothing induced her to break silence; and some tears, which would involuntarily burst from her eyes, were the sole symptoms of her inward sufferings discoverable by those in her service.

Once only, when tired out with the misplaced remonstrances of an old lady attached to her person, who wished to dissuade her from riding on horseback, under the impression that it would prevent her producing heirs to the crown,

"Mademoiselle," said she, "in God's name, leave me in peace; be assured that I can put no heir in danger."

The Dauphiness found at the Court of Louis XV, besides the three Princesses, the King's daughters, the Princes also, brothers of the Dauphin, who were receiving their education, and Clotilde and Elisabeth, still in the care of Madame de Marsan, governess of the children of France. The elder of the two latter Princesses, in 1777, married the Prince of Piedmont, afterwards King of Sardinia. This Princess was in her infancy so extremely large that the people nicknamed her *gros Madame*. The second Princess was the pious Elisabeth, the victim of her respect and tender attachment for the King, her brother. She was still scarcely out of her leading-strings at the period of the Dauphin's marriage. The Dauphiness showed her marked preference. The governess, who sought to advance the Princess to whom nature had been least favourable, was offended at the Dauphiness's partiality for Madame Elisabeth, and by her injudicious complaints weakened the friendship which yet subsisted between Madame Clotilde and Marie Antoinette. There even arose some degree of rivalry on the subject of education; and that which the Empress Maria Theresa bestowed on her daughters was talked of openly and unfavourably enough. The Abbé de Vermond thought himself affronted, took a part in the quarrel, and added his complaints and jokes to those of the Dauphiness on the criticisms of the governess; he even indulged himself in his turn in reflections on the tuition of Madame Clotilde. Everything becomes known at Court. Madame de Marsan was informed of all that had been said in the Dauphiness's circle, and was very angry with her on account of it.

From that moment a centre of intrigue, or rather gossip, against Marie Antoinette was established round Madame de Marsan's fireside; her most trifling actions were there construed ill; her gaiety, and the harmless amusements in which she sometimes indulged in her own apartments with the more youthful ladies of her train, and even with the women in her service, were stigmatised as criminal. Prince Louis de Rohan, sent through the influence of this clique ambassador to Vienna, was the echo there of these unmerited comments, and threw himself into a series of culpable accusations which he proffered under the guise of zeal. He ceaselessly represented the young Dauphiness as alienating all hearts by levities unsuitable to the dignity of the French Court. The Princess frequently received from the Court of Vienna remonstrances, of the origin of which she could not long remain in ignorance. From this period must be dated that aversion which she never ceased to manifest for the Prince de Rohan.

About the same time the Dauphiness received information of a letter written by Prince Louis to the Duc d'Aiguillon, in which the ambassador expressed himself in very free language respecting the intentions of Maria Theresa with relation to the partition of Poland. This letter of Prince Louis had been read at the Comtesse du Barry's; the levity of the ambassador's correspondence wounded the feelings and the dignity of the Dauphiness at Versailles, while at Vienna the representations which he made to Maria Theresa against the young Princess terminated in rendering the motives of his incessant complaints suspected by the Empress.

Maria Theresa at length determined on sending her private secretary, Baron de Neni, to Versailles, with directions to observe the conduct of the Dauphiness with attention, and form a just estimate of the opinion of the Court and of Paris with regard to that Princess. The Baron de Neni, after having devoted sufficient time and intelligence to the subject, undeceived his sovereign as to the exaggerations of the French ambassador; and the Empress had no difficulty in detecting, among the calumnies which he had conveyed to her under the specious excuse of anxiety for her august daughter, proofs of the enmity of a party which had never approved of the alliance of the House of Bourbon with her own.

At this period the Dauphiness, though unable to obtain any influence over the heart of her husband, dreading Louis XV, and justly mistrusting everything connected with Madame du Barry and the Duc d'Aiguillon, had not deserved the slightest reproach for that sort of levity which hatred and her misfortunes afterwards construed into crime. The Empress, convinced of the innocence of Marie Antoinette, directed the Baron de Neni to solicit the recall of the Prince de Rohan, and to inform the Minister for Foreign Affairs of all the motives which made her require it; but the House of Rohan interposed between its *protégé* and the Austrian envoy, and an evasive answer merely was given.

It was not until two months after the death of Louis XV that the Court of Vienna obtained his recall. The avowed grounds for requiring it were, first, the public gallantries of Prince Louis with some ladies of the Court and others, secondly, his surliness and haughtiness towards other foreign ministers, which would have had more serious consequences, especially with the ministers of England and Denmark, if the Empress herself had not interfered; thirdly, his contempt for religion in a country where it was particularly necessary to show respect for it. He had been seen frequently to dress himself in clothes of different colours, assuming the hunting uniforms of various noblemen whom he visited, with so much audacity that one day in particular, during the *Fête Dieu*, he and all his legation, in green uniforms laced with gold, broke through a procession which impeded them, in order to make their way to a hunting party at the Prince de Paar's; and fourthly, the immense debts contracted by him and his people, which were tardily and only in part discharged.

The succeeding marriages of the Comte de Provence and the Comte d'Artois with two daughters of the King of Sardinia procured society for the Dauphiness more suitable to her age, and altered her mode of life.

A pair of tolerably fine eyes drew forth, in favour of the Comtesse de Provence, upon her arrival at Versailles, the only praises which could reasonably be bestowed upon her. The Comtesse d'Artois, though not deformed, was very small; she had a fine complexion; her face, tolerably pleasing, was not remarkable for anything except the extreme length of the nose. But being good and generous, she was beloved by those about her, and even possessed some influence so long as she was the only Princess who had produced heirs to the crown.

From this time the closest intimacy subsisted between the three young families. They took their meals together, except on those days when they dined in public. This manner of living *en famille* continued until the Queen sometimes indulged herself in going to dine with the Duchesse de Polignac, when she was governess; but the evening meetings at supper were never interrupted; they took place at the house of the Comtesse de Provence. Madame Elisabeth made one of the party when she had finished her education, and sometimes Mesdames, the King's aunts, were invited. The custom, which had no precedent at Court, was the work of Marie Antoinette, and she maintained it with the utmost perseverance.

The Court of Versailles saw no change in point of etiquette during the reign of Louis XV. Play took place at the house of the Dauphiness, as being the first lady of the State. It had, from the death of Queen Maria Leczinska to the marriage of the Dauphin, been held at the abode of Madame Adélaïde. This removal, the result of an order of precedence not to be violated, was not the less displeasing to Madame Adélaïde, who established a separate party for play in her apartments, and scarcely ever went to that which not only the Court in general, but also the royal family, were expected to attend. The full-dress visits to the King on his *débotter* were continued. High mass was attended daily. The airings of the Princesses were nothing more than rapid races in berlins, during which they were accompanied by Body Guards, equerries, and pages on horseback. They galloped for some leagues from Versailles. Calashes were used only in hunting.

The young Princesses were desirous to infuse animation into their circle of associates by something useful as well as pleasant. They adopted the plan of learning and performing all the best plays of the French theatre. The Dauphin was the only spectator. The three Princesses, the two brothers of the King and Messieurs Campan, father and son, were the sole performers, but they endeavoured to keep this amusement as secret as an affair of State; they dreaded the censure of Mesdames, and they had no doubt that

Louis XV would forbid such pastimes if he knew of them. They selected for their performance a cabinet in the *entresol* which nobody had occasion to enter. A kind of proscenium, which could be taken down and shut up in a closet, formed the whole theatre. The Comte de Provence always knew his part with imperturbable accuracy; the Comte d'Artois knew his tolerably well, and recited elegantly; the Princesses acted badly. The Dauphiness acquitted herself in some characters with discrimination and feeling. The chief pleasure of this amusement consisted in all the costumes being elegant and accurate. The Dauphin entered into the spirit of these diversions, and laughed heartily at the comic characters as they came on the scene; from these amusements may be dated his discontinuance of the timid manner of his youth, and his taking pleasure in the society of the Dauphiness.

It was not till a long time afterwards that I learnt these particulars, M. Campan having kept the secret; but an unforeseen event had well-nigh exposed the whole mystery. One day the Queen desired M. Campan to go down into her closet to fetch something that she had forgotten; he was dressed for the character of Crispin, and was rouged. A private staircase led direct to the *entresol* through the dressing-room. M. Campan fancied he heard some noise, and remained still, behind the door, which was shut. A servant belonging to the wardrobe, who was, in fact, on the staircase, had also heard some noise, and, either from fear or curiosity, he suddenly opened the door; the figure of Crispin frightened him so that he fell down backwards, shouting with his might, "Help! help!" My father-in-law raised him up, made him recognize his voice, and laid upon him an injunction of silence as to what he had seen. He felt himself, however, bound to inform the Dauphiness of what had happened, and she was afraid that a similar occurrence might betray their amusements. They were therefore discontinued.

The Princess occupied her time in her own apartment in the study of music and the parts in plays which she had to learn; the latter exercise, at least, produced the beneficial effect of strengthening her memory and familiarising her with the French language.

While Louis XV reigned, the enemies of Marie Antoinette made no attempt to change public opinion with regard to her. She was always popular with the French people in general, and particularly with the inhabitants of Paris, who went on every opportunity to Versailles, the majority of them attracted solely by the pleasure of seeing her. The courtiers did not fully enter into the popular enthusiasm which the Dauphiness had inspired; the disgrace of the Duc de Choiseul had removed her real support from her; and the party which had the ascendency at Court since the exile of that minister was, politically, as much opposed to her family as to herself. The Dauphiness was therefore surrounded by enemies at Versailles.

Nevertheless everybody appeared outwardly desirous to please her; for the age of Louis XV, and the apathetic character of the Dauphin, sufficiently warned courtiers of the important part reserved for the Princess during the following reign, in case the Dauphin should become attached to her.

IV

ABOUT the beginning of May, 1774, Louis XV, the strength of whose constitution had promised a long enough life, was attacked by confluent smallpox of the worst kind. Mesdames at this juncture inspired the Dauphiness with a feeling of respect and attachment, of which she gave them repeated proofs when she ascended the throne. In fact, nothing was more admirable nor more affecting than the courage with which they braved that most horrible disease. The air of the palace was infected; more than fifty persons took the smallpox, in consequence of having merely loitered in the galleries of Versailles, and ten died of it.

The end of the monarch was approaching. His reign, peaceful in general, had inherited strength from the power of his predecessor; on the other hand, his own weakness had been preparing misfortune for whoever should reign after him. The scene was about to change; hope, ambition, joy, grief, and all those feelings which variously affected the hearts of the courtiers, sought in vain to disguise themselves under a calm exterior. It was easy to detect the different motives which induced them every moment to repeat to everyone the question: "How is the King?" At length, on the 10th of May, 1774, the mortal career of Louis XV terminated. The Comtesse du Barry had, a few days previously, withdrawn to Ruelle, to the Duc d'Aiguillon's. Twelve or fifteen persons belonging to the Court thought it their duty to visit her there; their liveries were observed, and these visits were for a long time grounds for disfavour. More than six years after the King's death one of these persons being spoken of in the circle of the royal family, I heard it remarked, "That was one of the fifteen Ruelle carriages."

The whole Court went to the Château; the *œil-de-bœuf* was filled with courtiers, and the palace with the inquisitive. The Dauphin had settled that he would depart with the royal family the moment the King should breathe his last sigh. But on such an occasion decency forbade that positive orders for departure should be passed from mouth to mouth. The heads of the stables, therefore, agreed with the people who were in the King's room, that the latter should place a lighted taper near a window, and that at the instant of the King's decease one of them should extinguish it.

The taper was extinguished. On this signal the Body Guards, pages, and equerries mounted on horseback, and all was ready for setting off. The Dauphin was with the Dauphiness. They were expecting together the intelligence of the death of Louis XV. A dreadful noise, absolutely like thunder, was heard in the outer apartment; it was the crowd of courtiers who were deserting the dead sovereign's antechamber, to come and do homage to the new power of Louis

XVI. This extraordinary tumult informed Marie Antoinette and her husband that they were called to the throne; and, by a spontaneous movement, which deeply affected those around them, they threw themselves on their knees; both, pouring forth a flood of tears, exclaimed: *"O God! Guide us, protect us; we are too young to reign."*

The Comtesse de Noailles entered, and was the first to salute Marie Antoinette as Queen of France. She requested their Majesties to condescend to quit the inner apartments for the grand *salon*, to receive the Princes and all the great officers, who were desirous to do homage to their new sovereigns. Marie Antoinette received these first visits leaning upon her husband, with her handkerchief held to her eyes; the carriages drove up, the guards and equerries were on horseback. The Château was deserted; every one hastened to fly from contagion, which there was no longer any inducement to brave.

On leaving the chamber of Louis XV, the Duc de Ville-quier, first gentleman of the bedchamber for the year, ordered M. Andouillé, the King's chief surgeon, to open the body and embalm it. The chief surgeon would inevitably have died in consequence. "I am, ready," replied Andouillé, "but while I operate you shall hold the head; your office imposes this duty upon you." The Duke went off without saying a word, and the corpse was neither opened nor embalmed. A few under-servants and workmen continued with the pestiferous remains, and paid the last duty to their master; the surgeons directed that spirits of wine should be poured into the coffin.

The entire Court set off for Choisy at four o'clock; Mesdames the King's aunts in their private carriage, and the Princesses under tuition with the Comtesse de Marsan and the under-governesses. The King, the Queen, Monsieur, the King's brother, Madame, and the Comte and Comtesse d'Artois went in the same carriage. The solemn scene that had just passed before their eyes, the multiplied ideas offered to their imaginations by that which was just opening, had naturally inclined them to grief and reflection; but, by the Queen's own confession, this inclination, little suited to their age, wholly left them before they had gone half their journey; a word, drolly mangled by the Comtesse d'Artois, occasioned a general burst of laughter; and from that moment they dried their tears.

The communication between Choisy and Paris was incessant ; never was a Court seen in greater agitation. What influence will the royal aunts have,—and the Queen? What fate is reserved for the Comtesse du Barry? Whom will the young King choose for his ministers? All these questions were answered in a few days. It was determined that the King's youth required a confidential person near him; and that there should be a prime minister. All eyes were turned upon De Machault and De Maurepas, both of them much advanced in years. The first had retired to his estate near Paris; and the second to Pont Chartrain, to which place he had long been exiled. The letter recalling M. de Machault was written, when Madame Adélaïde obtained the preference of that important appointment for M. de Maurepas. The page to whose care the first letter had been actually consigned was recalled.[1]

1. This fact has been doubted: but I am able to assert, that Louis XVI desired M. Campan to recall the page, whom he found ready to mount his horse, and whom he desired to come back again, to return the letter to the king himself; and that the queen said upon the subject to my father-in-law, "If the letter had gone, M. de Machault would have been Prime Minister; for the king would never have consented to write a second letter in contradiction of his first intention."

The Duc d'Aiguillon had been too openly known as the private friend of the King's mistress; he was dismissed. M. de Vergennes, at that time ambassador of France at Stockholm, was appointed Minister for Foreign Affairs; Comte du Muy, the intimate friend of the Dauphin, the father of Louis XVI, obtained the War Department. The Abbé Terray in vain said, and wrote, that he had boldly done all possible injury to the creditors of the State during the reign of the late King; that order was restored in the finances; that nothing but what was beneficial to all parties remained to be done; and that the new Court was about to enjoy the advantages of the regenerating part of his plan of finance; all these reasons, set forth in five or six memorials, which he sent in succession to the King and Queen, did not avail to keep him in office. His talents were admitted, but the odium which his operations had necessarily brought upon his character, combined with the immorality of his private life, forbade his further stay at Court; he was succeeded by M. de Clugny. De Maupeou, the chancellor, was exiled; this caused universal joy. Lastly, the reassembling of the Parliaments produced the strongest sensation; Paris was in a delirium of joy, and not more than one person in a hundred foresaw that the spirit of the ancient magistracy would be still the same; and that in a short time it would make new attempts upon the royal authority.

Madame du Barry had been exiled to Pont-aux-Dames. This was a measure rather of necessity than of severity; a short period of compulsory retreat was requisite in order completely to break off her connections with State affairs.

The possession of Louveciennes and a considerable pension were continued to her. [1]

Everybody expected the recall of M. de Choiseul; the regret occasioned by his absence among the numerous friends when he had left at Court, the attachment of the young Princess who was indebted to him for her elevation to the throne of France, and all concurring circumstances, seemed to foretell his return; the Queen earnestly entreated it of the King, but she met with an insurmountable and unforeseen obstacle. The King, it is said, had imbibed the strongest prejudices against that minister, [2] from secret memoranda penned by his father, and which had been committed to the care of the Duc de La Vauguyon, with an injunction to place them in his hands as soon as he should be old enough to study, the art of reigning. It was by these memoranda that the esteem which he had conceived for the Maréchal du Muy was inspired, and we may add that Madame Adélaïde, who at this early period power-fully influenced the decisions of the young monarch, con-firmed the impressions they had made.

---

1. The Comtesse du Barry never forgot the mild treatment she experienced from the court of Louis XVI; during the most violent convulsions of the Revolution, she signified to the Queen that there was not in all France a female more grieved at the sufferings of her sovereign than herself; that the honour she had for years enjoyed, of living near the throne, and the unbounded kindness of the King and Queen had so sincerely attached her to the cause of royalty, that she entreated the Queen to hon-our her by disposing of all she possessed. Though they did not accept her offer, their Majesties were affected by her gratitude. The Comtesse du Barry was, as is well known, one of the victims of the Revolution. She betrayed the lowest degree of weakness, and the most ardent desire to live. She was the only woman who wept upon the scaffold, and implored for mercy. Her beauty and tears made an impression on the populace, and the execution was hurried to a conclusion.

2. These prejudices did not arise from the pretended crime, of which slander had accused this minis-ter; but principally from the suppression of the Jesuits, in which he had in fact taken an active part.

The Queen conversed with M. Campan on the regret she felt at having been unable to procure the recall of M. de Choiseul, and disclosed the cause of it to him. The Abbé de Vermond, who, down to the time of the death of Louis XV, had been on terms of the strictest friendship with M. Campan, called upon him on the second day after the arrival of the Court at Choisy, and, assuming a serious air, said, "Monsieur, the Queen was indiscreet enough yesterday to speak to you of a minister to whom she must of course be attached, and whom his friends ardently desire to have near her; you are aware that we must give up all expectation of seeing the Duke at Court; you know the reasons why; but you do not know that the young Queen, having mentioned the conversation in question to me, it was my duty, both as her preceptor and her friend, to remonstrate severely with her on her indiscretion in communicating to you those particulars of which you are in possession. I am now come to tell you that if you continue to avail yourself of the good nature of your mistress to initiate yourself in secrets of State, you will have me for your most inveterate enemy. The Queen should find here no other confidant than myself respecting things that ought to remain secret."[1] M. Campan answered that he did not covet the important and dangerous character at the new Court which the Abbé wished to appropriate; and that he should confine himself to the duties of his office, being sufficiently satisfied with the continued kindness with which the Queen honoured him. Notwithstanding this, however, he informed

---

1. The Abbé de Vermond was not blamable for preventing the Queen talking to one of her servants about matters of importance; but he was so, for saying that he himself ought to be the depositary of the most momentous secrets.

the Queen, on the very same evening, of the injunction he had received. She owned that she had mentioned their conversation to the Abbé; that he had indeed seriously scolded her, in order to make her feel the necessity of being secret in concerns of State; and she added, "The Abbé cannot like you, my dear Campan; he did not expect that I should, on my arrival in France, find in my household a man who would suit me so exactly as you have done.[1] I know that he has taken umbrage at it; that is enough. I know, too, that you are incapable of attempting anything to injure him in my esteem; an attempt which would besides be vain, for I have been too long attached to him. As to yourself, be easy on the score of the Abbé's hostility, which shall not in any way hurt you."

The Abbé de Vermond having made himself master of the office of sole confidant to the Queen, was nevertheless agitated whenever he saw the young King; he could not be ignorant that the Abbé had been promoted by the Duc de Choiseul, and was believed to favour the Encyclopedists,

---

1. The Abbé de Vermond was indeed not aware that the young princess would find in her household a well-informed man, capable of amusing her, by interesting and lively anecdotes of the courts of Louis XV the Regent, and even of Louis XIV. The abbé had taken pains at Vienna to prepossess the dauphiness against M. Moreau, an aged advocate in the councils, and historiographer of France, whose talents had promoted him to the office of librarian to her. On the day after the arrival of the dauphiness at Versailles, the Comtesse de Noailles asked her what orders she had to give for M. Moreau. She replied, that the only order she had for him was to give up the key of her library to M. Campan, whom she installed into his office; adding that he might retain the title which the King had conferred upon him, but that she did not accept of his services. Her *dame d'honneur* exclaimed against this determination, and spoke very highly of M. Moreau's talents; but the princess was so prejudiced against him that she insisted upon the execution of her order, and added that she would speak to the King about the matter; that she knew M. Moreau had a double share of talent, and that she desired to have no people about her but those on whom she could rely. It is probable that the dauphiness had been informed of the connection of M. Moreau with the Duc d'Aiguillon, and some members of that minister's party.

against whom Louis XVI entertained a secret prejudice, although he suffered them to gain so great an ascendency during his reign. The Abbé had, moreover, observed that the King had never, while Dauphin, addressed a single word to him; and that he very frequently only answered him with a shrug of the shoulders. He therefore determined on writing to Louis XVI, and intimating that he owed his situation at Court solely to the confidence with which the late King had honoured him; and that as habits contracted during the Queen's education placed him continually in the closest intimacy with her, he could not enjoy the honour of remaining near her Majesty without the King's consent. Louis XVI sent back his letter, after writing upon it these words: "I approve the Abbé de Vermond continuing in his office about the Queen."

V

AT the period of his grandfather's death, Louis XVI began to be exceedingly attached to the Queen. The first period of so deep a mourning not admitting of indulgence in the diversion of hunting, he proposed to her walks in the gardens of Choisy; they went out like husband and wife, the young King giving his arm to the Queen, and accompanied by a very small suite. The influence of this example had such an effect upon the courtiers that the next day several couples, who had long, and for good reasons, been disunited, were seen walking upon the terrace with the same apparent conjugal intimacy. Thus they spent whole hours, braving the intolerable wearisomeness of their protracted *tête-à-têtes*, out of mere obsequious imitation.

The devotion of Mesdames to the King their father throughout his dreadful malady had produced that effect upon their health which was generally apprehended. On the fourth day after their arrival at Choisy they were attacked by pains in the head and chest, which left no doubt as to the danger of their situation. It became necessary instantly to send away the young royal family; and the Château de la Muette, in the Bois de Boulogne, was selected for their reception. Their arrival at that residence, which was very near Paris, drew so great a concourse of people into its neighbourhood, that even at daybreak the crowd had begun to assemble round the gates. Shouts of *"Vive le Roi!"* were scarcely interrupted for a moment between six o'clock in the morning and sunset. The unpopularity the late King had drawn upon himself during his latter years, and the hopes to which a new reign gives birth, occasioned these transports of joy.

A fashionable jeweller made a fortune by the sale of mourning snuff-boxes, whereon the portrait of the young Queen, in a black frame of shagreen, gave rise to the pun: "Consolation in chagrin." All the fashions, and every article of dress, received names expressing the spirit of the moment. Symbols of abundance were everywhere represented, and the head-dresses of the ladies were surrounded by ears of wheat. Poets sang of the new monarch; all hearts, or rather all heads, in France were filled with enthusiasm. Never did the commencement of any reign excite more unanimous testimonials of love and attachment. It must be observed, however, that, amidst all this intoxication, the anti-Austrian party never lost sight of the young Queen, but kept on the watch, with the malicious desire to injure her through such errors as might arise from her youth and inexperience.

Their Majesties had to receive at La Muette the condolences of the ladies who had been presented at Court, who all felt themselves called on to pay homage to the new sovereigns. Old and young hastened to present themselves on the day of general reception; little black bonnets with great wings, shaking heads, low curtsies, keeping time with the motions of the head, made, it must be admitted, a few venerable dowagers appear somewhat ridiculous; but the Queen, who possessed a great deal of dignity, and a high respect for decorum, was not guilty of the grave fault of losing the state she was bound to preserve. An indiscreet piece of drollery of one of the ladies of the palace, however, procured her the imputation of doing so. The Marquise de Clermont-Tonnerre, whose office required that she should continue standing behind the Queen, fatigued by the length of the ceremony, seated herself on the floor, concealed behind the fence formed by the hoops of the Queen and the ladies of the palace. Thus seated, and wishing to attract attention and to appear lively, she twitched the dresses of those ladies, and played a thousand other tricks. The contrast of these childish pranks with the solemnity which reigned over the rest of the Queen's chamber disconcerted her Majesty; she several times placed her fan before her face to hide an involuntary smile, and the severe old ladies pronounced that the young Queen had derided all those respectable persons who were pressing forward to pay their homage to her; that she liked none but the young; that she was deficient in decorum; and that not one of them would attend her Court again. The epithet *moqueuse* was applied to her; and there is no epithet less favourably received in the world.

The next day a very ill-natured song was circulated; the stamp of the party to which it was attributable might easily be seen upon it. I remember only the following chorus:

" Little Queen, you must not be
So saucy, with your twenty years ;

Your ill-used courtiers soon will see
You pass, once more, the barriers.
Fal lal lal, fal lal la."

The errors of the great, or those which ill-nature chooses to impute to them, circulate in the world with the greatest rapidity, and become historical traditions, which every one delights to repeat. More than fifteen years after this occurrence I heard some old ladies in the most retired part of Auvergne relating all the particulars of the day of public condolence for the late King, on which, as they said, the Queen had laughed in the faces of the sexagenarian duchesses and princesses who had thought it their duty to appear on the occasion.

The King and the Princes, his brothers, determined to avail themselves of the advantages held out by inoculation, as a safeguard against the illness under which their grandfather had just fallen; but the utility of this new discovery not being then generally acknowledged in France, many persons were greatly alarmed at the step; those who blamed it openly threw all the responsibility of it upon the Queen, who alone, they said, could have ventured to give such rash advice, inoculation being at this time established in the Northern Courts. The operation upon the King and his brothers, performed by Doctor Jauberthou, was fortunately quite successful.

When the convalescence of the Princes was perfectly established, the excursions to Marly became cheerful enough. Parties on horseback and in calashes were formed continually. The Queen was desirous to afford herself one very innocent gratification; she had never seen the day break; and having now no other consent than that of the King to seek, she intimated her wish to him. He agreed that she should go, at three o'clock in the morning, to the eminences of the gardens of Marly; and, unfortunately, little disposed to partake in her amusements, he himself went to bed. Foreseeing some inconveniences possible in this nocturnal party, the Queen determined on having a number of people with her; and even ordered her waiting women to accompany her. All precautions were ineffectual to prevent the effects of calumny, which thenceforward sought to diminish the general attachment that she had inspired. A few days afterwards, the most wicked libel that appeared during the earlier years of her reign was circulated in Paris. The blackest colours were employed to paint an enjoyment so harmless that there is scarcely a young woman living in the country who has not endeavoured to procure it for herself. The verses which appeared on this occasion were entitled "Sunrise."[1]

The Duc d'Orléans, then Duc de Chartres, was among those who accompanied the young Queen in her nocturnal ramble: he appeared very attentive to her at this epoch; but it was the only moment of his life in which there was any advance towards intimacy between the Queen and himself. The King disliked the character of the Duc de Chartres, and the Queen always excluded him from her private society. It is therefore without the slightest foundation that some writers have attributed to feelings of jealousy or wounded self-love the hatred which he displayed towards the Queen during the latter years of their existence.

---

1. It was thus, with libels and ill-natured ballads, that the enemies of Marie Antoinette hailed the first days of her reign. They exerted themselves every way to render her unpopular. Their aim was, beyond all doubt, to have her sent back to Germany; and there was not a moment to be lost in its accomplishment. That the indifference of the King towards his amiable and beautiful wife had lasted so long, was already a matter of wonder; day after day it was to be expected that the seductive charms of Marie Antoinette would undo all their machinations.

It was on this first journey to Marly that Bœhmer, the jeweller, appeared at Court,—a man whose stupidity and avarice afterwards fatally affected the happiness and reputation of Marie Antoinette. This person had, at great expense, collected six pear-formed diamonds of a prodigious size; they were perfectly matched and of the finest water. The earrings which they composed had, before the death of Louis XV, been destined for the Comtesse du Barry.

Bœhmer, by the recommendation of several persons about the Court, came to offer these jewels to the Queen. He asked four hundred thousand francs for them. The young Princess could not withstand her wish to purchase them; and the King having just raised the Queen's income, which, under the former reign, had been but two hundred thousand livres, to one hundred thousand crowns a year, she wished to make the purchase out of her own purse, and not burden the royal treasury with the payment. She proposed to Bœhmer to take off the two buttons which formed the tops of the clusters, as they could be replaced by two of her own diamonds. He consented, and then reduced the price of the earrings to three hundred and sixty thousand francs; the payment for which was to be made by instalments, and was discharged in the course of four or five years by the Queen's first *femme de chambre*, deputed to manage the funds of her privy purse. I have omitted no details as to the manner in which the Queen first became possessed of these jewels, deeming them very needful to place in its true light the too famous circumstance of the necklace, which happened near the end of her reign.

It was also on this first journey to Marly that the Duchesse de Chartres, afterwards Duchesse d'Orléans, introduced into the Queen's household Mademoiselle Bertin, a milliner who became celebrated at that time for the total change she effected in the dress of the French ladies.

It may be said that the mere admission of a milliner into the house of the Queen was followed by evil consequences to her Majesty. The skill of the milliner, who was received into the household, in spite of the custom which kept persons of her description out of it, afforded her the opportunity of introducing some new fashion every day. Up to this time the Queen had shown very plain taste in dress; she now began to make it a principal occupation; and she was of course imitated by other women.

All wished instantly to have the same dress as the Queen, and to wear the feathers and flowers to which her beauty, then in its brilliancy, lent an indescribable charm. The expenditure of the younger ladies was necessarily much increased; mothers and husbands murmured at it; some few giddy women contracted debts; unpleasant domestic scenes occurred; in many families coldness or quarrels arose; and the general report was,—that the Queen would be the ruin of all the French ladies.

Fashion continued its fluctuating progress; and headdresses, with their superstructures of gauze, flowers, and feathers, became so lofty that the women could not find carriages high enough to admit them; and they were often seen either stooping, or holding their heads out of the windows. Others knelt down in order to manage these elevated objects of ridicule with less danger. Innumerable caricatures, exhibited in all directions, and some of which artfully gave the features of the Queen, attacked the extravagance of fashion, but with very little effect. It changed only, as is always the case, through the influence of inconstancy and time.

The Queen's toilet was a masterpiece of etiquette; everything was done in a prescribed form. Both the *dame d'honneur* and the *dame d'atours* usually attended and officiated, assisted by the first *femme de chambre* and two ordinary women. The *dame d'atours* put on the petticoat, and handed the gown to the Queen. The *dame d'honneur* poured out the water for her hands and put on her linen. When a princess of the royal family happened to be present while the Queen was dressing, the *dame d'honneur* yielded to her the latter act of office, but still did not yield it directly to the Princesses of the blood; in such a case the *dame d'honneur* was accustomed to present the linen to the first *femme de chambre*, who, in her turn, handed it to the Princess of the blood. Each of these ladies observed these rules scrupulously as affecting her rights. One winter's day it happened that the Queen, who was entirely undressed, was just going to put on her shift; I held it ready unfolded for her; the *dame d'honneur* came in, slipped off her gloves, and took it. A scratching was heard at the door; it was opened, and in came the Duchesse d'Orléans: her gloves were taken off, and she came forward to take the garment; but as it would have been wrong in the *dame d'honneur* to hand it to her she gave it to me, and I handed it to the Princess. More scratching: it was Madame la Comtesse de Provence; the Duchesse d'Orléans handed her the linen. All this while the Queen kept her arms crossed upon her bosom, and appeared to feel cold; Madame observed her uncomfortable situation, and, merely laying down her handkerchief without taking off her gloves, she put on the linen, and in doing so knocked the Queen's cap off. The Queen laughed to conceal her impatience, but not until she had muttered several times, "How disagreeable! how tiresome!"

All this etiquette, however inconvenient, was suitable to the royal dignity, which expects to find servants in all classes of persons, beginning even with the brothers and sisters of the monarch.

Speaking here of etiquette, I do not allude to majestic state, appointed for days of ceremony in all Courts. I mean those minute ceremonies that were pursued towards our Kings in their inmost privacies, in their hours of pleasure, in those of pain, and even during the most revolting of human infirmities.

These servile rules were drawn up into a kind of code; they offered to a Richelieu, a La Rochefoucauld and a Duras, in the exercise of their domestic functions, opportunities of intimacy useful to their interests; and their vanity was flattered by customs which converted the right to give a glass of water, to put on a dress, and to remove a basin, into honourable prerogatives.[1]

Princes thus accustomed to be treated as divinities naturally ended by believing that they were of a distinct nature, of a purer essence than the rest of mankind.

This sort of etiquette, which led our Princes to be treated in private as idols, made them in public martyrs to decorum. Marie Antoinette found in the Château of Versailles a multitude of established customs which appeared to her insupportable.

The ladies-in-waiting, who were all obliged to be sworn, and to wear full Court dresses, were alone entitled to remain in the room, and to attend in conjunction with

---

1. When the Queen took medicine, it was customary for the lady of honour to remove the basin from the bed.

the *dame d'honneur* and the tirewoman. The Queen abolished all this formality. When her head was dressed, she curtsied to all the ladies who were in her chamber, and, followed only by her own women, went into her closet, where Mademoiselle Bertin, who could not be admitted into the chamber, used to await her. It was in this inner closet that she produced her new and numerous dresses. The Queen was also desirous of being served by the most fashionable hairdresser in Paris. Now the custom which forbade all persons in inferior offices, employed by royalty, to exert their talents for the public, was no doubt intended to cut off all communication between the privacy of princes and society at large; the latter being always extremely curious respecting the most trifling particulars relative to the private life of the former. The Queen, fearing that the taste of the hairdresser would suffer if he should discontinue the general practice of his art, ordered him to attend as usual certain ladies of the Court and of Paris; and this multiplied the opportunities of learning details respecting the household, and very often of misrepresenting them.

One of the customs most disagreeable to the Queen was that of dining every day in public. Maria Leczinska had always submitted to this wearisome practice; Marie Antoinette followed it as long as she was Dauphiness. The Dauphin dined with her, and each branch of the family had its public dinner daily. The ushers suffered all decently dressed people to enter; the sight was the delight of persons from the country. At the dinner-hour there were none to be met upon the stairs but honest folks, who, after having seen the Dauphiness take her soup, went to see the Princes eat their *bouilli*, and then ran themselves out of breath to behold Mesdames at their dessert.[1]

Very ancient usage, too, required that the Queens of France should appear in public surrounded only by women; even at meal-times no persons of the other sex attended to serve at table; and although the King ate publicly with the Queen, yet he himself was served by women with everything which was presented to him directly at table. The *dame d'honneur*, kneeling, for her own accommodation, upon a low stool, with a napkin upon her arm, and four women in full dress, presented the plates to the King and Queen. The *dame d'honneur* handed them drink. This service had formerly been the right of the maids of honour. The Queen, upon her accession to the throne, abolished the usage altogether. She also freed herself from the necessity of being followed in the Palace of Versailles by two of her women in Court dresses, during those hours of the day when the ladies-in-waiting were not with her. From that time she was accompanied only by a single *valet de chambre* and two footmen. All the changes made by Marie Antoinette were of the same description; a disposition gradually to substitute the simple customs of Vienna for those of Versailles was more injurious to her than she could possibly have imagined.

When the King slept in the Queen's apartment he always rose before her; the exact hour was commuicated to the head *femme de chambre*, who entered, preceded by a

---

1. It will be imagined that the charms of conversation, cheerfulness, and good-natured freedom, which in France contribute to the pleasures of the table, were strangers to these ceremonious repasts. In fact it was necessary to have been habituated from infancy to eat in public, in order to avoid loss of appetite from being the object to which the eyes of so many strangers were directed.

servant of the bedchamber bearing a taper; she crossed the room and unbolted the door which separated the Queen's apartment from that of he King. She there found the first *valet de chambre* for the quarter, and a servant of the chamber. They entered, opened the bed curtains on the King's side, md presented him slippers generally, as well as the dressing-gown, which he put on, of gold or silver stuff. The first *valet de chambre* took down a short sword which was always laid within the railing on the King's side. When the King slept with the Queen, this sword was brought upon the arm-chair appropriated to the King, and which was placed near the Queen's bed, within the gilt railing which surrounded the bed. The first *femme de chambre* conducted the King to the door, bolted it again, and, leaving the Queen's chamber, did not return until the hour appointed by her Majesty the evening before. At night the Queen went to bed before the King; the first *femme de chambre* remained seated at the foot of her bed until the arrival of his Majesty, in order, as in the morning, to see the King's attendants out and bolt the door after them. The Queen awoke habitually at eight o'clock, and breakfasted at nine, frequently in bed, and sometimes after she had risen, at a table placed opposite her couch.

In order to describe the Queen's private service intelligibly, it must be recollected that *service* of every kind was *honour*, and had not any other denomination. *To do the honours of the service* was to present the service to a person of superior rank, who happened to arrive at the moment it was about to be performed. Thus, supposing the Queen asked for a glass of water, the servant of the chamber handed to the first woman a silver gilt waiter, upon which were placed a covered goblet and a small decanter; but should the lady of honour come in, the first woman was obliged to present the waiter to her, and if Madame or the Comtesse de'Artois came in at the moment, the waiter went again from the lady of honour into the hands of the Princess before it reached the Queen. It must be observed, however, that if a princess of the blood instead of a princess of the family entered, the service went directly from the first woman to the princess of the blood, the lady of honour being excused from transferring to any but princesses of the royal family. Nothing was presented directly to the Queen; her handkerchief or her gloves were placed upon a long salver of gold or silver gilt, which was placed as a piece of furniture of ceremony upon a side-table, and was called a *gantière*. The first woman presented to her in this manner all that she asked for, unless the tirewoman, the lady of honour, or a princess were present, and then the gradation pointed out in the instance of the glass of water was always observed.

Whether the Queen breakfasted in bed or up, those entitled to the *petites entrées* were equally admitted; this privilege belonged of right to her chief physician, chief surgeon, physician in ordinary, reader, closet secretary, the King's four first *valets de chambre* and their reversioners, and the King's chief physicians and surgeons. There were frequently from ten to twelve persons at this first *entrée*. The lady of honour or the superintendent, if present, placed the breakfast equipage upon the bed; the Princesse de Lamballe frequently performed that office.

As soon as the Queen rose, the wardrobe woman was admitted to take away the pillows and prepare the bed to be made by some of the *valets de chambre*. She undrew the curtains, and the bed was not generally made until the Queen was gone to mass. Generally, excepting at St. Cloud, where the Queen bathed in an apartment below her own, a slipper bath was rolled into her room, and her bathers brought, everything that was necessary for the bath. The Queen bathed in a large gown of English flannel buttoned down to the bottom; its sleeves throughout, as well as the collar, were lined with linen. When she came out of the bath the first woman held up a cloth to conceal her entirely from the sight of her women, and then threw it over her shoulders. The bathers wrapped her in it and dried her completely. She then put on a long and wide open chemise, entirely trimmed with lace, and afterwards a white taffety bed-gown. The wardrobe woman warmed the bed; the slippers were of dimity, trimmed with lace. Thus dressed, the Queen went to bed again, and the bathers and servants of the chamber took away the bathing apparatus. The Queen, replaced in bed, took a book or her tapestry work. On her bathing mornings she breakfasted in the bath. The tray was placed on the cover of the bath. These minute details are given here only to do justice to the Queen's scrupulous modesty. Her temperance was equally remarkable; she breakfasted on coffee or chocolate; at dinner ate nothing but white meat, drank water only, and supped on broth, a wing of a fowl, and small biscuits, which she soaked in a glass of water.

The tirewoman had under her order a principal under-tirewoman, charged with the care and preservation of all the Queen's dresses; two women to fold and press such articles as required it; two valets, and a porter of the wardrobe. The latter brought every morning into the Queen's apartments baskets covered with taffety, containing all that she was to wear during the day, and large cloths of green taffety covering the robes and the full dresses. The valet of the wardrobe on duty presented every morning a large book to the first *femme de chambre*, containing patterns of the gowns, full dresses, undresses, etc. Every pattern was marked, to show to which sort it belonged. The first *femme de chambre* presented this book to the Queen on her awaking, with a pincushion; her Majesty stuck pins in those articles which she chose for the day,—one for the dress, one for the afternoon undress, and one for the full evening dress for card or supper parties in the private apartments. The book was then taken back to the wardrobe, and all that was wanted for the day was soon after brought in in large taffety wrappers. The wardrobe woman, who had the care of the linen, in her turn brought in a covered basket containing two or three chemises and handkerchiefs. The morning basket was called *prêt du jour*. In the evening she brought in one containing the nightgown and nightcap, and the stockings for the next morning; this basket was called *prêt de la nuit*. They were in the department of the lady of honour, the tirewoman having nothing to do with the linen. Nothing was put in order or taken care of by the Queen's women. As soon as the toilet was over, the valets and porter belonging to the wardrobe were called in, and they carried all away in a heap, in the taffety wrappers, to the tirewoman's wardrobe, where all were folded up again, hung up, examined, and cleaned with so much regularity and care that even the cast-off clothes scarcely looked as if they had been worn. The tirewoman's wardrobe consisted of three large rooms surrounded with closets, some furnished with drawers and others with shelves; there were also large tables in each of these rooms, on which the gowns and dresses were spread out and folded up.

For the winter the Queen had generally twelve full dresses, twelve undresses called fancy dresses, and twelve rich hoop petticoats for the card and supper parties in the smaller apartments.

She had as many for the summer; those for the spring served likewise for the autumn. All these dresses were discarded at the end of each season, unless, indeed, she retained some that she particularly liked. I am not speaking of muslin or cambric gowns, or others of the same kind—they were lately introduced; but such as these were not renewed at each returning season, they were kept several years. The chief women were charged with the care and examination of the diamonds; this important duty was formerly confided to the tirewoman, but for many years had been included in the business of the first *femmes de chambre*.

The public toilet took place at noon. The toilet-table was drawn forward into the middle of the room. This piece of furniture was generally the richest and most ornamented of all in the apartment of the Princesses. The Queen used it in the same manner and place for undressing herself in the evening. She went to bed in corsets trimmed with ribbon, and sleeves trimmed with lace, and wore a large neck handkerchief. The Queen's combing cloth was presented by her first woman if she was alone at the commencement of the toilet; or, as well as the other articles, by the ladies of honour if they were come. At noon the women who had been in attendance four and twenty hours were relieved by two women in full dress; the first woman went also to dress herself. The *grandes entrées* were admitted during the toilet; sofas were placed in circles for the superintendent, the ladies of honour, and tirewomen, and the governess of the children of France when she came there; the duties of the ladies of the bed-chamber, having nothing to do with any kind of domestic or private functions, did not begin until the hour of going out to mass; they waited in the great closet, and entered when the toilet was over. The Princes of the blood, captains of the Guards, and all great officers having the entry paid their court at the hour of the toilet. The Queen saluted by nod-ding her head or bending her body, or leaning upon her toilet-table as if moving to rise; the last mode of salutation was for the Princes of the blood. The King's brothers also came very generally to pay their respects to her Majesty while her hair was being dressed. In the earlier years of the reign the first part of the dressing was performed in the bedchamber and according to the laws of etiquette; that is to say, the lady of honour put on the chemise and poured out the water for the hands, the tirewoman put on the skirt of the gown or full dress, adjusted the handkerchief, and tied on the necklace. But when the young Queen became more seriously devot-ed to fashion, and the head-dress attained so extravagant a height that it became necessary to put on the chemise from below,—when, in short, she determined to have her milli-ner, Mademoiselle Bertin, with her whilst she was dressing, whom the ladies would have refused to admit to any share in the honour of attending on the Queen, the dressing in the bedchamber was discontinued, and the Queen, leaving her toilet, withdrew into her closet to dress.

On returning into her chamber, the Queen, standing about the middle of it, surrounded by the superintendent, the ladies of honour and tirewomen, her ladies of the palace, the *chevalier d'honneur*, the chief equerry, her clergy ready to at-tend her to mass, and the Princesses of the royal family who happened to come, accompanied by all their chief attendants and, ladies, passed in order into the gallery as in going to mass. The Queen's signatures were generally given at the moment of entry into the chamber. The secretary for orders presented the pen. Presentations of colonels on taking leave were usually made at this time. Those of ladies, and such as had a right to the tabouret, or sitting in the royal presence, were made on Sunday evenings before card-playing began, on their coming in from paying their respects. Ambassadors were introduced to the Queen on Tuesday mornings, accompanied by the introducer of ambassadors on duty, and by M. de Sequeville, the secretary for the ambassadors. The introducer in waiting usually came to the Queen at her toilet to apprise her of the presentations of foreigners which would be made. The usher of the chamber, stationed at the entrance, opened the folding doors to none but the Princes and Princesses of the royal family, and announced them aloud. Quitting his post, he came forward to name to the lady of honour the persons who came to be presented, or who came to take leave; that lady again named them to the Queen at the moment they saluted her; if she and the tirewoman were absent, the first woman took the place and did that duty. The ladies of the bedchamber, chosen solely as companions for the Queen, had no domestic duties to fulfil, however opinion might dignify such offices. The King's letter in appointing them, among other instructions of etiquette, ran thus: "Having chosen you to bear the Queen company." There were hardly any emoluments accruing from this place.

The Queen heard mass with the King in the tribune, facing the grand altar and the choir, with the exception of the days of high ceremony, when their chairs were placed below upon velvet carpets fringed with gold. These days were marked by the name of *grand chapel days*.

The Queen named the collector beforehand, and informed her of it through her lady of honour, who was besides desired to send the purse to her. The collectors were almost always chosen from among those who had been recently presented. After returning from mass the Queen dined every Sunday with the King only, in public in the cabinet of the nobility, a room leading to her chamber. Titled ladies having the honours sat during the dinner upon folding-chairs placed on each side of the table. Ladies without titles stood round the table; the captain of the Guards and the first gentlemen of the chamber were behind the King's chair; behind that of the Queen were her first *maître d'hôtel*, her *chevalier d'honneur*, and the chief equerry. The Queen's *maître d'hôtel* was furnished with a large staff, six or seven feet in length, ornamented with golden *fleurs-de-lis*, and surmounted by *fleurs-de-lis* in the form of a crown. He entered the room with this badge of his office to announce that the Queen was served. The comptroller put into his hands the card of the dinner; in the absence of the *maître d'hôtel* he presented it to the Queen himself, otherwise he only did him the honours of the service. The *maître d'hôtel* did not leave his place, he merely gave the orders for serving up and removing; the comptroller and gentlemen serving placed the various dishes upon the table, receiving them from the inferior servants.

The Prince nearest to the crown presented water to wash the King's hands at the moment he placed himself at table, and a princess did the same service to the Queen.

The table service was formerly performed for the Queen by the lady of honour and four women in full dress; this part of the women's service was transferred to them on the suppression of the office of maids of honour. The Queen put an end to this etiquette in the first year of her reign. When the dinner was over the Queen returned without the King to her apartment with her women, and took off her hoop and train.

This unfortunate Princess, against whom the opinions of the French people were at length so much excited, possessed qualities which deserved to obtain the greatest popularity. None could doubt this who, like myself, had heard her with delight describe the partriarchal manners of the House of Lorraine. She was accustomed to say that, by transplanting their manners into Austria, the Princes of that house had laid the foundation of the unassailable popularity enjoyed by the imperial family. She frequently related to me the interesting manner in which the Ducs de Lorraine levied the taxes. "The sovereign Prince," said she, "went to church; after the sermon he rose, waved his hat in the air, to show that he was about to speak, and then mentioned the sum whereof he stood in need. Such was the zeal of the good Lorrainers that men have been known to take away linen or household utensils without the knowledge of their wives, and sell them to add the value to their contribution. It sometimes happened, too, that the Prince received more money than he had asked for, in which case he restored the surplus."

All who were acquainted with the Queen's private qualities knew that she equally deserved attachment and esteem. Kind and patient to excess in her relations with her household, she indulgently considered all around her, and interested herself in their fortunes and in their pleasures. She had, among her women, young girls from the Maison de St. Cyr, all well born; the Queen forbade them the play when the performances were not suitable; sometimes, when old plays were to be represented, if she found she could not with certainty trust to her memory, she would take the trouble to read them in the morning, to enable her to decide whether the girls should or should not go to see them,—rightly considering herself bound to watch over their morals and conduct.

VI

D URING the first few months of his reign Louis
XVI dwelt at La Muette, Marly, and Compiègne.
When settled at Versailles he occupied himself
with a general examination of his grandfather's papers. He
had promised the Queen to communicate to her all that he
might discover relative to the history of the man with the
iron mask, who, he thought, had become so inexhaustible
a source of conjecture only in consequence of the interest
which the pen of a celebrated writer had excited respecting
the detention of a prisoner of State, who was merely a man
of whimsical tastes and habits.

I was with the Queen when the King, having finished
his researches, informed her that he had not found anything
among the secret papers elucidating the existence of this
prisoner; that he had conversed on the matter with M. de
Maurepas, whose age made him contemporary with the epoch during which the story must have been known to the

ministers; and that M. de Maurepas had assured him he was merely a prisoner of a very dangerous character, in consequence of his disposition for intrigue. He was a subject of the Duke of Mantua, and was enticed to the frontier, arrested there, and kept prisoner, first at Pignerol, and afterwards in the Bastille. This transfer took place in consequence of the appointment of the governor of the former place to the government of the latter. It was for fear the prisoner should profit by the inexperience of a new governor that he was sent with the Governor of Pignerol to the Bastille.

Such was, in fact, the truth about the man on whom people have been pleased to fix an iron mask. And thus was it related in writing, and published by M.— twenty years ago. He had searched the archives of the Foreign Office, and laid the real story before the public; but the public, prepossessed in favour of a marvellous version, would not acknowledge the authenticity of his account. Every man relied upon the authority of Voltaire; and it was believed that a natural or a twin brother of Louis XIV lived many years in prison with a mask over his face. The story of this mask, perhaps, had its origin in the old custom, among both men and women in Italy, of wearing a velvet mask when they exposed themselves to the sun. It is possible that the Italian captive may have sometimes shown himself upon the terrace of his prison with his face thus covered. As to the silver plate which this celebrated prisoner is said to have thrown from his window, it is known that such a circumstance did happen, but it happened at Valzin, in the time of Cardinal Richelieu. This anecdote has been mixed up with the inventions respecting the Piedmontese prisoner.

In this survey of the papers of Louis XV by his grandson some very curious particulars relative to his private treasury were found. Shares in various financial companies afforded him a revenue, and had in course of time produced him a capital of some amount, which he applied to his secret expenses. The King collected his vouchers of title to these shares, and made a present of them to M. Thierry de Ville d'Avray, his chief *valet de chambre*.

The Queen was desirous to secure the comfort of Mesdames, the daughters of Louis XV who were held in the highest respect. About this period she contributed to furnish them with a revenue sufficient to provide them an easy, pleasant existence. The King gave them the Château of Bellevue; and added to the produce of it, which was given up to them, the expenses of their table and equipage, and payment of all the charges of their household, the number of which was even increased. During the lifetime of Louis XV, who was a very selfish prince, his daughters, although they had attained forty years of age, had no other place of residence than their apartments in the Château of Versailles; no other walks than such as they could take in the large park of that palace; and no other means of gratifying their taste for the cultivation of plants but by having boxes and vases, filled with them, in their balconies or their closets. They had, therefore, reason to be much pleased with the conduct of Marie Antoinette, who had the greatest influence in the King's kindness towards his aunts.

Paris did not cease, during the first years of the reign, to give proofs of pleasure whenever the Queen appeared at any of the plays of the capital. At the representation of "Iphigenia in Aulis," the actor who sang the words, "Let us

THE PRIVATE LIFE OF MARIE ANTOINETTE

sing, let us celebrate our Queen!" which were repeated by
the chorus, directed by a respectful movement the eyes of
the whole assembly upon her Majesty. Reiterated cries of
Bis! and clapping of hands, were followed by such a burst of
enthusiasm that many of the audience added their voices to
those of the actors in order to celebrate, it might too truly be
said, another Iphigenia. The Queen, deeply affected, covered
her eyes with her handkerchief; and this proof of sensibility
raised the public enthusiasm to a still higher pitch.

The King gave Marie Antoinette Petit Trianon.[1]
Henceforward she amused herself with improving the
gardens, without allowing any addition to the building, or
any change in the furniture, which was very shabby, and
remained, in 1789, in the same state as during the reign of
Louis XV. Everything there, without exception, was preserved; and the Queen slept in a faded bed, which had been
used by the Comtesse du Barry. The charge of extravagance,
generally made against the Queen, is the most unaccount-
able of all the popular errors respecting her character.[2] She
had exactly the contrary failing; and I could prove that she
often carried her economy to a degree of parsimony actually
blamable, especially in a sovereign. She took a great liking

1. The seat called Petit Trianon, which was built for Louis XV, is not remarkably handsome as a
building. The luxuriance of the hot-houses rendered the place agreeable to that prince. He spent a
few days there several times in the year. It was while he was setting off from Versailles for Petit Trianon, that he was struck in the side by the knife of Damiens; and it was there that he was attacked
by smallpox, of which disorder he died on the 10th of May, 1774.

2. This charge of prodigality, so unjustly laid against the Queen, was spread with such industry
throughout France and all Europe, that is must have been a part of the scheme for rendering the
court solely responsible for the bad state of the finances.

for Trianon, and used to go there alone, followed by a valet; but she found attendants ready to receive her,—a *concierge* and his wife, who served her as *femme de chambre*, women of the wardrobe, footmen, etc.

When she first took possession of Petit Trianon, it was reported that she changed the name of the seat which the King had given her, and called it *Little Vienna*, or *Little Schœnbrunn*. A person who belonged to the Court, and was silly enough to give this report credit, wishing to visit Petit Trianon with a party, wrote to M. Campan, requesting the Queen's permission to do so. In his note he called Trianon *Little Vienna*. Similar requests were usually laid before the Queen just as they were made: she chose to give the permissions to see her gardens herself, liking to grant these little favours. When she came to the words I have quoted she was very much offended, and exclaimed, angrily, that there were too many fools ready to aid the malicious; that she had been told of the report circulated, which pretended that she had thought of nothing but her own country, and that she kept an Austrian heart, while the interests of France alone ought to engage her. She refused the request so awkwardly made, and desired M. Campan to reply that Trianon was not to be seen for some time, and that the Queen was astonished that any man in good society should believe she would do so ill-judged a thing as to change the French names of her palaces to foreign ones.

Before the Emperor Joseph II's first visit to France the Queen received a visit from the Archduke Maximilian in 1775. A stupid act of the ambassador, seconded on the part of the Queen by the Abbé de Vermond, gave rise at that period to a discussion which offended the Princes of the blood and the chief nobility of the kingdom. Travelling incognito, the young Prince claimed that the first visit was not due from him to the Princes of the blood; and the Queen supported his pretension.

From the time of the Regency, and on account of the residence of the family of Orléans in the bosom of the capital, Paris had preserved a remarkable degree of attachment and respect for that branch of the royal house; and although the crown was becoming more and more remote from the Princes of the House of Orléans, they had the advantage (a great one with the Parisians) of being the descendants of Henri IV. An affront to that popular family was a serious ground of dislike to the Queen. It was at this period that the circles of the city, and even of the Court, expressed themselves bitterly about her levity, and her partiality for the House of Austria. The Prince for whom the Queen had embarked in an important family quarrel—and a quarrel involving national prerogatives—was, besides, little calculated to inspire interest. Still young, uninformed, and deficient in natural talent, he was always making blunders.

He went to the Jardin du Roi; M. de Buffon, who received him there, offered him a copy of his works; the Prince declined accepting the book, saying to M. de Buffon, in the most polite manner possible, "I should be very sorry to deprive you of it." It may be supposed that the Parisians were much entertained with this answer.

The Queen was exceedingly mortified at the mistakes made by her brother; but what hurt her most was being accused of preserving an Austrian heart, Marie Antoinette had more than once to endure that imputation during the long course of her misfortunes. Habit did not stop the tears such injustice caused; but the first time she was suspected of not loving France, she gave way to her indignation. All that she could say on the subject was useless; by seconding the pretensions of the Archduke she had put arms into her enemies' hands; they were labouring to deprive her of the love of the people, and endeavoured, by all possible means, to spread a belief that the Queen sighed for Germany, and preferred that country to France.

Marie Antoinette had none but herself to rely on for preserving the fickle smiles of the Court and the public. The King, too indifferent to serve her as a guide, as yet had conceived no love for her, notwithstanding the intimacy that grew between them at Choisy. In his closet Louis XVI was immersed in deep study. At the Council he was busied with the welfare of his people; hunting and mechanical occupations engrossed his leisure moments, and he never thought on the subject of an heir.

The coronation took place at Rheims, with all the accustomed pomp. At this period the people's love for Louis XVI burst forth in transports not to be mistaken for party demonstrations or idle curiosity. He replied to this enthusiasm by marks of confidence, worthy of a people happy in being governed by a good King; he took a pleasure in repeatedly walking without guards, in the midst of the crowd which pressed around him, and called down blessings on his head. I remarked the impression made at this time by an observation of Louis XVI. On the day of his coronation he put his hand up to his head, at the moment of the crown being placed upon it, and said, "It pinches me." Henri III, had exclaimed, "It pricks me." Those who were near the King were struck with the similarity between these two exclamations, though not of a class likely to be blinded by the superstitious fears of ignorance.

While the Queen, neglected as she was, could not even hope for the happiness of being a mother, she had the mortification of seeing the Comtesse d'Artois give birth to the Duc d'Angoulême.

Custom required that the royal family and the whole Court should be present at the *accouchement* of the Princesses; the Queen was therefore obliged to stay a whole day in her sister-in-law's chamber. The moment the Comtesse d'Artois was informed a prince was born, she put her hand to her forehead and exclaimed with energy, "My God, how happy I am!" The Queen felt very differently at this involuntary and natural exclamation. Nevertheless, her behaviour was perfect. She bestowed all possible marks of tenderness upon the young mother, and would not leave her until she was again put into bed; she afterwards passed along the staircase, and through the hall of the guards, with a calm demeanour, in the midst of an immense crowd. The *poissardes*, who had assumed a right of speaking to sovereigns in their own vulgar language, followed her to the very doors of her apartments, calling out to her with gross expressions, that she ought to produce heirs. The Queen reached her inner room, hurried and agitated; she shut herself up to weep with me alone, not from jealousy of her sister-in-law's happiness,—of that she was incapable,—but from sorrow at her own situation.

Deprived of the happiness of giving an heir to the crown, the Queen endeavoured to interest herself in the children of the people of her household. She had long been desirous to bring up one of them herself, and to make it the constant object of her care. A little village boy, four or five years old, full of health, with a pleasing countenance, remarkably large blue eyes, and fine light hair, got under the feet of the Queen's horses, when she was taking an airing in a calash, through the hamlet of St. Michel, near Louveciennes. The coachman and postilions stopped the horses, and the child was rescued without the slightest injury. Its grandmother rushed out of the door of her cottage to take it; but the Queen, standing up in her calash and extending her arms, called out that the child was hers, and that destiny had given it to her, to console her, no doubt, until she should have the happiness of having one herself. "Is his mother alive?" asked the Queen. "No, Madame; my daughter died last winter, and left five small children upon my hands." "I will take this one, and provide for all the rest; do you consent?" "Ah, Madame, they are too fortunate," replied the cottager; "but Jacques is a bad boy. I hope he will stay with you!" The Queen, taking little Jacques upon her knee, said that she would make him used to her, and gave orders to proceed. It was necessary, however, to shorten the drive, so violently did Jacques scream, and kick the Queen and her ladies.

The arrival of her Majesty at her apartments at Versailles, holding the little rustic by the hand, astonished the whole household; he cried out with intolerable shrillness that he wanted his grandmother, his brother Louis, and his sister Marianne; nothing could calm him. He was taken away by the wife of a servant, who was appointed to attend him as nurse. The other children were put to school. Little Jacques, whose family name was Armand, came back to the Queen two days afterwards; a white frock trimmed with lace, a rose-coloured sash with silver fringe, and a hat decorated with feathers, were now substituted for the woollen cap, the little red frock, and the wooden shoes. The child was really very beautiful. The Queen was enchanted with him; he was brought to her every morning at nine o'clock; he breakfasted and dined with her, and often even with the King. She liked to call him *my child*,[1] and lavished caresses upon him, still maintaining a deep silence respecting the regrets which constantly occupied her heart.

This child remained with the Queen until the time when Madame was old enough to come home to her august mother, who had particularly taken upon herself the care of her education.

The Queen talked incessantly of the qualities which she admired in Louis XVI, and gladly attributed to herself the slightest favourable change in his manner; perhaps she displayed too unreservedly the joy she felt, and the share she appropriated in the improvement. One day Louis XVI saluted her ladies with more kindness than usual, and the Queen laughingly said to them, "Now confess, ladies, that for one so badly taught as a child, the King has saluted you with very good grace!"

The Queen hated M. de La Vauguyon; she accused him alone of those points in the habits, and even the sentiments, of the King which hurt her. A former first woman of the bed-chamber to Queen Maria Leczinska had continued in office near the young Queen. She was one of those people who are fortunate enough to spend their lives in the service of kings

1. This little unfortunate was nearly twenty in 1792; the incendiary endeavours of the people, and the fear of being thought a favoured creature of the Queen, had made him the most sanguinary terrorist of Versailles. He was killed at the battle of Jemmapes.

without knowing anything of what is passing at Court. She was a great devotee; the Abbé Grisel, an ex-Jesuit, was her director. Being rich from her savings and an income of 50,000 livres, she kept a very good table; in her apartment, at the Grand Commun, the most distinguished persons who still adhered to the Order of Jesuits often assembled. The Duc de La Vauguyon was intimate with her; their chairs at the Eglise des Récollets were placed near each other; at high mass and at vespers they sang the "Gloria in Excelsis" and the "Magnificat" together; and the pious virgin, seeing in him only one of God's elect, little imagined him to be the declared enemy of a Princess whom she served and revered. On the day of his death she ran in tears to relate to the Queen the piety, humility, and repentance of the last moments of the Duc de La Vauguyon. He had called his people together, she said, to ask their pardon. "For what?" replied the Queen, sharply; "he has placed and pensioned off all his servants; it was of the King and his brothers that the holy man you bewail should have asked pardon, for having paid so little attention to the education of princes on whom the fate and happiness of twenty-five millions of men depend. Luckily," added she, "the King and his brothers, still young, have incessantly laboured to repair the errors of their preceptor."

The progress of time, and the confidence with which the King and the Princes, his brothers, were inspired by the change in their situation since the death of Louis XV, had developed their characters. I will endeavour to depict them.

The features of Louis XVI were noble enough, though somewhat melancholy in expression; his walk was heavy and unmajestic; his person greatly neglected; his hair, whatever might be the skill of his hairdresser, was soon in disorder.

His voice, without being harsh, was not agreeable; if he grew animated in speaking he often got above his natural pitch, and became shrill. The Abbé de Radonvilliers, his preceptor, one of the Forty of the French Academy, a learned and amiable man, had given him and Monsieur a taste for study. The King had continued to instruct himself; he knew the English language perfectly; I have often heard him translate some of the most difficult passages in Milton's poems. He was a skilful geographer, and was fond of drawing and colouring maps; he was well versed in history, but had not perhaps sufficiently studied the spirit of it. He appreciated dramatic beauties, and judged them accurately. At Choisy, one day, several ladies expressed their dissatisfaction because the French actors were going to perform one of Molière's pieces. The King inquired why they disapproved of the choice. One of them answered that everybody must admit that Molière had *very bad taste*; the King replied that many things might be found in Molière contrary to fashion, but that it appeared to him difficult to point out any in bad taste. This Prince combined with his attainments the attributes of a good husband, a tender father, and an indulgent master.

Unfortunately he showed too much predilection for the mechanical arts; masonry and lock-making so delighted him that he admitted into his private apartment a common locksmith, with whom he made keys and locks; and his hands, blackened by that sort of work, were often, in my presence, the subject of remonstrances and even sharp reproaches from the Queen, who would have chosen other amusements for her husband.

Austere and rigid with regard to himself alone, the King observed the laws of the Church with scrupulous exactness.

He fasted and abstained throughout the whole of Lent. He thought it right that the Queen should not observe these customs with the same strictness. Though sincerely pious, the spirit of the age had disposed his mind to toleration. Turgot, Malesherbes, and Necker judged that this Prince, modest and simple in his habits, would willingly sacrifice the royal prerogative to the solid greatness of his people. His heart, in truth, disposed him towards reforms; but his prejudices and fears, and the clamours of pious and privileged persons, intimidated him, and made him abandon plans which his love for the people had suggested.

Monsieur had more dignity of demeanour than the King; but his corpulence rendered his gait inelegant. He was fond of pageantry and magnificence. He cultivated the *belles lettres*, and under assumed names often contributed verses to the *Mercury* and other papers.

His wonderful memory was the handmaid of his wit, furnishing him with the happiest quotations. He knew by heart a varied repertoire, from the finest passages of the Latin classics to the Latin of all the prayers, from the works of Racine to the vaudeville of "Rose et Colas."

The Comte d'Artois had an agreeable countenance, was well made, skilful in bodily exercises, lively, impetuous, fond of pleasure, and very particular in his dress. Some happy observations made by him were repeated with approval, and gave a favourable idea of his heart. The Parisians liked the open and frank character of this Prince, which they considered national, and showed real affection for him.

The dominion that the Queen gained over the King's mind, the charms of a society in which Monsieur displayed his wit, and to which the Comte d'Artois gave life by the vivacity of youth, gradually softened that ruggedness of manner in Louis XVI which a better-conducted education might have prevented. Still, this defect often showed itself, and, in spite of his extreme simplicity, the King inspired those who had occasion to speak to him with diffidence. Courtiers, submissive in the presence of their sovereign, are only the more ready to caricature him; with little good breeding, they called those answers they so much dreaded, *les coups de boutoir du Roi.*

Methodical in all his habits, the King always went to bed at eleven precisely. One evening the Queen was going with her usual circle to a party, either at the Duc de Duras's or the Princesse de Guéménée's. The hand of the clock was slily put forward to hasten the King's departure by a few minutes; he thought bed-time was come, retired, and found none of his attendants ready to wait on him. This joke became known in all the drawing-rooms of Versailles, and was disapproved of there. Kings have no privacy. Queens have no boudoirs. If those who are in immediate attendance upon sovereigns be not themselves disposed to transmit their private habits to posterity, the meanest valet will relate what he has seen or heard; his gossip circulates rapidly, and forms public opinion, which at length ascribes to the most august persons characters which, however untrue they may be, are almost always indelible.

VII

T HE winter following the confinement of the Comtesse d'Artois was very severe; the recollections of the pleasure which sleighing-parties had given the Queen in her childhood made her wish to introduce similar ones in France. This amusement had already been known in that Court, as was proved by sleighs being found in the stables which had been used by the Dauphin, the father of Louis XVI. Some were constructed for the Queen in a more modern style. The Princes also ordered several; and in a few days there was a tolerable number of these vehicles. They were driven by the princes and noblemen of the Court. The noise of the bells and balls with which the harness of the horses was furnished, the elegance and whiteness of their plumes, the varied forms of the carriages, the gold with which they were all ornamented, rendered these parties delightful to the eye. The winter was very favourable to them, the snow remaining on the ground nearly six weeks;

the drives in the park afforded a pleasure shared by the spectators. No one imagined that any blame could attach to so innocent an amusement. But the party were tempted to extend their drives as far as the Champs-Elyséés ; a few sleighs even crossed the boulevards; the ladies being masked, the Queen's enemies took the opportunity of saying that she had traversed the streets of Paris in a sleigh.

This became a matter of moment. The public discovered in it a predilection for the habits of Vienna; but all that Marie Antoinette did was criticised.

Sleigh-driving, savouring of the Northern Courts, had no favour among the Parisians. The Queen was informed of this; and although all the sleighs were preserved, and several subsequent winters lent themselves to the amusement, she would not resume it.

It was at the time of the sleighing-parties that the Queen became intimately acquainted with the Princesse de Lamballe, who made her appearance in them wrapped in fur, with all the brilliancy and freshness of the age of twenty,—the emblem of spring, peeping from under sable and ermine. Her situation, moreover, rendered her peculiarly interesting; married, when she was scarcely past childhood, to a young prince, who ruined himself by the contagious example of the Duc d'Orléans, she had had nothing to do from the time of her arrival in France but to weep. A widow at eighteen, and childless, she lived with the Duc de Penthièvre as an adopted daughter. She had the tenderest respect and attachment for that venerable Prince; but the Queen, though doing justice to his virtues, saw that the Duc de Penthièvre's way of life, whether at Paris or at his country-seat, could neither afford his young daughter-in-law the amusements suited to her time of life, nor ensure her in the future an establishment such as she was deprived of by her widowhood. She determined, therefore, to establish her at Versailles; and for her sake revived the office of superintendent, which had been discontinued at Court since the death of Mademoiselle de Clermont. It is said that Maria Leczinska had decided that this place should continue vacant, the superintendent having so extensive a power in the houses of queens as to be frequently a restraint upon their inclinations. Differences which soon took place between Marie Antoinette and the Princesse de Lamballe respecting the official prerogatives of the latter, proved that the wife of Louis XV had acted judiciously in abolishing the office; but a kind of treaty made between the Queen and the Princess smoothed all difficulties. The blame for too strong an assertion of claims fell upon a secretary of the superintendent, who had been her adviser; and everything was so arranged that a firm friendship existed between these two Princesses down to the disastrous period which terminated their career.

Notwithstanding the enthusiasm which the splendour, grace, and kindness of the Queen generally inspired, secret intrigues continued in operation against her. A short time after the ascension of Louis XVI to the throne, the minister of the King's household was informed that a most offensive libel against the Queen was about to appear. The lieutenant of police deputed a man named Goupil, a police inspector, to trace this libel; he came soon after to say that he had found out the place where the work was being printed, and that it was at a country house near Yverdun. He had already got possession of two sheets, which contained the most atrocious calumnies, conveyed with a degree of art which might make them very dangerous to the Queen's reputation. Goupil said that he could obtain the rest, but that he should want a considerable sum for that purpose. Three thousand louis were given him, and very soon afterwards he brought the whole manuscript and all that had been printed to the lieutenant of police. He received a thousand louis more as a reward for his address and zeal; and a much more important office was about to be given him, when another spy, envious of Goupil's good fortune, gave information that Goupil himself was the author of the libel; that, ten years before, he had been put into the Bicêtre for swindling; and that Madame Goupil had been only three years out of the Salpétrière, where she had been placed under another name. This Madame Goupil was very pretty and very intriguing; she had found means to form an intimacy with Cardinal de Rohan, whom she led, it is said, to hope for a reconciliation with the Queen. All this affair was hushed up; but it shows that it was the Queen's fate to be incessantly attacked by the meanest and most odious machinations.

Another woman, named Cahouette de Villers, whose husband held an office in the Treasury, being very irregular in conduct, and of a scheming turn of mind, had a mania for appearing in the eyes of her friends at Paris as a person in favour at Court, to which she was not entitled by either birth or office. During the latter years of the life of Louis XV she had made many dupes, and picked up considerable sums by passing herself off as the King's mistress. The fear of irritating Madame du Barry was, according to her, the only thing which prevented her enjoying that title openly. She came regularly to Versailles, kept herself concealed in a furnished lodging, and her dupes imagined she was secretly summoned to Court.

This woman formed the scheme of getting admission, if possible, to the presence of the Queen, or at least causing it to be believed that she had done so. She adopted as her lover Gabriel de Saint Charles, intendant of her Majesty's finances,—an office, the privileges of which were confined to the right of entering the Queen's apartment on Sunday. Madame de Villers came every Saturday to Versailles with M. de Saint Charles, and lodged in his apartment. M. Campan was there several times. She painted tolerably well, and she requested him to do her the favour to present to the Queen a portrait of her Majesty which she had just copied. M. Campan knew the woman's character, and refused her. A few days after, he saw on her Majesty's couch the portrait which he had declined to present to her; the Queen thought it badly painted, and gave orders that it should be carried back to the Princesse de Lamballe, who had sent it to her. The ill success of the portrait did not deter the manœuvrer from following up her designs; she easily procured through M. de Saint Charles patents and orders signed by the Queen; she then set about imitating her writing, and composed a great number of notes and letters, as if written by her Majesty, in the tenderest and most familiar style. For many months she showed them as great secrets to several of her particular friends. Afterwards, she made the Queen appear to write to her, to procure various fancy articles. Under the pretext of wishing to execute her Majesty's commissions accurately, she gave these letters to the tradesmen to read, and succeeded in having it said, in many houses, that the Queen had a particular regard for her. She then enlarged her scheme, and represented the Queen as desiring to borrow 200,000 francs which she had need of, but which she did not wish to ask of the King from his private funds. This letter, being shown to M. Beranger, *fermier-général* of the finances, took effect;

he thought himself fortunate in being able to render this assistance to his sovereign, and lost no time in sending the 200,000 francs to Madame de Villers. This first step was followed by some doubts, which he communicated to people better informed than himself of what was passing at Court; they added to his uneasiness; he then went to M. de Sartine, who unravelled the whole plot. The woman was sent to St. Pelagie; and the unfortunate husband was ruined, by replacing the sum borrowed, and by paying for the jewels fraudulently purchased in the Queen's name. The forged letters were sent to her Majesty; I compared them in her presence with her own handwriting, and the only distinguishable difference was a little more regularity in the letters.

This trick, discovered and punished with prudence and without passion, produced no more sensation out of doors than that of the Inspector Goupil.

A year after the nomination of Madame de Lamballe to the post of superintendent of the Queen's household, balls and quadrilles gave rise to the intimacy of her Majesty with the Comtesse Jules de Polignac. This lady really interested Marie Antoinette. She was not rich, and generally lived upon her estate at Claye. The Queen was astonished at not having seen her at Court earlier. The confession that her want of fortune had even prevented her appearance at the celebration of the marriages of the Princes added to the interest which she had inspired.

The Queen was full of consideration, and took delight in counteracting the injustice of fortune. The Countess was induced to come to Court by her husband's sister, Madame Diane de Polignac, who had been appointed lady of honour to the Comtesse d'Artois. The Comtesse Jules was really fond of a tranquil life; the impression she made at Court affected her but little; she felt only the attachment manifested for her by the Queen. I had occasion to see her from the commencement of her favour at Court; she often passed whole hours with me, while waiting for the Queen. She conversed with me freely and ingenuously about the honour, and at the same time the danger, she saw in the kindness of which she was the object. The Queen sought for the sweets of friendship; but can this gratification, so rare in any rank, exist between a Queen and a subject,—when they are surrounded, moreover, by snares laid by the artifice of courtiers? This pardonable error was fatal to the happiness of Marie Antoinette.

The retiring character of the Comtesse Jules, afterwards Duchesse de Polignac, cannot be spoken of too favourably; but if her heart was incapable of forming ambitious projects, her family and friends in her fortune beheld their own, and endeavoured to secure the favour of the Queen.

The Comtesse de Diane, sister of M. de Polignac, and the Baron de Besenval and M. de Vaudreuil, particular friends of the Polignac family, made use of means, the success of which was infallible. One of my friends (Comte de Moustier), who was in their secret, came to tell me that Madame de Polignac was about to quit Versailles suddenly; that she would take leave of the Queen only in writing; that the Comtesse Diane and M. de Vaudreuil had dictated her letter, and the whole affair was arranged for the purpose of stimulating the attachment of Marie Antoinette. The next day, when I went up to the palace, I found the Queen with a letter in her hand, which she was reading with much emotion; it was the letter from the Comtesse Jules; the Queen showed it to me.

The Countess expressed in it her grief at leaving a princess who had loaded her with kindness. The narrowness of her fortune compelled her to do so; but she was much more strongly impelled by the fear that the Queen's friendship, after having raised up dangerous enemies against her, might abandon her to their hatred, and to the regret of having lost the august favour of which she was the object.

This step produced the full effect that had been expected from it. A young and sensitive queen cannot long bear the idea of contradiction. She busied herself in settling the Comtesse Jules near her, by making such a provision for her as should place her beyond anxiety. Her character suited the Queen; she had merely natural talents, no pedantry, no affectation of knowledge. She was of middle size; her complexion very fair, her eyebrows and hair dark brown, her teeth superb, her smile enchanting, and her whole person graceful. She was seen almost always in a demi-toilet, remarkable only for neatness and good taste. I do not think I ever once saw diamonds about her, even at the climax of her fortune, when she had the rank of Duchess at Court. I have always believed that her sincere attachment for the Queen, as much as her love of simplicity, induced her to avoid everything that might cause her to be thought a wealthy favourite. She had not one of the failings which usually accompany that position. She loved the persons who shared the Queen's affections, and was entirely free from jealousy. Marie Antoinette flattered herself that the Comtesse Jules and the Princesse de Lamballe would be her especial friends, and that she should possess a society formed according to her own taste. "I will receive them in my closet, or at Trianon," said she; "I will enjoy the comforts of private life, which exist not for us, unless we have the good sense to secure them for ourselves." The happiness the Queen thought to secure was destined to turn to vexation. All those courtiers who were not admitted to this, intimacy became so many jealous and vindictive enemies.

It was necessary to make a suitable provision for the Countess. The place of first equerry, in reversion after the Comte de Tessé, given to Comte Jules unknown to the titular holder, displeased the family of Noailles. This family had just sustained another mortification, the appointment of the Princesse de Lamballe having in some degree rendered necessary the resignation of the Comtesse de Noailles, whose husband was thereupon made a marshal of France. The Princesse de Lamballe, although she did not quarrel with the Queen, was alarmed at the establishment of the Comtesse Jules at Court, and did not form, as her Majesty had hoped, a part of that intimate society, which was in turn composed of Mesdames Jules and Diane de Polignac, d'Andlau and de Châlon, and Messieurs de Guignes, de Coigny, d'Adhémar, de Besenval, lieutenant-colonel of the Swiss, de Polignac, de Vaudreuil, and de Guiche; the Prince de Ligne and the Duke of Dorset, the English ambassador, were also admitted.

It was a long time before the Comtesse Jules maintained any great state at Court. The Queen contented herself with giving her very fine apartments at the top of the marble staircase. The salary of first equerry, the trifling emoluments derived from M. dePolignac's regiment, added to their slender patrimony, and perhaps some small pension, at that time formed the whole fortune of the favourite. I never saw the Queen make her a present of value; I was even astonished one day at hearing her Majesty mention, with pleasure, that the

Countess had gained ten thousand francs in the lottery. "She was in great want of it," added the Queen.

Thus the Polignacs were not settled at Court in any degree of splendour which could justify complaints from others, and the substantial favours bestowed upon that family were less envied than the intimacy between them and their *protégés* and the Queen. Those who had no hope of entering the circle of the Comtesse Jules were made jealous by the opportunities of advancement it afforded.

However, at the time I speak of, the society around the Comtesse Jules was fully engaged in gratifying the young Queen. Of this the Marquis de Vaudreuil was a conspicuous member; he was a brilliant man, the friend and protector of men of letters and celebrated artists.

The Baron de Besenval added to the bluntness of the Swiss all the adroitness of a French courtier. His fifty years and gray hairs made him enjoy among women the confidence inspired by mature age, although he had not given up the thought of love affairs. He talked of his native mountains with enthusiasm. He would at any time sing the "Ranz des Vaches" with tears in his eyes, and was the best story-teller in the Comtesse Jules's circle. The last new song or *bonmot* and the gossip of the day were the sole topics of conversation in the Queen's parties. Wit was banished from them. The Comtesse Diane, more inclined to literary pursuits than her sister-in-law, one day recommended her to read the "Iliad" and "Odyssey." The latter replied, laughing, that she was perfectly acquainted with the Greek poet, and said to prove it:

" Homere était aveugle et jouait du hautbois."
(Homer was blind and played on the hautboy.)

The Queen found this sort of humour very much to her taste, and said that no pedant should ever be her friend.

Before the Queen fixed her assemblies at Madame de Polignac's, she occasionally passed the evening at the house of the Duc and Duchesse de Duras, where a brilliant party of young persons met together. They introduced a taste for trifling games, such as question and answer, *guerre panpan*, blind man's buff, and especially a game called *descampativos*. The people of Paris, always criticising, but always imitating the customs of the Court, were infected with the mania for these childish sports. Madame de Genlis, sketching the follies of the day in one of her plays, speaks of these famous *descampativos*; and also of the rage for making a friend, called the *inséparable*, until a whim or the slightest difference might occasion a total rupture.

VIII

T HE Duc de Choiseul had reappeared at Court on the ceremony of the King's coronation for the first time after his disgrace under Louis XV in 1770. The state of public feeling on the subject gave his friends hope of seeing him again in administration, or in the Council of State; but the opposite party was too firmly seated at Versailles, and the young Queen's influence was outweighed, in the mind of the King, by long-standing prejudices; she therefore gave up for ever her attempt to reinstate the Duke. Thus this Princess, who has been described as so ambitious, and so strenuously supporting the interest of the House of Austria, failed twice in the only scheme which could forward the views constantly attributed to her; and spent the whole of her reign surrounded by enemies of herself and her house.

Marie Antoinette took little pains to promote literature and the fine arts. She had been annoyed in consequence of having ordered a performance of the "Connétable de Bourbon," on the celebration of the marriage of Madame Clotilde with the Prince of Piedmont. The Court and the people of Paris censured as indecorous the naming characters in the piece after the reigning family, and that with which the new alliance was formed. The reading of this piece by the Comte de Guibert in the Queen's closet had produced in her Majesty's circle that sort of enthusiasm which obscures the judgment. She promised herself she would have no more readings. Yet, at the request of M. de Cubières, the King's equerry, the Queen agreed to hear the reading of a comedy written by his brother. She collected her intimate circle, Messieurs de Coigny, de Vaudreuil, de Besenval, Mesdames de Polignac, de Châlon, etc., and to increase the number of judges, she admitted the two Parnys, the Chevalier de Bertin[1], my father-in-law, and myself. Molé[2] read for the author. I never could satisfy myself by what magic the skillful reader gained our unanimous approbation of a ridiculous work. Surely the delightful voice of Molé, by awakening our recollection of the dramatic beauties of the French stage, prevented the wretched lines of Dorat Cubières from striking on our ears. I can assert that the exclamation *Charming! Charming!* repeatedly interrupted the reader. The piece was admitted for performance at Fontainebleau; and for the first time the King had the curtain dropped before the end of the play. It was called the "Dramomane" or "Dramaturge."

---

1. The Chevalier de Parny was already known for his heroic poems, and the Chevalier de Bertin by some well-received verses.

2. An actor who was the delight of the Théâtre Français. He preceded Fleury, and took the same line of character.

All the characters died of eating poison in a pie. The Queen, highly disconcerted at having recommended this absurd production, announced that she would never hear another reading; and this time she kept her word.

The tragedy of "Mustapha and Zéangir," by M. de Chamfort, was highly successful at the Court theatre at Fontainebleau. The Queen procured the author a pension of 1,200 francs, but his play failed on being performed at Paris.

The spirit of opposition which prevailed in that city delighted in reversing the verdicts of the Court. The Queen determined never again to give any marked countenance to new dramatic works. She reserved her patronage for musical composers, and in a few years their art arrived at a perfection it had never before attained in France.

It was solely to gratify the Queen that the manager of the Opéra brought the first company of comic actors to Paris. Gluck, Piccini, and Sacchini were attracted there in succession. These eminent composers were treated with great distinction at Court. Immediately on his arrival in France, Gluck was admitted to the Queen's toilet, and she talked to him all the time he remained with her. She asked him one day whether he had nearly brought his grand opera of "Armide" to a conclusion, and whether it pleased him. Gluck replied very coolly, in his German accent, "Madame, it will soon be finished, and really it will be *superb*." There was a great outcry against the confidence with which the composer had spoken of one of his own productions. The Queen defended him warmly; she insisted that he could not be ignorant of the merit of his works; that he well knew they were generally admired, and that no doubt he was afraid lest a modesty, merely dictated by politeness, should look like affectation in him.

The Queen did not confine her admiration to the lofty style of the French and Italian operas; she greatly valued Grétry's music, so well adapted to the spirit and feeling of the words. A great deal of the poetry set to music by Grétry is by Marmontel. The day after the first performance of "Zemira and Azor," Marmontel and Grétry were presented to the Queen as she was passing through the gallery of Fontainebleau to go to mass. The Queen congratulated Grétry on the success of the new opera, and told him that she had dreamed of the enchanting effect of the trio by Zemira's father and sisters behind the magic mirror. Grétry, in a transport of joy, took Marmontel in his arms, "Ah! my friend," cried he, "excellent music may be made of this." "And execrable words," coolly observed Marmontel, to whom her Majesty had not addressed a single compliment.

The most indifferent artists were permitted to have the honour of painting the Queen. A full-length portrait, representing her in all the pomp of royalty, was exhibited in the gallery of Versailles. This picture, which was intended for the Court of Vienna, was executed by a man who does not deserve even to be named, and disgusted all people of taste. It seemed as if this art had, in France, retrograded several centuries.

The Queen had not that enlightened judgment, or even that mere taste, which enables princes to foster and protect great talents. She confessed frankly that she saw no merit in any portrait beyond the likeness. When she went to the Louvre, she would run hastily over all the little "genre" pictures, and come out, as she acknowledged, without having once raised her eyes to the grand compositions.

There is no good portrait of the Queen, save that by Werthmüller, chief painter to the King of Sweden, which was sent to Stockholm, and that by Madame Lebrun, which was saved from the revolutionary fury by the commissioners for the care of the furniture at Versailles. The composition of the latter picture resembles that of Henriette of France, the wife of the unfortunate Charles I, painted by Vandyke. Like Marie Antoinette, she is seated, surrounded by her children, and that resemblance adds to the melancholy interest raised by this beautiful production.

While admitting that the Queen gave no direct encouragement to any art but that of music, I should be wrong to pass over in silence the patronage conferred by her and the Princes, brothers of the King, on the art of printing.

To Marie Antoinette we are indebted for a splendid quarto edition of the works of Metastasio; to Monsieur, the King's brother, for a quarto Tasso, embellished with engravings after Cochin; and to the Comte d'Artois for a small collection of select works, which is considered one of the *chefs-d'œuvre* of the press of the celebrated Didot.

In 1775, on the death of the Maréchal du Muy, the ascendency obtained by the sect of innovators occasioned M. de Saint-Germain to be recalled to Court and made Minister of War. His first care was the destruction of the King's military household establishment, an imposing and effectual rampart round the sovereign power.

When Chancellor Maupeou obtained from Louis XV the destruction of the Parliament and the exile of all the ancient magistrates, the Mousquetaires were charged with the execution of the commission for this purpose; and at the stroke of midnight, the presidents and members were all arrested, each by two Mousquetaires. In the spring of 1775 a popular insurrection had taken place in consequence of the high price of bread. M. Turgot's new regulation, which permitted unlimited trade in corn, was either its cause or the pretext for it; and the King's household troops again rendered the greatest services to public tranquillity.

I have never been able to discover the true cause of the support given to M. de Saint-Germain's policy by the Queen, unless in the marked favour shown to the captains and officers of the Body Guards, who by this reduction became the only soldiers of their rank entrusted with the safety of the sovereign; or else in the Queen's strong prejudice against the Duc d'Aiguillon, then commander of the light-horse. M. de Saint-Germain, however, retained fifty *gens d'armes* and fifty light-horse to form a royal escort on state occasions; but in 1787 the King reduced both these military bodies. The Queen then said with satisfaction that at last she should see no more red coats in the gallery of Versailles.

From 1775 to 1781 were the gayest years of the Queen's life. In the little journeys to Choisy, performances frequently took place at the theatre twice in one day; grand opera and French or Italian comedy at the usual hour; and at eleven at night they returned to the theatre for parodies in which the best actors of the Opéra presented themselves in whimsical parts and costumes. The celebrated dancer Guimard always took the leading characters in the latter performance; she danced better than she acted; her extreme leanness, and her weak, hoarse voice added to the burlesque in the parodied characters of Ernelinde and Iphigénie.

The most magnificent fête ever given to the Queen was one prepared for her by Monsieur, the King's brother, at Brunoy. That Prince did me the honour to admit me, and I followed her Majesty into the gardens, where she found in the first copse knights in full armour asleep at the foot of trees, on which hung their spears and shields. The absence of the beauties who had incited the nephews of Charlemagne and the gallants of that period to lofty deeds was supposed to occasion this lethargic slumber. But when the Queen appeared at the entrance of the copse they were on foot in an instant, and melodious voices announced their eagerness to display their valour. They then hastened into a vast arena, magnificently decorated in the exact style of the ancient tournaments. Fifty dancers dressed as pages presented to the knights twenty-five superb black horses, and twenty-five of a dazzling whiteness, all most richly caparisoned. The party led by Augustus Vestris wore the Queen's colours. Picq, ballet-master at the Russian Court, commanded the opposing band. There was running at the negro's head, tilting, and, lastly, combats *à outrance*, perfectly well imitated. Although the spectators were aware that the Queen's colours could not but be victorious, they did not the less enjoy the apparent uncertainty.

Nearly all the agreeable women of Paris were ranged upon the steps which surrounded the area of the tourney. The Queen, surrounded by the royal family and the whole Court, was placed beneath an elevated canopy. A play, followed by a ballet-pantomime and a ball, terminated the fête. Fireworks and illuminations were not spared. Finally, from a prodigiously high scaffold, placed on a rising ground, the words *Vive Louis! Vive Marie Antoinette!* were shown in the air in the midst of a very dark but calm night.

Pleasure was the sole pursuit of every one of this young family, with the exception of the King. Their love of it was perpetually encouraged by a crowd of those officious people who, by anticipating the desires and even the passions of princes, find means of showing their zeal, and hope to gain or maintain favour for themselves.

Who would have dared to check the amusements of a queen, young, lively, and handsome? A mother or a husband alone would have had the right to do it; and the King threw no impediment in the way of Marie Antoinette's inclinations. His long indifference had been followed by admiration and love. He was a slave to all the wishes of the Queen, who, delighted with the happy change in the heart and habits of the King, did not sufficiently conceal the ascendency she was gaining over him.

The King went to bed every night at eleven precisely; he was very methodical, and nothing was allowed to interfere with his rules. The noise which the Queen unavoidably made when she returned very late from the evenings which she spent with the Princesse de Guéménée or the Duc de Duras, at last annoyed the King, and it was amicably agreed that the Queen should apprise him when she intended to sit up late. He then began to sleep in his own apartment, which had never before happened from the time of their marriage.

During the winter the Queen attended the Opéra balls with a single lady of the palace, and always found there Monsieur and the Comte d'Artois. Her people concealed their liveries under gray cloth greatcoats. She never thought she was recognized, while all the time she was known to the whole assembly, from the first moment she entered the theatre; they pretended, however, not to recognize her, and some masquerade manœuvre was always adopted to give her the pleasure of fancying herself incognito.

Louis XVI determined once to accompany the Queen to a masked ball; it was agreed that the King should hold not only the *grand* but the *petit coucher*, as if actually going to bed. The Queen went to his apartment through the inner corridors of the palace, followed by one of her women with a black domino; she assisted him to put it on, and they went alone to the chapel court, where a carriage waited for them, with the captain of the Guard of the quarter, and a lady of the palace. The King was but little amused, spoke only to two or three persons, who knew him immediately, and found nothing to admire at the masquerade but Punches and Harlequins, which served as a joke against him for the royal family, who often amused themselves with laughing at him about it.

An event, simple in itself, brought dire suspicion upon the Queen. She was going out one evening with the Duchesse de Luynes, lady of the palace, when her carriage broke down at the entrance into Paris; she was obliged to alight; the Duchess led her into a shop, while a footman called a *fiacre*. As they were masked, if they had but known how to keep silence, the event would never have been known; but to ride in a *fiacre* is so unusual an adventure for a queen that she had hardly entered the Opéra-house when she could not help saying to some persons whom she met there: "That I should be in a *fiacre*. Is it not droll?"

From that moment all Paris was informed of the adventure of the *fiacre*. It was said that everything connected with it was mysterious; that the Queen had kept an assignation in a private house with the Duc de Coigny. He was indeed very well received at Court, but equally so by the King and Queen. These accusations of gallantry once set afloat, there were no longer any bounds to the calumnies circulated at Paris. If, during the chase or at cards, the Queen spoke to Lord Edward Dillon, De Lambertye, or others, they were so many favoured lovers. The people of Paris did not know that none of those young persons were admitted into the Queen's private circle of friends; the Queen went about Paris in disguise, and had made use of a *fiacre*; and a single instance of levity gives room for the suspicion of others.

Conscious of innocence, and well knowing that all about her must do justice to her private life, the Queen spoke of these reports with contempt, contenting herself with the supposition that some folly in the young men mentioned had given rise to them. She therefore left off speaking to them or even looking at them. Their vanity took alarm at this, and revenge induced them either to say, or to leave others to think, that they were unfortunate enough to please no longer. Other young coxcombs, placing themselves near the private box which the Queen occupied incognito when she attended the public theatre at Versailles, had the presumption to imagine that they were noticed by her; and I have known such notions entertained merely on account of the Queen's requesting one of those gentlemen to inquire behind the scenes whether it would be long before the commencement of the second piece.

The list of persons received into the Queen's closet which I gave in the preceding chapter was placed in the hands of the ushers of the chamber by the Princesse de Lamballe; and the persons there enumerated could present themselves to enjoy the distinction only on those days when the Queen chose to be with her intimates in a private manner; and this was only when she was slightly indisposed. People of the first rank at Court sometimes requested special audiences of her; the Queen then received them in a room within that called the closet of the women on duty, and these women announced them in her Majesty's apartment.

The Duc de Lauzun had a good deal of wit, and chivalrous manners. The Queen was accustomed to see him at the King's suppers, and at the house of the Princesse de Guéménée, and always showed him attention. One day he made his appearance at Madame de Guéménée's in uniform, and with the most magnificent plume of white heron's feathers that it was possible to behold. The Queen admired the plume, and he offered it to her through the Princesse de Guéménée. As he had worn it the Queen had not imagined that he could think of giving it to her; much embarrassed with the present which she had, as it were, drawn upon herself, she did not like to refuse it, nor did she know whether she ought to make one in return; afraid, if she did give anything, of giving either too much or too little, she contented herself with once letting M. de Lauzun see her adorned with the plume. In his secret "Memoirs" the Duke attaches an importance to his present, which proves him utterly unworthy of an honour accorded only to his name and rank.

A short time afterwards he solicited an audience; the Queen granted it, as she would have done to any other courtier of equal rank. I was in the room adjoining that in which he was received; a few minutes after his arrival the Queen reopened the door, and said aloud, and in an angry tone of voice, "Go, monsieur." M. de Lauzun bowed low, and withdrew. The Queen was much agitated. She said to me: "That man shall never again come within my doors." A few years before the Revolution of 1789 the Maréchal de Biron died. The

Duc de Lauzun, heir to his name, aspired to the important post of colonel of the regiment of French guards. The Queen, however, procured it for the Duc de Châtelet. The Duc de Biron espoused the cause of the Duc d'Orléans, and became one of the most violent enemies of Marie Antoinette.

It is with reluctance that I enter minutely on a defence of the Queen against two infamous accusations with which libellers have dared to swell their envenomed volumes. I mean the unworthy suspicions of too strong an attachment for the Comte d'Artois, and of the motives for the tender friendship which subsisted between the Queen, the Princesse de Lamballe, and the Duchesse de Polignac. I do not believe that the Comte d'Artois was, during his own youth and that of the Queen, so much smitten as has been said with the loveliness of his sister-in-law; I can affirm that I always saw that Prince maintain the most respectful demeanour towards the Queen; that she always spoke of his good-nature and cheerfulness with that freedom which attends only the purest sentiments; and that none of those about the Queen ever saw in the affection she manifested toward the Comte d'Artois more than that of a kind and tender sister for her youngest brother. As to the intimate connection between Marie Antoinette and the ladies I have named, it never had, nor could have, any other motive than the very innocent wish to secure herself two friends in the midst of a numerous Court; and notwithstanding this intimacy, that tone of respect observed by persons of the most exalted rank towards majesty never ceased to be maintained.

The Queen, much occupied with the society of Madame de Polignac, and an unbroken series of amusements, found less time for the Abbé de Vermond; he therefore resolved to retire from Court. The world did him the honour to believe that he had hazarded remonstrances upon his august pupil's frivolous employment of her time, and that he considered himself, both as an ecclesiastic and as instructor, now out of place at Court. But the world was deceived: his dissatisfaction arose purely from the favour shown to the Comtesse Jules. After a fortnight's absence we saw him at Versailles again, resuming his usual functions.

The Queen could express herself with winning graciousness to persons who merited her praise. When M. Loustonneau was appointed to the reversion of the post of first surgeon to the King, he came to make his acknowledgments. He was much beloved by the poor, to whom he had chiefly devoted his talents, spending nearly thirty thousand francs a year on indigent sufferers. The Queen replied to his thanks by saying: "You are satisfied, Monsieur; but I am far from being so with the inhabitants of Versailles. On the news of your appointment the town should have been illuminated.""How so, Madame?" asked the astonished surgeon, who was very modest. "Why," replied the Queen, "if the poor whom you have succoured for the past twenty years had each placed a single candle in their windows it would have been the most beautiful illumination ever witnessed."

The Queen did not limit her kindness to friendly words. There was frequently seen in the apartments of Versailles a veteran captain of the grenadiers of France, called the Chevalier d'Orville, who for four years had been soliciting from the Minister of War the post of major, or of King's lieutenant. He was known to be very poor; but he supported his lot without complaining of this vexatious delay in rewarding his honourable services. He regularly attended the

Maréchal de Ségur, at the hour appointed for receiving the numerous solicitations in his department. One day the Marshal said to him "You are still at Versailles, M. d'Orville?" "Monsieur," he replied, "you may observe that by this board of the flooring where I regularly place myself; it is already worn down several lines by the weight of my body." The Queen frequently stood at the window of her bedchamber to observe with her glass the people walking in the park. Sometimes she inquired the names of those who were unknown to her. One day she saw the Chevalier d'Orville passing, and asked me the name of that knight of Saint Louis, whom she had seen everywhere for a long time past. I knew who he was, and related his history. "That must be put an end to," said the Queen, with some vivacity. "Such an example of indifference is calculated to discourage our soldiers." Next day, in crossing the gallery to go to mass, the Queen perceived the Chevalier d'Orville; she went directly towards him. The poor man fell back in the recess of a window, looking to the right and left to discover the person whom the Queen was seeking, when she thus addressed him: "M. d'Orville, you have been several years at Versailles, soliciting a majority or a King's lieutenancy. You must have very powerless patrons." "I have none, Madame," replied the Chevalier, in great confusion. "Well! I will take you under my protection. Tomorrow at the same hour be here with a petition, and a memorial of your services." A fortnight after, M. d'Orville was appointed King's lieutenant, either at La Rochelle or at Rochefort.

IX

FROM the time of Louis XVI's accession to the throne, the Queen had been expecting a visit from her brother, the Emperor Joseph II. That Prince was the constant theme of her discourse. She boasted of his intelligence, his love of occupation, his military knowledge, and the perfect simplicity of his manners. Those about her Majesty ardently wished to see at Versailles a prince so worthy of his rank. At length the coming of Joseph II, under the title of Count Falkenstein, was announced, and the very day on which he would be at Versailles was mentioned.[1] The first embraces between the Queen and her august brother took place in the presence of all the Queen's household. The sight of their emotion was extremely affecting.

---

1. The Queen received the Emperor at Versailles, and did not go to meet him in a cabriolet, as is said in some of the collections of anecdotes respecting the court of Louis XVI; especially in a very respectable work in which this false anecdote is inserted; as is likewise in the *English Spy*, from which it was probably taken.

THE PRIVATE LIFE OF MARIE ANTOINETTE

The Emperor was at first generally admired in France; learned men, well-informed officers, and celebrated artists appreciated the extent of his information. He made less impression at Court, and very little in the private circle of the King and Queen. His eccentric manners, his frankness, often degenerating into rudeness, and his evidently affected simplicity,—all these characteristics caused him to be looked upon as a prince rather singular than admirable. The Queen spoke to him about the apartment she had prepared for him in the Château; the Emperor answered that he would not accept it, and that while travelling he always lodged at a *cabaret* (that was his very expression); the Queen insisted, and assured him that he should be at perfect liberty, and placed out of the reach of noise. He replied that he knew the Château of Versailles was very large, and that so many scoundrels lived there that he could well find a place; but that his *valet de chambre* had made up his camp-bed in a lodging-house, and there he would stay.

He dined with the King and Queen, and supped with the whole family. He appeared to take an interest in the young Princesse Elisabeth, then just past childhood, and blooming in all the freshness of that age. An intended marriage between him and this young sister of the King was reported at the time, but I believe it had no foundation in truth.

The table was still served by women only, when the Queen dined in private with the King, the royal family, or crowned heads.[1] I was present at the Queen's dinner almost

---

1. The custom was, that even supposing dinner to have commenced, if a princess of the blood arrived, and she was asked to sit down at the Queen's table, the comptrollers and gentlemen-in-waiting came immediately to attend, and the Queen's women withdrew. These had succeeded

every day. The Emperor would talk much and fluently; he expressed himself in French with facility, and the singularity of his expressions added a zest to his conversation. I have often heard him say that he liked *spectaculous* objects, when he meant to express such things as formed a show, or a scene worthy of interest. He disguised none of his prejudices against the etiquette and customs of the Court of France; and even in the presence of the King made them the subject of his sarcasms. The King smiled, but never made any answer; the Queen appeared pained. The Emperor frequently terminated his observations upon the objects in Paris which he had admired by reproaching the King for suffering himself to remain in ignorance of them. He could not conceive how such a wealth of pictures should remain shut up in the dust of immense stores;[1] and told him one day that but for the practice of placing some of them in the apartments of Versailles he would not know even the principal *chef-d'œuvre*

---

the maids of honour in several parts of their service and had preserved some of their privileges. One day the Duchesse d'Orléans arrived at Fontainebleu, at the Queen's dinner-hour. The Queen invited her to the table, and herself motioned to her women to leave the room, and let the men take their places. Her Majesty said she was resolved to continue a privilege which kept places of that description honourable, and rendered them a fit resort for ladies of nobility without fortune. Madame de Misery, a Baronne de Biache, the Queen's first lady-of-the-chamber, to whom I was made reversioner, was a daughter of M. the Comte de Chemant, and her grandmother was a Montmorency. M. the Prince de Tingry, in the presence of the Queen, used to call her "cousin." The ancient household of the kings of France conferred prerogatives acknowledged in the state. Many of the offices were tenable only by those of noble blood, and were sold at from 40,000 to 300,000 francs. A collection of edicts of the kings in favour of the prerogatives and right of precedence of the persons holding office in the king's household is still in existence.

1. The Emperor loudly censured the practice existing at that time, of allowing shopkeepers to erect shops near the outward walls of all the palaces, and to establish something like a fair upon the staircases in the galleries of Versailles and Fontainebleau, and even up to each landing-place of the great staircases.

that he possessed.[1] He also reproached him for not having visited the Hôtel des Invalides nor the Ecole Militaire; and even went so far as to tell him before us that he ought not only to know what Paris contained, but to travel in France, and reside a few days in each of his large towns.

At last the Queen was really hurt at the Emperor's remarks, and gave him a few lectures upon the freedom with which he allowed himself to lecture others. One day she was busied in signing warrants and orders for payment for her household, and was conversing with M. Augeard, her secretary for such matters, who presented the papers one after another to be signed, and replaced them in his portfolio. While this was going forward, the Emperor walked about the room; all at once he stood still, to reproach the Queen rather severely for signing all those papers without reading them, or, at least, without running her eye over them; and he spoke most judiciously to her upon the danger of signing her name inconsiderately. The Queen answered that very wise principles might be very ill applied; that her secretary, who deserved her implicit confidence, was at that moment laying before her nothing but orders for payment of the quarter's expenses of her household, registered in the Chamber of Accounts; and that she ran no risk of incautiously giving her signature.

The Queen's toilet was likewise a never-failing subject for animadversion with the Emperor. He blamed her for having introduced too many new fashions; and teased her about her use of rouge. One day, while she was laying on more of it than usual, before going to the play, he pointed out

1. Shortly after the Emperor's departure, the Comte d'Angivillers laid before the King plans for the erection of the Museum, which was then begun.

a lady who was in the room, and who was, in truth, highly painted. "A little more under the eyes," said the Emperor to the Queen; "lay on the rouge like a fury, as that lady does." The Queen entreated her brother to refrain from his jokes, or at all events to address them, when they were so outspoken, to her alone.

The Queen had made an appointment to meet her brother at the Italian theatre; she changed her mind, and went to the French theatre, sending a page to the Italian theatre to request the Emperor to come to her there. He left his box, lighted by the comedian Clairval, and attended by M. de la Ferté, comptroller of the Queen's privy purse, who was much hurt at hearing his Imperial Majesty, after kindly expressing his regret at not being present during the Italian performance, say to Clairval, "Your young Queen is very giddy; but, luckily, you Frenchmen have no great objection to that."

I was with my father-in-law in one of the Queen's apartments when the Emperor came to wait for her there, and, knowing that M. Campan was librarian, he conversed with him about such books as would of course be found in the Queen's library. After talking of our most celebrated authors, he casually said, "There are doubtless no works on finance or on administration here?"

These words were followed by his opinion on all that had been written on those topics, and the different systems of our two famous ministers, Sully and Colbert; on errors which were daily committed in France, in points essential to the prosperity of the Empire; and on the reform he himself would make at Vienna. Holding M. Campan by the button, he spent more than an hour talking vehemently, and without the slightest reserve, about the French Government.

My father-in-law and myself maintained profound silence, as much from astonishment as from respect; and when we were alone we agreed not to speak of this interview.

The Emperor was fond of describing the Italian Courts that he had visited. The jealous quarrels between the King and Queen of Naples amused him highly; he described to the life the manner and speech of that sovereign, and the simplicity with which he used to go and solicit the first chamberlain to obtain permission to return to the nuptial bed, when the angry Queen had banished him from it. The time which he was made to wait for this reconciliation was calculated between the Queen and her chamberlain, and always proportioned to the gravity of the offence. He also related several very amusing stories relative to the Court of Parma, of which he spoke with no little contempt. If what this Prince said of those Courts, and even of Vienna, had been written down, the whole would have formed an interesting collection. The Emperor told the King that the Grand Duke of Tuscany and the King of Naples being together, the former said a great deal about the changes he had effected in his State. The Grand Duke had issued a mass of new edicts, in order to carry the precepts of the economists into execution, and trusted that in so doing he was labouring for the welfare of his people. The King of Naples suffered him to go on speaking for a long time, and then casually asked how many Neapolitan families there were in Tuscany. The Duke soon reckoned them up, as they were but few. "Well, brother," replied the King of Naples, "I do not understand the indifference of your people towards your great reforms; for I have four times the number of Tuscan families settled in my States than you have of Neapolitan families in yours."

The Queen being at the Opéra with the Emperor, the latter did not wish to show himself; but she took him by the hand, and gently drew him to the front of the box. This kind of presentation to the public was most warmly received. The performance was "Iphigenia in Aulis," and for the second time the chorus, "*Chantons, celebrons notre Reine!*" was called for with universal plaudits.

A fête of a novel description was given at Petit Trianon. The art with which the English garden was not illuminated, but lighted, produced a charming effect. Earthen lamps, concealed by boards painted green, threw light upon the beds of shrubs and flowers, and brought out their varied tints. Several hundred burning fagots in the moat behind the Temple of Love made a blaze of light, which rendered that spot the most brilliant in the garden. After all, this evening's entertainment had nothing remarkable about it but the good taste of the artists, yet it was much talked of. The situation did not allow the admission of a great part of the Court; those who were uninvited were dissatisfied; and the people, who never forgive any fêtes but those they share in, so exaggerated the cost of this little fête as to make it appear that the fagots burnt in the moat had required the destruction of a whole forest. The Queen being informed of these reports, was determined to know exactly how much wood had been consumed; and she found that fifteen hundred fagots had sufficed to keep up the fire until four o'clock in the morning.

After staying a few months the Emperor left France, promising his sister to come and see her again. All the officers of the Queen's chamber had many opportunities of serving him during his stay, and expected that he would make them presents before his departure. Their oath of office positively forbade them to receive a gift from any foreign prince; they had therefore agreed to refuse the Emperor's presents at first, but to ask the time necessary for obtaining permission to accept them. The Emperor, probably informed of this custom, relieved the good people from their difficulty by setting off without making a single present.

About the latter end of 1777 the Queen, being alone in her closet, sent for my father-in-law and myself, and, giving us her hand to kiss, told us that, looking upon us both as persons deeply interested in her happiness, she wished to receive our congratulations,— that at length she was the Queen of France, and that she hoped soon to have children; that till now she had concealed her grief, but that she had shed many tears in secret.

Dating from this happy but long-delayed moment, the King's attachment to the Queen assumed every characteristic of love. The good Lassone, first physician to the King and Queen, frequently spoke to me of the uneasiness that the King's indifference, the cause of which he had been so long in overcoming, had given him, and appeared to me at that time to entertain no anxiety except of a very different description.

In the winter of 1778 the King's permission for the return of Voltaire, after an absence of twenty-seven years, was obtained. A few strict persons considered this concession on the part of the Court very injudicious. The Emperor, on leaving France, passed by the Château of Ferney without stopping there. He had advised the Queen not to suffer Voltaire to be presented to her. A lady belonging to the Court learned the Emperor's opinion on that point, and reproached him with his want of enthusiasm towards the greatest genius of the age. He replied that for the good of the people he should always endeavour to profit by the knowledge of the philosophers; but that his own business of sovereign would always prevent his ranking himself amongst that sect. The clergy also took steps to hinder Voltaire's appearance at Court. Paris, however, carried to the highest pitch the honours and enthusiasm shown to the great poet.

It was very unwise to let Paris pronounce with such transport an opinion so opposite to that of the Court. This was pointed out to the Queen, and she was told that, without conferring on Voltaire the honour of a presentation, she might see him in the State apartments. She was not averse to following this advice, and appeared embarrassed solely about what she should say to him. She was recommended to talk about nothing but the "Henriade," "Mérope," and "Zaira." The Queen replied that she would still consult a few other persons in whom she had great confidence. The next day she announced that it was irrevocably decided Voltaire should not see any member of the royal family,—his writings being too antagonistic to religion and morals. "It is, however, strange," said the Queen, "that while we refuse to admit Voltaire into our presence as the leader of philosophical writers, the Maréchale de Mouchy should have presented to me some years ago Madame Geoffrin, who owed her celebrity to the title of foster-mother of the philosophers."

On the occasion of the duel of the Comte d'Artois with the Prince de Bourbon the Queen determined privately to see the Baron de Besenval, who was to be one of the witnesses, in order to communicate the King's intentions. I have read with infinite pain the manner in which that simple fact is perverted in the first volume of M. de Besenval's "Memoirs." He is right in saying that M. Campan led him through the upper corridors of the Château, and introduced him into an apartment unknown to him; but the air of romance given to the interview is equally culpable and ridiculous. M. de Besenval says that he found himself, without knowing how he came there, in an apartment unadorned, but very conveniently furnished, of the existence of which he was till then utterly ignorant. He was astonished, he adds, not that the Queen should have so many facilities, but that she should have ventured to procure them. Ten printed sheets of the woman Lamotte's libels contain nothing so injurious to the character of Marie Antoinette as these lines, written by a man whom she honoured by undeserved kindness. He could not have had any opportunity of knowing the existence of the apartments, which consisted of a very small antechamber, a bedchamber, and a closet. Ever since the Queen had occupied her own apartment, these had been appropriated to her Majesty's lady of honour in cases of illness, and were actually so used when the Queen was confined. It was so important that it should not be known the Queen had spoken to the Baron before the duel that she had determined to go through her inner room into this little apartment, to which M. Campan was to conduct him. When men write of recent times they should be scrupulously exact, and not indulge in exaggerations or inventions.

The Baron de Besenval appears mightily surprised at the Queen's sudden coolness, and refers it to the fickleness of her disposition. I can explain the reason for the change by repeating what her Majesty said to me at the time; and I will not alter one of her expressions. Speaking of the strange presumption of men, and the reserve with which women ought always to treat them, the Queen added that age did not deprive them of the hope of pleasing, if they retained any agreeable qualities; that she had treated the Baron de Besenval as a brave Swiss, agreeable, polished, and witty, whose gray hairs had induced her to look upon him as a man whom she might see without harm; but that she had been much deceived. Her Majesty, after having enjoined me to the strictest secrecy, told me that, finding herself alone with the Baron, he began to address her with so much gallantry that she was thrown into the utmost astonishment, and that he was mad enough to fall upon his knees, and make her a declaration in form. The Queen added that she said to him: "Rise, monsieur; the King shall be ignorant of an offence which would disgrace you for ever;" that the Baron grew pale and stammered apologies; that she left her closet without saying another word, and that since that time she hardly ever spoke to him. "It is delightful to have friends," said the Queen; "but in a situation like mine it is sometimes difficult for the friends of our friends to suit us."

In the beginning of the year 1778 Mademoiselle d'Eon obtained permission to return to France, on condition that she should appear there in female dress. The Comte de Vergennes entreated my father, M. Genet, chief clerk of Foreign Affairs, who had long known the Chevalier d'Eon, to receive that strange personage at his house, to guide and restrain, if possible, her ardent disposition. The Queen, on learning her arrival at Versailles, sent a footman to desire my father to bring her into her presence; my father thought it his duty first to inform the Minister of her Majesty's wish. The Comte de Vergennes expressed himself pleased with my father's prudence, and desired that he would accompany him to the Queen. The Minister had a few minutes audience; her

Majesty came out of her closet with him, and condescended to express to my father the regret she felt at having troubled him to no purpose; and added, smiling, that a few words from M. de Vergennes had for ever cured her of her curiosity. The discovery in London of the true sex of this pretended woman makes it probable that the few words uttered by the Minister contained a solution of the enigma.

The Chevalier d'Eon had been useful in Russia as a spy of Louis XV. While very young he had found means to introduce himself at the Court of the Empress Elizabeth, and served that sovereign in the capacity of reader. Resuming afterwards his military dress, he served with honour and was wounded. Appointed chief secretary of legation, and afterwards minister plenipotentiary at London, he unpardonably insulted Comte de Guerchy, the ambassador. The official order for the Chevalier's return to France was actually delivered to the King's Council; but Louis XV delayed the departure of the courier who was to be its bearer, and sent off another courier privately, who gave the Chevalier d'Eon a letter in his own writing, in which he said, "I know that you have served me as effectually in the dress of a woman as in that which you now wear. Resume it instantly; withdraw into the city; I warn you that the King yesterday signed an order for your return to France; you are not safe in your hotel, and you would here find too powerful enemies." I heard the Chevalier d'Eon repeat the contents of this letter, in which Louis XV thus separated himself from the King of France, several times at my father's. The Chevalier, or rather the *Chevalière* d'Eon had preserved all the King's letters. Messieurs de Maurepas and de Vergennes wished to get them out of his hands, as they were afraid he would print them. This eccentric being had long solicited permission to return to France; but it was necessary to find a way of sparing the family he had offended the insult they would see in his return; he was therefore made to resume the costume of that sex to which in France everything is pardoned. The desire to see his native land once more determined him to submit to the condition, but he revenged himself by combining the long train of his gown and the three deep ruffles on his sleeves with the attitude and conversation of a grenadier, which made him very disagreeable company.

At last, the event so long desired by the Queen, and by all those who wished her well, took place; her Majesty became *enceinte*. The King was in ecstasies. Never was there a more united or happier couple. The disposition of Louis XVI entirely altered, and became prepossessing and conciliatory; and the Queen was amply compensated for the uneasiness which the King's indifference during the early part of their union had caused her.

The summer of 1778 was extremely hot. July and August passed, but the air was not cooled by a single storm. The Queen spent whole days in close rooms, and could not sleep until she had breathed the fresh night air, walking with the Princesses and her brothers upon the terrace under her apartments. These promenades at first gave rise to no remark; but it occurred to some of the party to enjoy the music of wind instruments during these fine summer nights. The musicians belonging to the chapel were ordered to perform pieces suited to instruments of that description, upon steps constructed in the middle of the garden. The Queen, seated on one of the terrace benches, enjoyed the effect of this music, surrounded by all the royal family with the exception of the King, who joined them but twice, disliking to change his hour of going to bed.

Nothing could be more innocent than these parties; yet Paris, France, nay, all Europe, were soon canvassing them in a manner most disadvantageous to the reputation of Marie Antoinette. It is true that all the inhabitants of Versailles enjoyed these serenades, and that there was a crowd near the spot from eleven at night until two or three in the morning. The windows of the ground floor occupied by Monsieur and Madame were kept open, and the terrace was perfectly well lighted by the numerous wax candles burning in the two apartments. Lamps were likewise placed in the garden, and the lights of the orchestra illuminated the rest of the place.

I do not know whether a few incautious women might not have ventured farther, and wandered to the bottom of the park; it may have been so; but the Queen, Madame, and the Comtesse d'Artois were always arm-in-arm, and never left the terrace. The Princesses were not remarkable when seated on the benches, being dressed in cambric muslin gowns, with large straw hats and muslin veils, a costume universally adopted by women at that time; but when standing up their different figures always distinguished them; and the persons present stood on one side to let them pass. It is true that when they seated themselves upon the benches private individuals would sometimes, to their great amusement, sit down by their side.

A young clerk in the War Department, either not knowing or pretending not to know the Queen, spoke to her of the beauty of the night, and the delightful effect of the music. The Queen, fancying she was not recognised, amused herself by keeping up the incognito, and they talked of several private families of Versailles, consisting of persons belonging to the King's household or her own. After a few minutes the Queen and Princesses rose to walk, and on leaving the bench curtsied to the clerk The young man knowing, or having subsequently discovered, that he had been conversing with the Queen, boasted of it in his office. He was merely desired to hold his tongue; and so little attention did he excite that the Revolution found him still only a clerk.

Another evening one of Monsieur's body-guard seated himself near the Princesses, and, knowing them, left the place where he was sitting, and placed himself before the Queen, to tell her that he was very fortunate in being able to seize an opportunity of imploring the kindness of his sovereign; that he was "soliciting at Court"—at the word *soliciting* the Queen and Princesses rose hastily and withdrew into Madame's apartment.[1] I was at the Queen's residence that day. She talked of this little occurrence all the time of her *coucher*; though she only complained that one of Monsieur's guards should have had the effrontery to speak to her. Her Majesty added that he ought to have respected her incognito; and that that was not the place where he should have ventured to make a request. Madame had recognised him, and talked of making a complaint to his captain; the Queen opposed it, attributing his error to his ignorance and provincial origin.

The most scandalous libels were based on these two insignificant occurrences, which I have related with scrupulous exactness. Nothing could be more false than those calumnies. It must be confessed, however, that such meetings

1. Soulavie has most criminally perverted these two facts.

were liable to ill consequences. I ventured to say as much to the Queen, and informed her that one evening, when her Majesty beckoned to me to go and speak to her, I thought I recognised on the bench on which she was sitting two wom- en deeply veiled, and keeping profound silence; that those women were the Comtesse du Barry and her sister-in-law; and that my suspicions were confirmed, when, at a few paces from the seat, and nearer to her Majesty, I met a tall footman belonging to Madame du Barry, whom I had seen in her ser- vice all the time she resided at Court.

My advice was disregarded. Misled by the pleasure she found in these promenades, and secure in the consciousness of blameless conduct, the Queen would not see the lamen- table results which must necessarily follow. This was very unfortunate; for besides the mortifications they brought upon her, it is highly probable that they prompted the vile plot which gave rise to the Cardinal de Rohan's fatal error.

Having enjoyed these evening promenades about a month, the Queen ordered a private concert within the col- onnade which contained the group of Pluto and Proser- pine. Sentinels were placed at all the entrances, and ordered to admit within the colonnade only such persons as should produce tickets signed by my father-in-law. A fine concert was performed there by the musicians of the chapel and the female musicians belonging to the Queen's chamber. The Queen went with Mesdames de Polignac, de Châlon and d'Andlau, and Messieurs de Polignac, de Coigny, de Besenval, and de Vaudreuil; there were also a few equerries present. Her Majesty gave me permission to attend the concert with some of my female relations. There was no music upon the terrace. The crowd of inquisitive people, whom the sentinels kept at a distance from the enclosure of the colonnade went away highly discontented; the small number of persons admitted no doubt occasioned jealousy, and gave rise to offensive comments which were caught up by the public with avidity.[1] I do not pretend to apologise for the kind of amusements with which the Queen indulged herself during this and the following summer; the consequences were so lamentable that the error was no doubt very great; but what I have said respecting the character of these promenades may be relied on as true.

When the season for evening walks was at an end, odious couplets were circulated in Paris; the Queen was treated in them in the most insulting manner; her situation ranked among her enemies persons attached to the only prince who for several years had appeared likely to give heirs to the crown. People uttered the most inconsiderate language; and those improper conversations took place in societies wherein the imminent danger of violating to so criminal an extent both truth and the respect due to sovereigns ought to have been better understood. A few days before the Queen's confinement a whole volume of manuscript songs, concerning her and all the ladies about her remarkable for rank or station, was thrown down in the œil-de-bœuf. This manuscript was immediately put into the hands of the King, who was highly incensed at it, and said that he had himself been at those promenades; that he had seen nothing connected with them but what was perfectly harmless; that such songs would disturb the harmony of twenty families in the Court and city; that it was a capital crime to have made any against the Queen

1. This anecdote is in the same manner detestably perverted in Soulavie's infamous collection; yet his six volumes are, unfortunately, admitted into libraries, and particularly into the libraries of foreigners.

herself; and that he wished the author of the infamous libels to be discovered and punished. A fortnight afterwards it was known publicly that the verses were by M. Champcenetz de Riquebourg,[1] who was not even reprimanded.

I knew for a certainty that the King spoke to M. de Maurepas, before two of his most confidential servants, respecting the risk which he saw the Queen ran from these night walks upon the terrace of Versailles, which the public ventured to censure thus openly, and that the old minister had the cruelty to advise that she should be suffered to go on; she possessed talent; her friends were very ambitious, and longed to see her take a part in public affairs; and to let her acquire the reputation of levity would do no harm. M. de Vergennes was as hostile to the Queen's influence as M. de Maurepas, it may therefore be fairly presumed, since the Prime Minister durst point out to his King an advantage to be gained by the Queen's discrediting herself, that he and M. de Vergennes employed all means within the reach of powerful ministers in order to ruin her in the opinion of the public.

The Queen's *accouchement* approached; *Te Deums* were snug and prayers offered up in all the cathedrals. On the 11th of December, 1778, the royal family, the Princes of the blood, and the great officers of State passed the night in the rooms adjoining the Queen's bedchamber. Madame, the King's daughter, came into the world before mid-day on the 19th of December. The etiquette of allowing all

---

1. This Monsieur Champcenetz de Riquebourg was known as the author of a great many songs, some of which are very well written. Lively and satirical by nature, he did not lose either his cheerfulness or his carelessness before the revolutionary tribunal; where after hearing his own sentence of condemnation read, he asked his judges if he might not be allowed to find a substitute.

persons indiscriminately to enter at the moment of the delivery of a queen was observed with such exaggeration that when the *accoucheur* said aloud, "*La Reine va s'accoucher*," the persons who poured into the chamber were so numerous that the rush nearly destroyed the Queen. During the night the King had taken the precaution to have the enormous tapestry screens which surrounded her Majesty's bed secured with cords; but for this they certainly would have been thrown down upon her. It was impossible to move about the chamber, which was filled with so motley a crowd that one might have fancied himself in some place of public amusement. Two Savoyards got upon the furniture for a better sight of the Queen, who was placed opposite the fireplace.

The noise and the sex of the infant, with which the Queen was made acquainted by a signal previously agreed on, as it is said, with the Princesse de Lamballe, or some error of the *accoucheur*, brought on symptoms which threatened fatal consequences; the *accoucheur* exclaimed, "Give her air—warm water—she must be bled in the foot!" The windows were stopped up; the King opened them with a strength which his affection for the Queen gave him at the moment. They were of great height and pasted over with strips of paper all round. The basin of hot water not being brought quickly enough, the *accoucheur* desired the chief surgeon to use his lancet without waiting for it. He did so; the blood streamed out freely, and the Queen opened her eyes. The Princesse de Lamballe was carried through the crowd in a state of insensibility. The *valets de chambre* and pages dragged out by the collar such inconsiderate persons as would not leave the room. This cruel custom was abolished afterwards. The Princes of the family, the Princes of the blood, the chancellor, and the ministers are surely sufficient to attest the legitimacy of an hereditary prince. The Queen was snatched from the very jaws of death; she was not conscious of having been bled, and on being replaced in bed asked why she had a linen bandage upon her foot.

The delight which succeeded the moment of fear was equally lively and sincere. We were all embracing each other, and shedding tears of joy. The Comte d'Esterhazy and the Prince de Poix, to whom I was the first to announce that the Queen was restored to life, embraced me in the midst of the cabinet of nobles. We little imagined, in our happiness at her escape from death, for how much more terrible a fate our beloved Princess was reserved.

X

URING the alarm for the life of the Queen, regret at not possessing an heir to the throne was not even thought of. The King himself was wholly occupied with the care of preserving an adored wife. The young Princess was presented to her mother. "Poor little one," said the Queen, "you were not wished for, but you are not on that account less dear to me. A son would have been rather the property of the State. You shall be mine; you shall have my undivided care, shall share all my happiness, and console me in all my troubles."

The King despatched a courier to Paris, and wrote letters himself to Vienna, by the Queen's bedside; and part of the rejoicings ordered took place in the capital.

A great number of attendants watched near the Queen during the first nights of her confinement. This custom distressed her; she knew how to feel for others, and ordered large armchairs for her women, the backs of which were capable of being let down by springs, and which served perfectly well instead of beds. M. de Lassone, the chief physician, the chief surgeon, the chief apothecary, the principal officers of the buttery, etc., were likewise nine nights without going to bed. The royal children were watched for a long time, and one of the women on duty remained, nightly, up and dressed, during the first three years from their birth.

The Queen made her entry into Paris for the churching. One hundred maidens were portioned and married at Notre-Dame. There were few popular acclamations, but her Majesty was perfectly well received at the Opéra.

A few days after the Queen's recovery from her confinement, the Curé of the Magdelaine de la Cité at Paris wrote to M. Campan and requested a private interview with him; it was to desire he would deliver into the hands of the Queen a little box containing her wedding ring, with this note written by the Curé: "I have received under the seal of confession the ring which I send to your Majesty; with an avowal that it was stolen from you in 1771, in order to be used in sorceries, to prevent your having any children." On seeing her ring again the Queen said that she had in fact lost it about seven years before, while washing her hands, and that she had resolved to use no endeavour to discover the superstitious woman who had done her the injury.

The Queen's attachment to the Comtesse Jules increased every day; she went frequently to her house at Paris, and even took up her own abode at the Château de la Muette to be nearer during her confinement. She married Mademoiselle de Polignac, when scarcely thirteen years of age, to M. de Grammont, who, on account of this marriage, was made Duc de Guiche, and captain of the King's Guards, in reversion after the Duc de Villeroi. The Duchesse de Civrac, Madame Victoire's *dame d'honneur*, had been promised the place for the Duc de Lorges, her son. The number of discontented families at Court increased.

The title of favourite was too openly given to the Comtesse Jules by her friends. The lot of the favourite of a queen is not, in France, a happy one; the favourites of kings are treated, out of gallantry, with much greater indulgence.

A short time after the birth of Madame the Queen became again *enceinte*; she had mentioned it only to the King, to her physician, and to a few persons honoured with her intimate confidence, when, having overexerted her strength in pulling up one of the glasses of her carriage, she felt that she had hurt herself, and eight days afterwards she miscarried. The King spent the whole morning at her bedside, consoling her, and manifesting the tenderest concern for her. The Queen wept exceedingly; the King took her affectionately in his arms, and mingled his tears with hers. The King enjoined silence among the small number of persons who were informed of this unfortunate occurrence; and it remained generally unknown. These particulars furnish an accurate idea of the manner in which this august couple lived together.

The Empress Maria Theresa did not enjoy the happiness of seeing her daughter give an heir to the crown of France. That illustrious Princess died at the close of 1780, after having proved by her example that, as in the instance of Queen Blanche, the talents of a sovereign might be blended with the virtues of a pious princess. The King was deeply affected at the death of the Empress; and on the arrival of the courier from Vienna said that he could not bring himself to afflict the Queen by informing her of an event which grieved even him so much. His Majesty thought the Abbé de Vermond, who had possessed the confidence of Maria Theresa during his stay at Vienna, the most proper person to discharge this painful duty. He sent his first *valet de chambre*, M. de Chamilly, to the Abbé on the evening of the day he received the despatches from Vienna, to order him to come the next day to the Queen before her breakfast hour, to acquit himself discreetly of the afflicting commission with which he was charged, and to let his Majesty know the moment of his entering the Queen's chamber. It was the King's intention to be there precisely a quarter of an hour after him, and he was punctual to his time; he was announced; the Abbé came out; and his Majesty said to him, as he drew up at the door to let him pass, "I thank you, Monsieur l'Abbé, for the service you have just done me." This was the only time during nineteen years that the King spoke to him.

Within an hour after learning the event the Queen put on temporary mourning, while waiting until her Court mourning should be ready; she kept herself shut up in her apartments for several days; went out only to mass; saw none but the royal family; and received none but the Princesse de Lamballe and the Duchesse de Polignac. She talked incessantly of the courage, the misfortunes, the successes, and the virtues of her mother. The shroud and dress in which Maria Theresa was to be buried, made entirely by her own hands, were found ready prepared in one of her closets. She often regretted that the numerous duties of her august mother had prevented her from watching in person over the education of her daughters; and modestly said that she herself would have been more worthy if she had had the good

fortune to receive lessons directly from a sovereign so enlightened and so deserving of admiration.

The Queen told me one day that her mother was left a
widow at an age when her beauty was yet striking; that she
was secretly informed of a plot laid by her three principal
ministers to make themselves agreeable to her; of a compact made between them, that the losers should not feel any
jealousy towards him who should be fortunate enough to
gain his sovereign's heart; and that they had sworn that the
successful one should be always the friend of the other two.
The Empress being assured of this scheme, one day after
the breaking up of the council over which she had presided,
turned the conversation upon the subject of female sovereigns, and the duties of their sex and rank; and then applying
her general reflections to herself in particular, told them that
she hoped to guard herself all her life against weaknesses of
the heart; but that if ever an irresistible feeling should make
her alter her resolution, it should be only in favour of a man
proof against ambition, not engaged in State affairs, but attached only to a private life and its calm enjoyments,—in a
word, if her heart should betray her so far as to lead her to
love a man invested with any important office, from the moment he should discover her sentiments he would forfeit his
place and his influence with the public. This was sufficient;
the three ministers, more ambitious than amorous, gave up
their projects for ever.

On the 22d of October, 1781, the Queen gave birth
to a Dauphin. So deep a silence prevailed in the room that
the Queen thought her child was a daughter; but after the
Keeper of the Seals had declared the sex of the infant, the
King went up to the Queen's bed, and said to her, "Madame,

you have fulfilled my wishes and those of France: you are the mother of a Dauphin." The King's joy was boundless; tears streamed from his eyes; he gave his hand to every one present; and his happiness carried away his habitual reserve. Cheerful and affable, he was incessantly taking occasion to introduce the words, "my son," or "the Dauphin." As soon as the Queen was in bed, she wished to see the long-looked-for infant. The Princesse de Guéménée brought him to her. The Queen said there was no need for commending him to the Princess, but in order to enable her to attend to him more freely, she would herself share the care of the education of her daughter. When the Dauphin was settled in his apartment, he received the customary homages and visits. The Duc d'Angoulême, meeting his father at the entrance of the Dauphin's apartment, said to him, "Oh, papa! how little my cousin is!" "The day will come when you will think him great enough, my dear," answered the Prince, almost involuntarily.

The birth of the Dauphin appeared to give joy to all classes. Men stopped one another in the streets, spoke without being acquainted, and those who were acquainted embraced each other. In the birth of a legitimate heir to the sovereign every man beholds a pledge of prosperity and tranquillity.

The rejoicings were splendid and ingenious. The artificers and tradesmen of Paris spent considerable sums in order to go to Versailles in a body, with their various insignia. Almost every troop had music with it. When they arrived at the court of the palace, they there arranged themselves so as to present a most interesting living picture. Chimney-sweepers, quite as well dressed as those that appear upon the stage, carried an ornamented chimney, at the top of which was perched one of the smallest of their fraternity. The chairmen carried a sedan highly gilt, in which were to be seen a handsome nurse and a little Dauphin. The butchers made their appearance with their fat ox. Cooks, masons, blacksmiths, all trades were on the alert. The smiths hammered away upon an anvil, the shoemakers finished off a little pair of boots for the Dauphin, and the tailors a little suit of the uniform of his regiment. The King remained a long time upon a balcony to enjoy the sight. The whole Court was delighted with it. So general was the enthusiasm that (the police not having carefully examined the procession) the grave-diggers had the imprudence to send their deputation also, with the emblematic devices of their ill-omened occupation. They were met by the Princesse Sophie, the King's aunt, who was thrilled with horror at the sight, and entreated the King to have the audacious fellows driven out of the procession, which was then drawing up on the terrace.

The *dames de la halle* came to congratulate the Queen, and were received with the suitable ceremonies. Fifty of them appeared dressed in black silk gowns, the established full dress of their order, and almost all wore diamonds. The Princesse de Chimay went to the door of the Queen's bedroom to receive three of these ladies, who were led up to the Queen's bed. One of them addressed her Majesty in a speech written by M. de la Harpe. It was set down on the inside of a fan, to which the speaker repeatedly referred, but without any embarrassment. She was handsome, and had a remarkably fine voice. The Queen was affected by the address, and answered it with great affability—wishing a distinction to be made between these women and the poissardes, who always left a disagreeable impression on her mind. The King ordered a substantial repast for all these women. One of his Majesty's *maîtres d'hôtel*,[1] wearing his hat, sat as president and did the honours of the table. The public were admitted, and numbers of people had the curiosity to go.

The Gardes-du-Corps obtained the King's permission to give the Queen a dress ball in the great hall of the Opéra at Versailles. Her Majesty opened the ball in a minuet with a private selected by the corps, to whom the King granted the baton of an exempt. The fête was most splendid. All then was joy, happiness, and peace.

The Dauphin was a year old when the Prince de Gué-ménée's bankruptcy compelled the Princess, his wife, who was governess to the children of France, to resign her situation.

The Queen was at La Muette for the inoculation of her daughter. She sent for me, and condescended to say she wished to converse with me about a scheme which de-lighted her, but in the execution of which she foresaw some inconveniences. Her plan was to appoint the Duchesse de Polignac to the office lately held by the Princesse de Guémé-née. She saw with extreme pleasure the facilities which this appointment would give her for superintending the educa-tion of her children, without running any risk of hurting the pride of the governess; and that it would bring together the objects of her warmest affections,— her children and her friend. "The friends of the Duchesse de Polignac," con-tinued the Queen, "will be gratified by the splendour and importance conferred by the employment. As to the Duch-ess, I know her; the place by no means suits her simple and

1 Proofs of nobility, or at least of being noble in the third degree, were required for the office of *maître d'hôtel*.

154

quiet habits, nor the sort of indolence of her disposition. She will give me the greatest possible proof of her devotion if she yields to my wish." The Queen also spoke of the Princesse de Chimay and the Duchesse de Duras, whom the public pointed out as fit for the post; but she thought the Princesse de Chimay's piety too rigid; and as to the Duchesse de Duras, her wit and learning quite frightened her. What the Queen dreaded as the consequence of her selection of the Duchesse de Polignac was principally the jealousy of the courtiers; but she showed so lively a desire to see her scheme executed that I had no doubt she would soon set at naught all the obstacles she discovered. I was not mistaken; a few days afterwards the Duchess was appointed governess.

The Queen's object in sending for me was no doubt to furnish me with the means of explaining the feelings which induced her to prefer a governess disposed by friendship to suffer her to enjoy all the privileges of a mother. Her Majesty knew that I saw a great deal of company.

The Queen frequently dined with the Duchess after having been present at the King's private dinner. Sixty-one thousand francs were therefore added to the salary of the governess as a compensation for this increase of expense.

The Queen was tired of the excursions to Marly, and had no great difficulty in setting the King against them. He did not like the expense of them, for everybody was entertained there *gratis*. Louis XIV had established a kind of parade upon these excursions, differing from that of Versailles, but still more annoying. Card and supper parties occurred every day, and required much dress. On Sundays and holidays the fountains played, the people were admitted into the gardens, and there was as great a crowd as at the fêtes of St. Cloud.

Every age has its peculiar colouring; Marly showed that of Louis XIV even more than Versailles. Everything in the former place appeared to have been produced by the magic power of a fairy's wand. Not the slightest trace of all this splendour remains; the revolutionary spoilers even tore up the pipes which served to supply the fountains. Perhaps a brief description of this palace and the usages established there by Louis XIV may be acceptable.

The very extensive gardens of Marly ascended almost imperceptibly to the Pavilion of the Sun, which was occupied only by the King and his family. The pavilions of the twelve zodiacal signs bounded the two sides of the lawn. They were connected by bowers impervious to the rays of the sun. The pavilions nearest to that of the sun were reserved for the Princes of the blood and the ministers; the rest were occupied by persons holding superior offices at Court, or invited to stay at Marly. Each pavilion was named after fresco paintings, which covered its walls, and which had been executed by the most celebrated artists of the age of Louis XIV. On a line with the upper pavilion there was on the left a chapel; on the right a pavilion called La Perspective, which concealed a long suite of offices, containing a hundred lodging-rooms intended for the persons belonging to the service of the Court, kitchens, and spacious dining-rooms, in which more than thirty tables were splendidly laid out.

During half of Louis XV's reign the ladies still wore the *habit de cour de Marly*, so named by Louis XIV, and which differed little from that devised for Versailles. The French gown, gathered in the back, and with great hoops, replaced this dress, and continued to be worn till the end of the reign of Louis XVI. The diamonds, feathers, rouge, and embroidered stuffs spangled with gold, effaced all trace of a rural residence; but the people loved to see the splendour of their sovereign and a brilliant Court glittering in the shades of the woods.

After dinner, and before the hour for cards, the Queen, the Princesses, and their ladies, paraded among the clumps of trees, in little carriages, beneath canopies richly embroidered with gold, drawn by men in the King's livery. The trees planted by Louis XIV were of prodigious height, which, however, was surpassed in several of the groups by fountains of the clearest water; while, among others, cascades over white marble, the waters of which, met by the sunbeams, looked like draperies of silver gauze, formed a contrast to the solemn darkness of the groves.

In the evening nothing more was necessary for any well-dressed man to procure admission to the Queen's card parties than to be named and presented, by some officer of the Court, to the gentleman usher of the card-room. This room, which was very large, and of octagonal shape, rose to the top of the Italian roof, and terminated in a cupola furnished with balconies, in which ladies who had not been presented easily obtained leave to place themselves, and enjoy the sight of the brilliant assemblage.

Though not of the number of persons belonging to the Court, gentlemen admitted into this *salon* might request one of the ladies seated with the Queen at lansquenet or faro to bet upon her cards with such gold or notes as they presented to her. Rich people and the gamblers of Paris did not miss one of the evenings at the Marly *salon*, and there were always considerable sums won and lost. Louis XVI hated high play, and very often showed displeasure when the loss of large sums was mentioned. The fashion of wearing a black coat without being in mourning had not then been introduced, and the King gave a few of his *coups de boutoir* to certain chevaliers de St. Louis, dressed in this manner, who came to venture two or three louis, in the hope that fortune would favour the handsome duchesses who deigned to place them on their cards.

Singular contrasts are often seen amidst the grandeur of courts. In order to manage such high play at the Queen's faro table, it was necessary to have a banker provided with large sums of money; and this necessity placed at the table, to which none but the highest titled persons were admitted in general, not only M. de Chalabre, who was its banker, but also a retired captain of foot, who officiated as his second. A word, trivial, but perfectly appropriate to express the manner in which the Court was attended there, was often heard. Gentlemen presented at Court, who had not been invited to stay at Marly, came there notwithstanding, as they did to Versailles, and returned again to Paris; under such circumstances, it was said such a one had been to Marly only *en polisson*; and it appeared odd to hear a captivating marquis, in answer to the inquiry whether he was of the royal party at Marly, say, "No, I am only here *en polisson*;" meaning simply "I am here on the footing of all those whose nobility is of a later date than 1400." The Marly excursions were exceedingly expensive to the King. Besides the superior tables, those of the almoners, equerries, *maîtres d'hôtel*, etc., were all supplied with such a degree of magnificence as to allow of inviting strangers to them; and almost all the visitors from Paris were boarded at the expense of the Court.

The personal frugality of the unfortunate Prince who sank beneath the weight of the national debts thus favoured the Queen's predilection for her Petit Trianon; and for five or six years preceding the Revolution the Court very seldom visited Marly.

The King, always attentive to the comfort of his family, gave Mesdames, his aunts, the use of the Château de Bellevue, and afterwards purchased the Princesse de Guéménée's house, at the entrance to Paris, for Elisabeth.[1] The Comtesse de Provence bought a small house at Montreuil; Monsieur already had Brunoy; the Comtesse d'Artois built Bagatelle; Versailles became, in the estimation of all the royal family, the least agreeable of residences. They only fancied themselves at home in the plainest houses, surrounded by English gardens, where they better enjoyed the beauties of nature. The taste for cascades and statues was entirely past.

The Queen occasionally remained a whole month at Petit Trianon, and had established there all the ways of life in a château. She entered the sitting-room without driving the ladies from their pianoforte or embroidery. The gentlemen continued their billiards or backgammon without suffering her presence to interrupt them. There was but little room in the small Château of Trianon. Madame Elisabeth accompanied the Queen there, but the ladies of honour and ladies of the palace had no establishment at Trianon. When invited by the Queen, they came from Versailles to dinner. The King and Princes came regularly to sup. A white gown, a gauze kerchief, and a straw hat were the uniform dress of the Princesses. Examining all the manufactories of the hamlet, seeing the cows milked, and fishing in the lake delighted

---

1. Madame Elisabeth enjoyed this house for several years; but the King arranged that she should not sleep there until she was twenty-five years of age. The Revolution broke out before that time.

the Queen; and every year she showed increased aversion to the pompous excursions to Marly. The idea of acting comedies, as was then done in almost all country houses, followed on the Queen's wish to live at Trianon without ceremony. It was agreed that no young man except the Comte d'Artois should be admitted into the company of performers, and that the audience should consist only of the King, Monsieur, and the Princesses, who did not play; but in order to stimulate the actors a little, the first boxes were to be occupied by the readers, the Queen's ladies, their sisters and daughters, making altogether about forty persons.

The Queen laughed heartily at the voice of M. d'Adhémar, formerly a very fine one, but latterly become rather tremulous. His shepherd's dress in Colin, in the "Devin du Village," contrasted very ridiculously with his time of life, and the Queen said it would be difficult for malevolence itself to find anything to criticise in the choice of such a lover. The King was highly amused with these plays, and was present at every performance. Caillot, a celebrated actor, who had long quitted the stage, and Dazincourt, both of acknowledged good character, were selected to give lessons, the first in comic opera, of which the easier sorts were preferred, and the second in comedy. The office of hearer of rehearsals, prompter, and stage manager was given to my father-in-law. The Duc de Fronsac, first gentleman of the chamber, was much hurt at this. He thought himself called upon to make serious remonstrances upon the subject, and wrote to the Queen, who made him the following answer: "You cannot be first gentleman when we are the actors. Besides, I have already intimated to you my determination respecting Trianon. I hold no court there, I live like a private person, and M. Campan shall be always employed to execute orders relative to the private fêtes I choose to give there." This not putting a stop to the Duke's remonstrances, the King was obliged to interfere. The Duke continued obstinate, and insisted that he was entitled to manage the private amusements as much as those which were public. It became absolutely necessary to end the argument in a positive manner.

The diminutive Duc de Fronsac never failed, when he came to pay his respects to the Queen at her toilet, to turn the conversation upon Trianon, in order to make some ironical remarks on my father-in-law, of whom, from the time of his appointment, he always spoke as "my colleague Campan." The Queen would shrug her shoulders, and say, when he was gone, "It is quite shocking to find so 'little a man in the son of the Maréchal de Richelieu.'"

So long as no strangers were admitted to the performances they were but little censured; but the praise obtained by the performers made them look for a larger circle of admirers. The company, for a private company, was good enough, and the acting was applauded to the skies; nevertheless, as the audience withdrew, adverse criticisms were occasionally heard. The Queen permitted the officers of the Body Guards and the equerries of the King and Princes to be present at the plays. Private boxes were provided for some of the people belonging to the Court; a few more ladies were invited; and claims arose on all sides for the favour of admission. The Queen refused to admit the officers of the body guards of the Princes, the officers of the King's *Cent Suisses*, and many other persons, who were highly mortified at the refusal.

While delight at having given an heir to the throne of the Bourbons, and a succession of fêtes and amusements, filled up the happy days of Marie Antoinette, the public was engrossed by the Anglo-American war. Two kings, or rather their ministers, planted and propagated the love of liberty in the new world; the King of England, by shutting his ears and his heart against the continued and respectful representations of subjects at a distance from their native land, who had become numerous, rich, and powerful, through the resources of the soil they had fertilised; and the King of France, by giving support to this people in rebellion against their ancient sovereign. Many young soldiers, belonging to the first families of the country, followed La Fayette's example, and forsook luxury, amusement, and love, to go and tender their aid to the revolted Americans. Beaumarchais, secretly seconded by Messieurs de Maurepas and de Vergennes, obtained permission to send out supplies of arms and clothing. Franklin appeared at Court in the dress of an American agriculturist. His unpowdered hair, his round hat, his brown cloth coat formed a contrast to the laced and emboidered coats and the powder and perfume of the courtiers of Versailles. This novelty turned the light heads of the Frenchwomen. Elegant entertainments were given to Doctor Franklin, who, to the reputation of a man of science, added the patriotic virtues which invested him with the character of an apostle of liberty. I was present at one of these entertainments, when the most beautiful woman out of three hundred was selected to place a crown of laurels upon the white head of the American philosopher, and two kisses upon his cheeks. Even in the palace of Versailles Franklin's medallion was sold under the King's eyes, in the exhibition of Sèvres porcelain. The legend of this medallion was:

"Eripuit cœlo fulmen, sceptrumque tyrannis."

The King never declared his opinion upon an enthusiasm which his correct judgment no doubt led him to blame. The Queen spoke out more plainly about the part France was taking respecting the independence of the American colonies, and constantly opposed it. Far was she from foreseeing that a revolution at such a distance could excite one in which a misguided populace would drag her from her palace to a death equally unjust and cruel. She only saw something ungenerous in the method which France adopted of checking the power of England.

However, as Queen of France, she enjoyed the sight of a whole people rendering homage to the prudence, courage, and good qualities of a young Frenchman; and she shared the enthusiasm inspired by the conduct and military success of the Marquis de La Fayette. The Queen granted him several audiences on his first return from America, and, until the 10th of August, on which day my house was plundered, I preserved some lines from Gaston and Bayard, in which the friends of M. de La Fayette saw the exact outline of his character, written by her own hand :

> " Why talk of youth,
> When all the ripe experience of the old
> Dwells with him ? In his schemes profound and cool,
> He acts with wise precaution, and reserves
> For time of action his impetuous fire.
> To guard the camp, to scale the leaguered wall,
> Or dare the hottest of the fight, are toils

> That suit th' impetuous bearing of his youth;
> Yet like the gray-hair'd veteran he can shun
> The field of peril. Still before my eyes
> I place his bright example, for I love
> His lofty courage, and his prudent thought.
> Gifted like him, a warrior has no age."

These lines had been applauded and encored at the French theatre; everybody's head was turned. There was no class of persons that did not heartily approve of the support given openly by the French Government to the cause of American independence. The constitution planned for the new nation was digested at Paris, and while liberty, equality, and the rights of man were commented upon by the Condorcets, Baillys, Mirabeaus, etc., the minister Ségur published the King's edict, which, by repealing that of 1st November, 1750, declared all officers not noble by four generations incapable of filling the rank of captain, and denied all military rank to the *roturiers*, excepting sons of the chevaliers de St. Louis. The injustice and absurdity of this law was no doubt a secondary cause of the Revolution. To understand the despair and rage with which this law inspired the *Tiers Etat* one should have belonged to that honourable class. The provinces were full of *roturier* families, who for ages had lived as people of property upon their own domains, and paid the taxes. If these persons had several sons, they would place one in the King's service, one in the Church, another in the Order of Malta as a *chevalier servant d'armes*, and one in the magistracy; while the eldest preserved the paternal manor, and if he were situated in a country celebrated for wine, he would, besides selling his own produce, add a kind of commission trade in the wines of the canton. I have seen an individual of this justly respected class, who had been long employed in diplomatic business, and even honoured with the title of minister plenipotentiary, the son-in-law and nephew of colonels and town mayors, and, on his mother's side, nephew of a lieutenant-general with a cordon rouge, unable to introduce his sons as sous-lieutenants into a regiment of foot.

Another decision of the Court, which could not be announced by an edict, was that all ecclesiastical benefices, from the humblest priory up to the richest abbéy, should in future be appanages of the nobility. Being the son of a village surgeon, the Abbé de Vermond, who had great influence in the disposition of benefices, was particularly struck with the justice of this decree.

During the absence of the Abbé in an excursion he made for his health, I prevailed on the Queen to write a post-script to the petition of a curé, one of my friends, who was so-liciting a priory near his curacy, with the intention of retiring to it. I obtained it for him. On the Abbé's return he told me very harshly that I should act in a manner quite contrary to the King's wishes if I again obtained such a favour; that the wealth of the Church was for the future to be invariably de-voted to the support of the poorer nobility; that it was the in-terest of the State that it should be so; and a plebeian priest, happy in a good curacy, had only to remain curate.

Can we be astonished at the part shortly afterwards taken by the deputies of the Third Estate, when called to the States General?

XI

A BOUT the close of the last century several of the Northern sovereigns took a fancy for travelling. Christian III King of Denmark, visited the Court of France in 1763, during the reign of Louis XV. We have seen the King of Sweden and Joseph II at Versailles. The Grand Duke of Russia (afterwards Paul I), son of Catherine II, and the Princess of Wurtemberg, his wife, likewise resolved to visit France. They travelled under the titles of the Comte and Comtesse du Nord. They were presented on the 20th of May, 1782. The Queen received them with grace and dignity. On the day of their arrival at Versailles they dined in private with the King and Queen.

The plain, unassuming appearance of Paul I pleased Louis XVI. He spoke to him with more confidence and cheerfulness than he had spoken to Joseph II. The Comtesse du Nord was not at first so successful with the Queen. This lady was of a fine height, very fat for her age, with all the German

stiffness, well informed, and perhaps displaying her acquire-
ments with rather too much confidence. When the Comte
and Comtesse du Nord were presented the Queen was exceedingly nervous. She withdrew into her closet before she
went into the room where she was to dine with the illustrious travellers, and asked for a glass of water, confessing "she
had just experienced how much more difficult it was to play
the part of a queen in the presence of other sovereigns, or of
princes born to become so, than before courtiers." She soon
recovered from her confusion, and reappeared with ease and
confidence. The dinner was tolerably cheerful, and the conversation very animated.

Brilliant entertainments were given at Court in honour of the King of Sweden and the Comte du Nord. They
were received in private by the King and Queen, but they
were treated with much more ceremony than the Emperor,
and their Majesties always appeared to me to be very cautious before these personages. However, the King one day
asked the Russian Grand Duke if it were true that he could
not rely on the fidelity of any one of those who accompanied him. The Prince answered him without hesitation, and
before a considerable number of persons, that he should be
very sorry to have with him even a poodle that was much attached to him, because his mother would take care to have it
thrown into the Seine, with a stone round its neck, before he
should leave Paris. This reply, which I myself heard, horri-
fied me, whether it depicted the disposition of Catherine, or
only expressed the Prince's prejudice against her.

The Queen gave the Grand Duke a supper at Trianon,
and had the gardens illuminated as they had been for the
Emperor. The Cardinal de Rohan very indiscreetly ventured

to introduce himself there without the Queen's knowledge. Having been treated with the utmost coolness ever since his return from Vienna, he had not dared to ask her himself for permission to see the illumination; but he persuaded the porter of Trianon to admit him as soon as the Queen should have set off for Versailles, and his Eminence engaged to remain in the porter's lodge until all the carriages should have left the château. He did not keep his word, and while the porter was busy in the discharge of his duty, the Cardinal, who wore his red stockings and had merely thrown on a greatcoat, went down into the garden, and, with an air of mystery, drew up in two different places to see the royal family and suite pass by.

Her Majesty was highly offended at this piece of boldness, and next day ordered the porter to be discharged. There was a general feeling of disgust at the Cardinal's conduct, and of commiseration towards the porter for the loss of his place. Affected at the misfortune of the father of a family, I obtained his forgiveness; and since that time I have often regretted the feeling which induced me to interfere. The notoriety of the discharge of the porter of Trianon, and the odium that circumstance would have fixed upon the Cardinal, would have made the Queen's dislike to him still more publicly known, and would probably have prevented the scandalous and notorious intrigue of the necklace.

The Queen, who was much prejudiced against the King of Sweden, received him very coldly. All that was said of the private character of that sovereign, his connection with the Comte de Vergennes, from the time of the Revolution of Sweden, in 1772, the character of his favourite Armfeldt, and the prejudices of the monarch himself against the

Swedes who were well received at the Court of Versailles, formed the grounds of this dislike. He came one day uninvited and unexpected, and requested to dine with the Queen. The Queen received him in the little closet, and desired me to send for her clerk of the kitchen, that she might be informed whether there was a proper dinner to set before Comte d'Haga, and add to it if necessary. The King of Sweden assured her that there would be enough for him; and I could not help smiling when I thought of the length of the *menu* of the dinner of the King and Queen, not half of which would have made its appearance had they dined in private. The Queen looked significantly at me, and I withdrew. In the evening she asked me why I had seemed so astonished when she ordered me to add to her dinner, saying that I ought instantly to have seen that she was giving the King of Sweden a lesson for his presumption. I owned to her that the scene had appeared to me so much in the bourgeois style, that I involuntarily thought of the cutlets on the gridiron, and the omelette, which in families in humble circumstances serve to piece out short commons. She was highly diverted with my answer, and repeated it to the King, who also laughed heartily at it.

The peace with England satisfied all classes of society interested in the national honour. The departure of the English commissary from Dunkirk, who had been fixed at that place ever since the shameful peace of 1763 as inspector of our navy, occasioned an ecstasy of joy. The Government communicated to the Englishman the order for his departure before the treaty was made public. But for that precaution the populace would have probably committed some excess or other, in order to make the agent of English power feel the effects of the resentment which had constantly increased during his stay at that port. Those engaged in trade were the only persons dissatisfied with the treaty of 1783. That article which provided for the free admission of English goods annihilated at one blow the trade of Rouen and the other manufacturing towns throughout the kingdom. The English swarmed into Paris. A considerable number of them were presented at Court. The Queen paid them marked attention; doubtless she wished them to distinguish between the esteem she felt for their noble nation and the political views of the Government in the support it had afforded to the Americans. Discontent was, however, manifested at Court in consequence of the favour bestowed by the Queen on the English noblemen: these attentions were called infatuations. This was illiberal; and the Queen justly complained of such absurd jealousy.

The journey to Fontainebleau and the winter at Paris and at Court were extremely brilliant. The spring brought back those amusements which the Queen began to prefer to the splendour of fêtes. The most perfect harmony subsisted between the King and Queen; I never saw but one cloud between them. It was soon dispelled, and the cause of it is perfectly unknown to me.

My father-in-law, whose penetration and experience I respected greatly, recommended me, when he saw me placed in the service of a young queen, to shun all kinds of confidence. "It procures," said he, "but a very fleeting, and at the same time, dangerous sort of favour; serve with zeal to the best of your judgment, but never do more than obey. Instead of setting your wits to work to discover why an order or a commission which may appear of consequence is given to you, use them to prevent the possibility of your knowing anything of the matter." I had occasion to act on this wise advice. One morning at Trianon I went into the Queen's chamber; there were letters lying upon the bed, and she was weeping bitterly. Her tears and sobs were occasionally interrupted by exclamations of "Ah! that I were dead!— wretches! monsters! What have I clone to them?" I offered her orange-flower water and ether. "Leave me," said she, "if you love me; it would be better to kill me at once." At this moment she threw her arm over my shoulder and began weeping afresh. I saw that some weighty trouble oppressed her heart, and that she wanted a confidant. I suggested sending for the Duchesse de Polignac; this she strongly opposed. I renewed my arguments, and her opposition grew weaker. I disengaged myself from her arms, and ran to the antechamber, where I knew that an outrider always waited, ready to mount and start at a moment's warning for Versailles. I ordered him to go full speed, and tell the Duchesse de Polignac that the Queen was very uneasy, and desired to see her instantly. The Duchess always had a carriage ready. In less than ten minutes she was at the Queen's door. I was the only person there, having been forbidden to send for the other women. Madame de Polignac came in; the Queen held out her arms to her, the Duchess rushed towards her. I heard her sobs renewed and withdrew.

A quarter of an hour afterwards the Queen, who had become calmer, rang to be dressed. I sent her woman in; she put on her gown and retired to her boudoir with the Duchess. Very soon afterwards the Comte d'Artois arrived from Compiègne, where he had been with the King. He eagerly inquired where the Queen was; remained half an hour with her and the Duchess; and on coming out told me the Queen asked for me. I found her seated on the couch by the side of her friend; her features had resumed their usual cheerful and gracious appearance. She held out her hand to me, and said to the Duchess, "I know I have made her so uncomfortable this morning that I must set her poor heart at ease." She then added, "You must have seen, on some fine summer's day, a black cloud suddenly appear and threaten to pour down upon the country and lay it waste. The lightest wind drives it away, and the blue sky and serene weather are restored. This is just the image of what has happened to me this morning." She afterwards told me that the King would return from Compiègne after hunting there, and sup with her; that I must send for her purveyor, to select with him from his bills of fare all such dishes as the King liked best; that she would have no others served up in the evening at her table; and that this was a mark of attention that she wished the King to notice. The Duchesse de Polignac also took me by the hand, and told me how happy she was that she had been with the Queen at a moment when she stood in need of a friend. I never knew what could have created in the Queen so lively and so transient an alarm; but I guessed from the particular care she took respecting the King that attempts had been made to irritate him against her; that the malice of her enemies had been promptly discovered and counteracted by the King's penetration and attachment; and that the Comte d'Artois had hastened to bring her intelligence of it.

It was, I think, in the summer of 1787, during one of the Trianon excursions, that the Queen of Naples sent the Chevalier de Bressac to her Majesty on a secret mission relative to a projected marriage between the Hereditary Prince, her son, and Madame, the King's daughter; in the absence of the lady of honour he addressed himself to me. Although he said a great deal to me about the close confidence with which the Queen of Naples honoured him, and about his letter of credit, I thought he had the air of an adventurer.[1] He had, indeed, private letters for the Queen, and his mission was not feigned; he talked to me very rashly even before his admission, and entreated me to do all that lay in my power to dispose the Queen's mind in favour of his sovereign's wishes; I declined, assuring him that it did not become me to meddle with State affairs. He endeavoured, but in vain, to prove to me that the union contemplated by the Queen of Naples ought not to be looked upon in that light.

I procured M. de Bressac the audience he desired, but without suffering myself even to seem acquainted with the object of his mission. The Queen told me what it was; she thought him a person ill-chosen for the occasion; and yet she thought that the Queen, her sister, had done wisely in not sending a man worthy to be avowed,—it being impossible that what she solicited should take place. I had an opportunity on this occasion, as indeed on many others, of judging to what extent the. Queen valued and loved France and the dignity of our Court. She then told me that Madame, in marrying her cousin, the Duc d'Angoulême, would not lose her rank as daughter of the Queen; and that her situation would be far preferable to that of queen of any other country; and that

---

1. I know that he afterwards spent several years shut up in the Château de l'Œuf.

there was nothing in Europe to be compared to the Court of France; and that it would be necessary, in order to avoid exposing a French Princess to feelings of deep regret, in case she should be married to a foreign prince, to take her from the palace of Versailles at seven years of age, and send her immediately to the Court in which she was to dwell; and that at twelve would be too late; for recollections and comparisons would ruin the happiness of all the rest of her life. The Queen looked upon the destiny of her sisters as far beneath her own; and frequently mentioned the mortifications inflicted by the Court of Spain upon her sister, the Queen of Naples, and the necessity she was under of imploring the mediation of the King of France.

She showed me several letters that she had received from the Queen of Naples relative to her differences with the Court of Madrid respecting the Minister Acton. She thought him useful to her people, inasmuch as he was a man of considerable information and great activity. In these letters she minutely acquainted her Majesty with the nature of the affronts she had received, and represented Mr. Acton to her as a man whom malevolence itself could not suppose capable of interesting her otherwise than by his services. She had had to suffer the impertinences of a Spaniard named Las Casas, who had been sent to her by the King, her father-in-law, to persuade her to dismiss Mr. Acton from the business of the State, and from her intimacy. She complained bitterly to the Queen, her sister, of the insulting proceedings of this *chargé d'affaires*, whom she told, in order to convince him of the nature of the feelings which attached her to Mr. Acton, that she would have portraits and busts of him executed by the most eminent artists of Italy, and that she would then send them to the King of Spain, to prove that nothing but the desire to retain a man of superior capacity had induced her to bestow on him the favour he enjoyed. This Las Casas dared to answer her that it would be useless trouble; that the ugliness of a man did not always render him displeasing; and that the King of Spain had too much experience not to know that there was no accounting for the caprices of a woman.

This audacious reply filled the Queen of Naples with indignation, and her emotion caused her to miscarry on the same day. In consequence of the mediation of Louis XVI the Queen of Naples obtained complete satisfaction, and Mr. Acton continued Prime Minister.

Among the characteristics which denoted the goodness of the Queen, her respect for personal liberty should have a place. I have seen her put up with the most troublesome importunities from people whose minds were deranged rather than have them arrested. Her patient kindness was put to a very disagreeable trial by an ex-councillor of the Bordeaux Parliament, named Castelnaux; this man declared himself the lover of the Queen, and was generally known by that appellation. For ten successive years did he follow the Court in all its excursions. Pale and wan, as people who are out of their senses usually are, his sinister appearance occasioned the most uncomfortable sensations. During the two hours that the Queen's public card parties lasted, he would remain opposite her Majesty. He placed himself in the same manner before her at chapel, and never failed to be at the King's dinner or the dinner in public. At the theatre he invariably seated himself as near the Queen's box as possible. He always set off for Fontainebleau or St. Cloud the day before the Court, and when her Majesty arrived at her various residences, the first person she met on getting out of her carriage was this melancholy madman, who never spoke to any one. When the Queen stayed at Petit Trianon the passion of this unhappy man became still more annoying. He would hastily swallow a morsel at some eating-house, and spend all the rest of the day, even when it rained, in going round and round the garden, always walking at the edge of the moat. The Queen frequently met him when she was either alone or with her children; and yet she would not suffer any violence to be used to relieve her from this intolerable annoyance. Having one day given M. de Sèze permission to enter Trianon, she sent to desire he would come to me, and directed me to inform that celebrated advocate of M. de Castelnaux's derangement, and then to send for him that M. de Sèze might have some conversation with him. He talked to him nearly an hour, and made considerable impression upon his mind; and at last M. de Castelnaux requested me to inform the Queen positively that, since his presence was disagreeable to her, he would retire to his province. The Queen was very much rejoiced, and desired me to express her full satisfaction to M. de Sèze. Half an hour after M. de Sèze was gone the unhappy madman was announced. He came to tell me that he withdrew his promise, that he had not sufficient command of himself to give up seeing the Queen as often as possible. This new determination was a disagreeable message to take to her Majesty; but how was I affected at hearing her say, "Well, let him annoy me! but do not let him be deprived of the blessing of freedom." [1]

---

1. On the arrest of the King and Queen at Varennes, this unfortunate Castelnaux attempted to starve himself to death. The people in whose house he lived becoming uneasy at his absence, had

The direct influence of the Queen on affairs during the earlier years of the reign was shown only in her exertions to obtain from the King a revision of the decrees in two celebrated causes.[1] It was contrary to her principles to interfere in matters of justice, and never did she avail herself of her influence to bias the tribunals. The Duchesse de Praslin, through a criminal caprice, carried her enmity to her husband so far as to disinherit her children in favour of the family of M. de Guéménée. The Duchesse de Choiseul, who was warmly interested in this affair, one day entreated the Queen, in my presence, at least to condescend to ask the first president when the cause would be called on; the Queen replied that she could not even do that, for it would manifest an interest which it was her duty not to show.

If the King had not inspired the Queen with a lively feeling of love, it is quite certain that she yielded him respect and affection for the goodness of his disposition and the equity of which he gave so many proofs throughout his reign. One evening she returned very late; she came out of the King's closet, and said to M. de Misery and myself, drying her eyes, which were filled with tears, "You see me weeping,

---

the door of his room forced open, where he was found stretched senseless on the floor. I do not know what became of him after the 10th of August.

1. The Queen did not venture to meddle with those two causes further than to solicit a revision of them; for it was contrary to her principles to interfere in matters of justice, and never did she avail herself of her influence to bias the tribunals. The Duchesse de Praslin, through a criminal caprice, carried her enmity to her husband so far, as to disinherit her children in favour of the family of M. de Guéménée. The Duchesse de Choiseul, who was warmly interested in this affair, one day entreated the Queen, in my presence, at least to condescend to ask the First President when the cause would be called on; the Queen replied, that she could not even do that, for it would manifest an interest which it was her duty not to show.

but do not be uneasy at it: these are the sweetest tears that a wife can shed; they are caused by the impression which the justice and goodness of the King have made upon me; he has just complied with my request for a revision of the proceedings against Messieurs de Bellegarde and de Monthieu, victims of the Duc d'Aiguillon's hatred to the Duc de Choiseul. He has been equally just to the Duc de Guines in his affair with Tort. It is a happy thing for a queen to be able to admire and esteem him who has admitted her to a participation of his throne; and as to you, I congratulate you upon your having to live under the sceptre of so virtuous a sovereign."

The Queen laid before the King all the memorials of the Duc de Guines, who, during his embassy to England, was involved in difficulties by a secretary, who speculated in the public funds in London on his own account, but in such a manner as to throw a suspicion of it on the ambassador. Messieurs de Vergennes and Turgot, bearing but little goodwill to the Duc de Guines, who was the friend of the Duc de Choiseul, were not disposed to render the ambassador any service. The Queen succeeded in fixing the King's particular attention on this affair, and the innocence of the Duc de Guines triumphed through the equity of Louis XVI.

An incessant underhand war was carried on between the friends and partisans of M. de Choiseul, who were called the Austrians, and those who sided with Messieurs d'Aiguillon, de Maurepas, and de Vergennes, who, for the same reason, kept up the intrigues carried on at Court and in Paris against the Queen. Marie Antoinette, on her part, supported those who had suffered in this political quarrel, and it was this feeling which led her to ask for a revision of the proceedings against Messieurs de Bellegarde and de Monthieu.

The first, a colonel and inspector of artillery, and the second, proprietor of a foundry at St. Etienne, were, under the Ministry of the Duc d'Aiguillon, condemned to imprisonment for twenty years and a day for having withdrawn from the arsenals of France, by order of the Duc de Choiseul, a vast number of muskets, as being of no value except as old iron, while in point of fact the greater part of those muskets were immediately embarked and sold to the Americans. It appears that the Duc de Choiseul imparted to the Queen, as grounds of defence for the accused, the political views which led him to authorise that reduction and sale in the manner in which it had been executed. It rendered the case of Messieurs de Bellegarde and de Monthieu more unfavourable that the artillery officer who made the reduction in the capacity of inspector was, through a clandestine marriage, brother-in-law of the owner of the foundry, the purchaser of the rejected arms. The innocence of the two prisoners was, nevertheless, made apparent; and they came to Versailles with their wives and children to throw themselves at the feet of their benefactress. This affecting scene took place in the grand gallery, at the entrance to the Queen's apartment. She wished to restrain the women from kneeling, saying that they had only had justice done them; and that she ought to be congratulated upon the most substantial happiness attendant upon her station, that of laying such appeals before the King.

On every occasion, when the Queen had to speak in public, she used the most appropriate and elegant language, notwithstanding the difficulty a foreigner might be expected to experience. She answered all addresses herself, a custom which she learned at the Court of Maria Theresa. The Princesses of the House of Bourbon had long ceased to take the trouble of speaking in such cases. Madame Adé-laïde blamed the Queen for not doing as they did, assuring her that it was quite sufficient to mutter a few words that might sound like an answer, while the addressers, occupied with what they had themselves been saying, would always take it for granted that a proper answer had been returned. The Queen saw that idleness alone dictated such a proceeding, and that as the practice even of muttering a few words showed the necessity of answering in some way, it must be more proper to reply simply but clearly, and in the best style possible. Sometimes, indeed, when apprised of the subject of the address; she would write down her answer in the morning, not to learn it by heart, but in order to settle the ideas or sentiments she wished to introduce.

The influence of the Comtesse de Polignac increased daily; and her friends availed themselves of it to effect changes in the Ministry. The dismissal of M. de Montbarrey, a man without talents or character, was generally approved of. It was rightly attributed to the Queen. He had been placed in administration by M. de Maurepas, and maintained by his aged wife; both, of course, became more inveterate than ever against the Queen and the Polignac circle.

The appointment of M. de Ségur to the place of Minister of War, and of M. de Castries to that of Minister of Marine, were wholly the work of that circle. The Queen dreaded making ministers; her favourite often wept when the men of her circle compelled her to interfere. Men blame women for meddling in business, and yet in courts it is con-tinually the men themselves who make use of the influence of the women in matters with which the latter ought to have nothing to do.

When M. de Ségur was presented to the Queen on his new appointment, she said to me, "You have just seen a minister of my making. I am very glad, so far as regards the King's service, that he is appointed, for I think the selection a very good one; but I almost regret the part I have taken in it. I take a responsibility upon myself. I was fortunate in being free from any; and in order to relieve myself from this as much as possible I have just promised M. de Ségur, and that upon my word of honour, not to back any petition, nor to hinder any of his operations by solicitations on behalf of my *protégés*."

During the first administration of M. Necker, whose ambition had not then drawn him into schemes repugnant to his better judgment, and whose views appeared to the Queen to be very judicious, she indulged in hopes of the restoration of the finances. Knowing that M. de Maurepas wished to drive M. Necker to resign, she urged him to have patience until the death of an old man whom the King kept about him from a fondness for his first choice, and out of respect for his advanced age. She even went so far as to tell him that M. de Maurepas was always ill, and that his end could not be very distant. M. Necker would not wait for that event. The Queen's prediction was fulfilled. M. de Maurepas ended his days immediately after a journey to Fontainebleau in 1781.

M. Necker had retired. He had been exasperated by a piece of treachery in the old minister, for which he could not forgive him. I knew something of this intrigue at the time; it has since been fully explained to me by Madame la Maréchale de Beauvau. M. Necker saw that his credit at Court was declining, and fearing lest that circumstance should injure his financial operations, he requested the King to grant him some favour which might show the public that he had not lost the confidence of his sovereign. He concluded his letter by pointing out five requests— such an office, *or* such a mark of distinction, *or* such a badge of honour, and so on, and handed it to M. de Maurepas. The *ors* were changed into ands; *and* the King was displeased at M. Necker's ambition, and the assurance with which he displayed it. Madame la Maréchale de Beauvau assured me that the Maréchal de Castries saw the minute of M. Necker's letter, and that he likewise saw the altered copy.[1]

The interest which the Queen took in M. Necker died away during his retirement, and at last changed into strong prejudice against him. He wrote too much about the measures he would have pursued, and the benefits that would have resulted to the State from them. The ministers who succeeded him thought their operations embarrassed by the care that M. Necker and his partisans incessantly took to occupy the public with his plans; his friends were too ardent. The Queen discerned a party spirit in these combinations, and sided wholly with his enemies.

After those inefficient comptrollers-general, Messieurs Joly de Fleury and d'Ormesson, it became necessary to resort to a man of more acknowledged talent, and the Queen's friends, at that time combining with the Comte d'Artois and with M. de Vergennes, got M. de Calonne appointed. The Queen was highly displeased, and her close intimacy with the Duchesse de Polignac began to suffer for this.

Her Majesty, continuing to converse with me upon the difficulties she had met with in private life, told me that

1. I have this anecdote under that lady's hand.

ambitious men without merit sometimes found means to gain their ends by dint of importunity, and that she had to blame herself for having procured M. d'Adhémar's appointment to the London embassy, merely because he teased her into it at the Duchess's house. She added, however, that it was at a time of perfect peace with the English; that the Ministry knew the inefficiency of M. d'Adhémar as well as she did, and that he could do neither harm nor good.

Often in conversations of unreserved frankness the Queen owned that she had purchased rather dearly a piece of experience which would make her carefully watch over the conduct of her daughters-in-law, and that she would be particularly scrupulous about the qualifications of the ladies who might attend them; that no consideration of rank or favour should bias her in so important a choice. She attributed several of her youthful mistakes to a lady of great levity, whom she found in her palace on her arrival in France. She also determined to forbid the Princesses coming under her control the practice of singing with professors, and said, candidly, and with as much severity as her slanderers could have done, "I ought to have heard Garat sing, and never to have sung duets with him."

The indiscreet zeal of Monsieur Augeard contributed to the public belief that the Queen disposed of all the offices of finance. He had, without any authority for doing so, required the committee of *fermiers-général* to inform him of all vacancies, assuring them that they would be meeting the wishes of the Queen. The members complied, but not without murmuring. When the Queen became aware of what her secretary had done, she highly disapproved of it, caused her resentment to be made known to the *fermiers-général*, and abstained from asking for appointments,—making only one request of the kind, as a marriage portion for one of her attendants, a young woman of good family.

XII

THE Queen did not sufficiently conceal the dissatisfaction she felt at having been unable to prevent the appointment of M. de Calonne; she even one day went so far as to say at the Duchess's, in the midst of the partisans and protectors of that minister, that the finances of France passed alternately from the hands of an honest man without talent into those of a skilful knave. M. de Calonne was thus far from acting in concert with the Queen all the time that he continued in office; and, while dull verses were circulated about Paris describing the Queen and her favourite dipping at pleasure into the coffers of the comptroller-general, the Queen was avoiding all communication with him.

During the long and severe winter of 1783-84 the King gave three millions of livres for the relief of the indigent. M. de Calonne, who felt the necessity of making advances to the Queen, caught at this opportunity of showing her respect and devotion. He offered to place in her hands one million of the three, to be distributed in her name and under her direction. His proposal was rejected; the Queen answered that the charity ought to be wholly distributed in the King's name, and that she would this year debar herself of even the slightest enjoyments, in order to contribute all her savings to the relief of the unfortunate.

The moment M. de Calonne left the closet the Queen sent for me: "Congratulate me, my dear," said she; "I have just escaped a snare, or at least a matter which eventually might have caused me much regret." She related the conversation which had taken place word for word to me, adding, "That man will complete the ruin of the national finances, it is said that I placed him in his situation. The people are made to believe that I am extravagant; yet I have refused to suffer a sum of money from the royal treasury, although destined for the most laudable purpose, even to pass through my hands."

The Queen, making monthly retrenchments from the expenditure of her privy purse, and not having spent the gifts customary at the period of her confinement, was in possession of from five to six hundred thousand francs, her own savings. She made use of from two to three hundred thousand francs of this, which her first women sent to M. Lenoir, to the curés of Paris and Versailles, and to the Sœurs Hospitalières, and so distributed them among families in need. Desirous to implant in the breast of her daughter not only a desire to succour the unfortunate, but those qualities necessary for the due discharge of that duty, the Queen incessantly talked to her, though she was yet very young, about the sufferings of the poor during a season so inclement. The Princess already had a sum of from eight to ten thousand francs for charitable purposes, and the Queen made her distribute part of it herself.

Wishing to give her children yet another lesson of beneficence, she desired me on New Year's eve to get from Paris, as in other years, all the fashionable playthings, and have them spread out in her closet. Then taking her children by the hand, she showed them all the dolls and mechanical toys which were ranged there, and told them that she had intended to give them some handsome New Year's gifts, but that the cold made the poor so wretched that all her money was spent in blankets and clothes to protect them from the rigour of the season, and in supplying them with bread; so that this year they would only have the pleasure of looking at the new playthings. When she returned with her children into her sitting-room, she said there was still an unavoidable expense to be incurred; that assuredly many mothers would at that season think as she did,—that the toyman must lose by it; and therefore she gave him fifty louis to repay him for the cost of his journey, and console him for having sold nothing.

The purchase of St. Cloud, a matter very simple in itself, had, on account of the prevailing spirit, unfavourable consequences to the Queen.

The palace of Versailles, pulled to pieces in the interior by a variety of new arrangements, and mutilated in point of uniformity by the removal of the ambassadors' staircase, and of the peristyle of columns placed at the end of the marble court, was equally in want of substantial and ornamental repair. The King therefore desired M. Micque to lay before him several plans for the repairs of the palace. He consulted me on certain arrangements analogous to some of those adopted in the Queen's establishment, and in my presence asked M. Micque how much money would be wanted for the execution of the whole work, and how many years he would be in completing it. I forget how many millions were mentioned: M. Micque replied that six years would be sufficient time if the Treasury made the necessary periodical advances without any delay. "And how many years shall you require," said the King, "if the advances are not punctually made?" "Ten, Sire," replied the architect. "We must then reckon upon ten years," said his Majesty, "and put off this great undertaking until the year 1790; it will occupy the rest of the century." The King afterwards talked of the depreciation of property which took place at Versailles whilst the Regent removed the Court of Louis XV to the Tuileries, and said that he must consider how to prevent that inconvenience; it was the desire to do this that promoted the purchase of St. Cloud. The Queen first thought of it one day when she was riding out with the Duchesse de Polignac and the Comtesse Diane; she mentioned it to the King, who was much pleased with the thought,—the purchase confirming him in the intention, which he had entertained for ten years, of quitting Versailles.

The King determined that the ministers, public officers, pages, and a considerable part of his stabling should remain at Versailles. Messieurs de Breteuil and de Calonne were instructed to treat with the Duc d'Orléans for the purchase of St. Cloud; at first they hoped to be able to conclude the business by a mere exchange. The value of the Château de Choisy, de la Muette, and a forest was equivalent to the sum demanded by the House of Orléans; and in the exchange which the Queen expected she only saw a saving to be made instead of an increase of expense. By this arrangement the government of Choisy, in the hands of the Duc de Coigny, and that of La Muette, in the hands of the Maréchal de Soubise, would be suppressed. At the same time the two *concierges*, and all the servants employed in these two royal houses, would be reduced; but while the treaty was going forward Messieurs de Breteuil and de Calonne gave up the point of exchange, and some millions in cash were substituted for Choisy and La Muette.

The Queen advised the King to give her St. Cloud, as a means of avoiding the establishment of a governor; her plan being to have merely a *concierge* there, by which means the governor's expenses would be saved. The King agreed, and St. Cloud was purchased for the Queen. She provided the same liveries for the porters at the gates and servants at the château as for those at Trianon. The *concierge* at the latter place had put up some regulations for the household, headed, "By order of the Queen." The same thing was done at St. Cloud. The Queen's livery at the door of a palace where it was expected none but that of the King would be seen, and the words "By order of the Queen" at the head of the printed papers pasted near the iron gates, caused a great sensation, and produced a very unfortunate effect, not only among the common people, but also among persons of a superior class. They saw in it an attack upon the customs of monarchy, and customs are nearly equal to laws. The Queen heard of this, but she thought that her dignity would be compromised if she made any change in the form of these regulations, though they might have been altogether superseded without inconvenience. "My name is not out of place," said she, "in gardens belonging to myself; I may give orders there without infringing on the rights of the State." This was her only answer to the representations which a few faithful servants ventured to make on the subject. The discontent of the Parisians on this occasion probably induced

M. d'Espréménil, upon the first troubles about the Parliament, to say that it was *impolitic* and *immoral* to see palaces belonging to a Queen of France.[1]

The Queen was very much dissatisfied with the manner in which M. de Calonne had managed this matter. The Abbé de Vermond, the most active and persevering of that minister's enemies, saw with delight that the expedients of those from whom alone new resources might be expected were gradually becoming exhausted, because the period when the Archbishop of Toulouse would be placed over the finances was thereby hastened.

The royal navy had resumed an imposing attitude during the war for the independence of America; a glorious peace with England had compensated for the former attacks of our enemies upon the fame of France; and the throne was surrounded by numerous heirs. The sole ground of uneasiness was in the finances, but that uneasiness related only to the manner in which they were administered. In a word, France felt confident in its own strength and resources, when two events, which seem scarcely worthy of a place in history, but which have, nevertheless, an important one in that of the French Revolution, introduced a spirit of ridicule and contempt, not only against the highest ranks, but even

1. The Queen never forgot this affront of M. d'Espréménil's; she said, that as it was offered at a time when social order had not been disturbed, she felt the severest mortification at it. Shortly before the downfall of the throne, M. d'Espréménil, having openly espoused the King's side, was insulted in the garden of the Tuileries, by the Jacobins, and so ill-treated that he was carried home very ill. Somebody recommended the Queen, on account of the royalist principles he then professed, to send and inquire after him. She replied, that she was truly grieved at what had happened to M. d'Espréménil, but that mere policy should never induce her to show any particular solicitude for the man who had been the first to make so insulting an attack upon her character.

THE PRIVATE LIFE OF MARIE ANTOINETTE

against the most august personages. I allude to a comedy and a great swindling transaction.

Beaumarchais had long possessed a reputation in certain circles in Paris for his wit and musical talents, and at the theatres for dramas more or less indifferent, when his "Barbier de Séville" procured him a higher position among dramatic writers. His "Memoirs" against M. Göesman had amused Paris by the ridicule they threw upon a Parliament which was disliked; and his admission to an intimacy with M. de Maurepas procured him a degree of influence over important affairs. He then became ambitious of influencing public opinion by a kind of drama, in which established manners and customs should be held up to popular derision and the ridicule of the new philosophers. After several years of prosperity the minds of the French had become more generally critical; and when Beaumarchais had finished his monstrous but diverting "Mariage de Figaro," all people of any consequence were eager for the gratification of hearing it read, the censors having decided that it should not be performed. These readings of "Figaro" grew so numerous that people were daily-heard to say, "I have been (or I am going to be) at the reading of Beaumarchais's play." The desire to see it performed became universal; an expression that he had the art to use compelled, as it were, the approbation of the nobility, or of persons in power, who aimed at ranking among the magnanimous; he made his "Figaro" say that "none but little minds dreaded little books." The Baron de Breteuil, and all the men of Madame de Polignac's circle, entered the lists as the warmest protectors of the comedy. Solicitations to the King became so pressing that his Majesty determined to judge for himself of a work which so much engrossed public attention, and desired me to ask M. Le Noir, lieutenant of police, for the manuscript of the "Mariage de Figaro." One morning I received a note from the Queen ordering me to be with her at three o'clock, and not to come without having dined, for she would detain me some time. When I got to the Queen's inner closet I found her alone with the King; a chair and a small table were ready placed opposite to them, and upon the table lay an enormous manuscript in several books. The King said to me, "There is Beaumarchais's comedy; you must read it to us. You will find several parts troublesome on account of the erasures and references. I have already run it over, but I wish the Queen to be acquainted with the work. You will not mention this reading to any one."

I began. The King frequently interrupted me by praise or censure, which was always just. He frequently exclaimed, "That's in bad taste; this man continually brings the Italian *concetti* on the stage." At that soliloquy of Figaro in which he attacks various points of government, and especially at the tirade against State prisons, the King rose up and said, indignantly:

"That's detestable; that shall never be played; the Bastille must be destroyed before the license to act this play can be any other than an act of the most dangerous inconsistency. This man scoffs at everything that should be respected in a government."

"It will not be played, then?" said the Queen.

"No, certainly," replied Louis XVI; "you may rely upon that."

Still it was constantly reported that "Figaro" was about to be performed; there were even wagers laid upon the subject; I never should have laid any myself, fancying that I was better informed as to the probability than anybody else; if I had, however, I should have been completely deceived. The protectors of Beaumarchais, feeling certain that they would succeed in their scheme of making his work public in spite of the King's prohibition, distributed the parts in the "Mariage de Figaro" among the actors of the Théâtre Français. Beaumarchais had made them enter into the spirit of his characters, and they determined to enjoy at least one performance of this so-called *chef d'œuvre*. The first gentlemen of the chamber agreed that M. de la Ferté should lend the theatre of the Hôtel des Menus Plaisirs, at Paris, which was used for rehearsals of the opera; tickets were distributed to a vast number of leaders of society; and the day for the performance was fixed. The King heard of all this only on the very morning, and signed a *lettre de cachet*,[1] which prohibited the performance. When the messenger who brought the order arrived, he found a part of the theatre already filled with spectators, and the streets leading to the Hôtel des Menus Plaisirs filled with carriages; the piece was not performed. This prohibition of the King's was looked upon as an attack on public liberty.

The disappointment produced such discontent that the words *oppression* and *tyranny* were uttered with no less passion and bitterness at that time than during the days which immediately preceded the downfall of the throne. Beaumarchais was so far put off his guard by rage as to exclaim, "Well, gentlemen, he won't suffer it to be played here; but I swear it shall be played,—perhaps in the very choir

---

1. A lettre de cachet was any written order proceeding from the King's will. The term was not confined merely to orders for arrest.

of Notre-Dame!" There was something prophetic in these words. It was generally insinuated shortly afterwards that Beaumarchais had determined to suppress all those parts of his work which could be obnoxious to the Government; and on pretence of judging of the sacrifices made by the author, M. de Vaudreuil obtained permission to have this far-famed "Mariage de Figaro" performed at his country house. M. Campan was asked there; he had frequently heard the work read, and did not now find the alterations that had been announced; this he observed to several persons belonging to the Court, who maintained that the author had made all the sacrifices required. M. Campan was so astonished at these persistent assertions of an obvious falsehood that he replied by a quotation from Beaumarchais himself, and assuming the tone of Basilio in the "Barbier de Séville," he said, "Faith, gentlemen, I don't know who is deceived here; everybody is in the secret." They then came to the point, and begged him to tell the Queen positively that all which had been pronounced reprehensible in M. de Beaumarchais's play had been cut out. My father-in-law contented himself with replying that his situation at Court would not allow of his giving an opinion unless the Queen should first speak of the piece to him. The Queen said nothing to him about the matter. Shortly afterwards permission to perform this play was at length obtained. The Queen thought the people of Paris would be finely tricked when they saw merely an ill-conceived piece, devoid of interest, as it must appear when deprived of its satire. Under the persuasion that there was not a passage left capable of malicious or dangerous application, Monsieur attended the first performance in a public box. The mad enthusiasm of the public in favour of the piece and Monsieur's just displeasure are well known. The author was sent to prison soon afterwards, though his work was extolled to the skies, and though the Court durst not suspend its performance.

The Queen testified her displeasure against all who had assisted the author of the "Mariage de Figaro" to deceive the King into giving his consent that it should be represented. Her reproaches were more particularly directed against M. de Vaudreuil for having had it performed at his house. The violent and domineering disposition of her favourite's friend at last became disagreeable to her.

One evening, on the Queen's return from the Duchess's, she desired her *valet de chambre* to bring her billiard cue into her closet, and ordered me to open the box that contained it. I took out the cue, broken in two. It was of ivory, and formed of one single elephant's tooth; the butt was of gold and very tastefully wrought. "There," said she, "that is the way M. de Vaudreuil has treated a thing I valued highly. I had laid it upon the couch while I was talking to the Duchess in the *salon*; he had the assurance to make use of it, and in a fit of passion about a blocked ball, he struck the cue so violently against the table that he broke it in two. The noise brought me back into the billiard room; I did not say a word to him, but my looks showed him how angry I was. He is the more provoked at the accident, as he aspires to the post of Governor to the Dauphin. I never thought of him for the place. It is quite enough to have consulted my heart only in the choice of a governess; and I will not suffer that of a Governor to the Dauphin to be at all affected by the influence of my friends. I should be responsible for it to the nation. The poor man does not know that my determination is taken; for I have never expressed it to the Duchess. Therefore, judge of the sort of an evening he must have passed!"

XIII

S HORTLY after the public mind had been thrown into agitation by the performance of the "Mariage de Figaro," an obscure plot, contrived by swindlers, and matured in a corrupted society, attacked the Queen's character in a vital point and assailed the majesty of the throne.

I am about to speak of the notorious affair of the necklace purchased, as it was said, for the Queen by Cardinal de Rohan. I will narrate all that has come to my knowledge relating to this business; the most minute particulars will prove how little reason the Queen had to apprehend the blow by which she was threatened, and which must be attributed to a fatality that human providence could not have foreseen, but from which, to say the truth, she might have extricated herself with more skill.

I have already said that in 1774 the Queen purchased jewels of Bœhmer to the value of three hundred and sixty thousand francs, that she paid for them herself out of her own private funds, and that it required several years to enable her to complete the payment. The King afterwards presented her with a set of rubies and diamonds of a fine water, and subsequently with a pair of bracelets worth two hundred thousand francs. The Queen, after having her diamonds reset in new patterns, told Bœhmer that she found her jewel case rich enough, and was not desirous of making any addition to it. Still, this jeweller busied himself for some years in forming a collection of the finest diamonds circulating in the trade, in order to compose a necklace of several rows, which he hoped to induce her Majesty to purchase; he brought it to M. Campan, requesting him to mention it to the Queen, that she might ask to see it, and thus be induced to wish to possess it. This M. Campan refused to do, telling him that he should be stepping out of the line of his duty were he to propose to the Queen an expense of sixteen hundred thousand francs, and that he believed neither the lady of honour nor the tirewoman would take upon herself to execute such a commission. Bœhmer persuaded the King's first gentleman for the year to show this superb necklace to his Majesty, who admired it so much that he himself wished to see the Queen adorned with it, and sent the case to her; but she assured him she should much regret incurring so great an expense for such an article, that she had already very beautiful diamonds, that jewels of that description were now worn at Court not more than four or five times a year, that the necklace must be returned, and that the money would be much better employed in building a man-of-war. Bœhmer, in sad tribulation at finding his expectations delusive, endeavoured for some time, it is said, to dispose of his necklace among the various Courts of Europe.

A year after his fruitless attempts, Bœhmer again caused his diamond necklace to be offered to the King, proposing that it should be paid for partly by instalments, and partly in life annuities; this proposal was represented as highly advantageous, and the King, in my presence, mentioned the matter once more to the Queen. I remember the Queen told him that, if the bargain really was not bad, he might make it, and keep the necklace until the marriage of one of his children; but that, for her part, she would never wear it, being unwilling that the world should have to reproach her with having coveted so expensive an article. The King replied that their children were too young to justify such an expense, which would be greatly increased by the number of years the diamonds would remain useless, and that he would finally decline the offer. Bœhmer complained to everybody of his misfortune, and all reasonable people blamed him for collecting diamonds to so considerable an amount without any positive order for them. This man had purchased the office of jeweller to the Crown, which gave him some rights of entry at Court. After several months spent in ineffectual attempts to carry his point, and in idle complaints, he obtained an audience of the Queen, who had with her the young Princess, her daughter; her Majesty did not know for what purpose Bœhmer sought this audience, and had not the slightest idea that it was to speak to her again about an article twice refused by herself and the King.

Bœhmer threw himself upon his knees, clasped his hands, burst into tears, and exclaimed, "Madame, I am ruined and disgraced if you do not purchase my necklace. I cannot outlive so many misfortunes. When I go hence I shall throw myself into the river."

"Rise, Bœhmer," said the Queen, in a tone sufficiently severe to recall him to himself; "I do not like these rhapsodies; honest men have no occasion to fall on their knees to make their requests. If you were to destroy yourself I should regret you as a madman in whom I had taken an interest, but I should not be in any way responsible for that misfortune. Not only have I never ordered the article which causes your present despair, but whenever you have talked to me about fine collections of jewels I have told you that I should not add four diamonds to those which I already possessed. I told you myself that I declined taking the necklace; the King wished to give it to me, but I refused him also; never mention it to me again. Divide it and try to sell it piecemeal, and do not drown yourself. I am very angry with you for acting this scene of despair in my presence and before this child. Let me never see you behave thus again. Go." Bœhmer withdrew, overwhelmed with confusion, and nothing further was then heard of him.

When Madame Sophie was born the Queen told me M. de Saint-James, a rich financier, had apprised her that Bcehmer was still intent upon the sale of his necklace, and that she ought, for her own satisfaction, to endeavour to learn what the man had done with it; she desired me the first time I should meet him to speak to him about it, as if from the interest I took in his welfare. I spoke to him about his necklace, and he told me he had been very fortunate, having sold it at Constantinople for the favourite sultana. I communicated this answer to the Queen, who was delighted with it, but could not comprehend how the Sultan came to purchase his diamonds in Paris.

The Queen long avoided seeing Bœhmer, being fearful of his rash character; and her *valet de chambre*, who had the

care of her jewels, made the necessary repairs to her ornaments unassisted. On the baptism of the Duc d'Angoulême,
in 1785, the King gave him a diamond epaulet and buckles,
and directed Bœhmer to deliver them to the Queen. Bœhmer presented them on her return from mass, and at the
same time gave into her hands a letter in the form of a petition. In this paper he told the Queen that he was happy
to see her "in possession of the finest diamonds known in
Europe," and entreated her not to forget him. The Queen
read Bœhmer's address to her aloud, and saw nothing in it
but a proof of mental aberration; she lighted the paper at a
wax laper standing near her, as she had some letters to seal,
saying, "It is not worth keeping." She afterwards much regretted the loss of this enigmatical memorial. After having
burnt the paper, her Majesty said to me, "That man is born
to be my torment; he has always some mad scheme in his
head; remember, the first time you see him, to tell him that
I do not like diamonds now, and that I will buy no more so
long as I live; that if I had any money to spare I would rather
add to my property at St. Cloud by the purchase of the land
surrounding it; now, mind you enter into all these particulars and impress them well upon him." I asked her whether
she wished me to send for him; she replied in the negative,
adding that it would be sufficient to avail myself of the first
opportunity afforded by meeting him; and that the slightest
advance towards such a man would be misplaced.

On the 1st of August I left Versailles for my country
house at Crespy; on the 3d came Bœhmer, extremely uneasy at not having received any answer from the Queen, to
ask me whether I had any commission from her to him; I
replied that she had entrusted me with none; that she had

no commands for him, and I faithfully repeated all she had desired me to say to him.

"But," said Bœhmer, "the answer to the letter I presented to her,—to whom must I apply for that?"

"To nobody," answered I; "her Majesty burnt your memorial without even comprehending its meaning."

"Ah! madame," exclaimed he, "that is impossible; the Queen knows that she has money to pay me!"

"Money, M. Bœhmer? Your last accounts against the Queen were discharged long ago."

"Madame, you are not in the secret. A man who is ruined for want of payment of fifteen hundred thousand francs cannot be said to be satisfied."

"Have you lost your senses?" said I. "For what can the Queen owe you so extravagant a sum?"

"For my necklace, madame," replied Bœhmer, coolly.

"What!" I exclaimed, "that necklace again, which you have teased the Queen about so many years! Did you not tell me you had sold it at Constantinople?"

"The Queen desired me to give that answer to all who should speak to me on the subject," said the wretched dupe. He then told me that the Queen wished to have the necklace, and had had it purchased for her by Monseigneur, the Cardinal de Rohan.

"You are deceived," I exclaimed; "the Queen has not once spoken to the Cardinal since his return from Vienna; there is not a man at her Court less favourably looked upon."

"You are deceived yourself, madame," said Bœhmer; "she sees him so much in private that it was to his Eminence she gave thirty thousand francs, which were paid me as an instalment; she took them, in his presence, out of the little *secrétaire* of Sèvres porcelain next the fireplace in her boudoir."

"And the Cardinal told you all this?"

"Yes, madame, himself."

"What a detestable plot!" cried I.

"Indeed, to say the truth, madame, I begin to be much alarmed, for his Eminence assured me that the Queen would wear the necklace on Whit-Sunday, but I did not see it upon her, and it was that which induced me to write to her Majesty."

He then asked me what he ought to do. I advised him to go on to Versailles, instead of returning to Paris, whence he had just arrived; to obtain an immediate audience from the Baron de Breteuil, who, as head of the King's household, was the minister of the department to which Bœhmer belonged, and to be circumspect; and I added that he appeared to me extremely culpable,—not as a diamond merchant, but because being a sworn officer it was unpardonable of him to have acted without the direct orders of the King, the Queen, or the Minister. He answered, that he had not acted without direct orders; that he had in his possession all the notes signed by the Queen, and that he had even been obliged to show them to several bankers in order to induce them to extend the time for his payments. I urged his departure for Versailles, and he assured me he would go there immediately. Instead of following my advice, he went to the Cardinal, and it was of this visit of Bœhmer's that his Eminence made a memorandum, found in a drawer overlooked by the Abbé Georgel when he burnt, by order of the Cardinal, all the papers which the latter had at Paris. The memorandum was thus worded:"On this day, 3d August, Bœhmer went to Madame Campan's country house, and she told him that the Queen had never had his necklace, and that he had been deceived."

When Bœhmer was gone, I wanted to follow him, and go to the Queen; my father-in-law prevented me, and ordered me to leave the minister to elucidate such an important affair, observing that it was an infernal plot; that I had given Bœhmer the best advice, and had nothing more to do with the business. Bœhmer never said one word to me about the woman De Lamotte, and her name was mentioned for the first time by the Cardinal in his answers to the interrogatories put to him before the King. After seeing the Cardinal, Bœhmer went to Trianon, and sent a message to the Queen, purporting that I had advised him to come and speak to her. His very words were repeated to her Majesty, who said, "He is mad; I have nothing to say to him, and will not see him." Two or three days afterwards the Queen sent for me to Petit Trianon, to rehearse with me the part of Rosina, which she was to perform in the "Barbier de Séville." I was alone with her, sitting upon her couch; no mention was made of anything but the part. After we had spent an hour in the rehearsal, her Majesty asked me why I had sent Bœhmer to her; saying he had been in my name to speak to her, and that she would not see him. It was in this manner I learnt that he had not followed my advice in the slightest degree. The change of my countenance, when I heard the man's name, was very perceptible; the Queen perceived it, and questioned me. I entreated her to see him, and assured her it was of the utmost importance for her peace of mind; that there was a plot going on, of which she was not aware; and that it was a serious one, since engagements signed by herself were shown about to people who had lent Bœhmer money. Her surprise and vexation were great. She desired me to remain at Trianon, and sent off a courier to Paris, ordering Bœhmer to come to her upon some pretext which has escaped my recollection. He came next morning; in fact it was the day on which the play was performed, and that was the last amusement the Queen allowed herself at that retreat.

The Queen made him enter her closet, and asked him by what fatality it was that she was still doomed to hear of his foolish pretence of selling her an article which she had steadily refused for several years. He replied that he was compelled, being unable to pacify his creditors any longer. "What are your creditors to me?" said her Majesty. Bœhmer then regularly related to her all that he had been made to believe lad passed between the Queen and himself through the intervention of the Cardinal. She was equally incensed and surprised at each thing she heard. In vain did she speak; the jeweller, equally importunate and dangerous, repeated incessantly, "Madame, there is no longer time for feigning; condescend to confess that you have my necklace, and let some assistance be given to me, or my bankruptcy will soon bring the whole to light."

It is easy to imagine how the Queen must have suffered. On Bœhmer's going away, I found her in an alarming condition; the idea that any one could have believed that such a man as the Cardinal possessed her full confidence; that she should have employed him to deal with a tradesman without the King's knowledge, for a thing which she had refused to accept from the King himself, drove her to desperation. She sent first for the Abbé de Vermond, and then for the Baron de Breteuil. Their hatred and contempt for the Cardinal made them too easily forget that the lowest faults do not prevent the higher orders of the empire from being defended by those to whom they have the honour to belong; that a Rohan, a Prince of the Church, however culpable he might be, would be sure to have a considerable party which would naturally be joined by all the discontented persons of the Court, and all the *frondeurs* of Paris. They too easily believed that he would be stripped of all the advantages of his rank and order, and given up to the disgrace due to his irregular conduct; they deceived themselves.

I saw the Queen after the departure of the Baron and the Abbé; her agitation made me shudder. "Fraud must be unmasked," said she; "when the Roman purple and the title of Prince cover a mere money-seeker, a cheat who dares to compromise the wife of his sovereign, France and all Europe should know it." It is evident that from that moment the fatal plan was decided on. The Queen perceived my alarm; I did not conceal it from her. I knew too well that she had many enemies not to be apprehensive on seeing her attract the attention of the whole world to an intrigue that they would try to complicate still more. I entreated her to seek the most prudent and moderate advice. She silenced me by desiring me to make myself easy, and to rest satisfied that no imprudence would be committed.

On the following Sunday, the 15th of August, being the Assumption, at twelve o'clock, at the very moment when the Cardinal, dressed in his pontifical garments, was about to proceed to the chapel, he was sent for into the King's closet, where the Queen then was.

The King said to him, "You have purchased diamonds of Bœhmer?"

"Yes, Sire."

"What have you done with them?"

"I thought they had been delivered to the Queen."

"Who commissioned you?"

"A lady, called the Comtesse de Lamotte-Valois, who handed me a letter from the Queen; and I thought I was gratifying her Majesty by taking this business on myself."

The Queen here interrupted him, and said, "How, monsieur, could you believe that I should select you, to whom I have not spoken for eight years, to negotiate anything for me, and especially through the mediation of a woman whom I do not even know?"

"I see plainly," said the Cardinal, "that I have been duped. I will pay for the necklace; my desire to please your Majesty blinded me ; I suspected no trick in the affair, and I am sorry for it."

He then took ont of his pocket-book a letter from the Queen to Madame de Lamotte, giving him this commission. The King took it and, holding it towards the Cardinal, said:

"This is neither written nor signed by the Queen. How could a Prince of the House of Rohan, and a Grand Almoner of France, ever think that the Queen would sign *Marie Antoinette de France?* Everybody knows that queens sign only by their baptismal names. But, monsieur," pursued the King, handing him a copy of his letter to Bœhmer, "have you ever written such a letter as this ?"

Having glanced over it, the Cardinal said, "I do not remember having written it,"

"But what if the original, signed by yourself, were shown to you?"

"If the letter be signed by myself it is genuine." He was extremely confused, and repeated several times, "I have been deceived, Sire; I will pay for the necklace. I ask pardon of your Majesties."

"Then explain to me," resumed the King, "the whole of this enigma. I do not wish to find you guilty; I had rather you would justify yourself. Account for all the manœuvres with Bœhmer, these assurances and these letters."

The Cardinal then, turning pale, and leaning against the table, said, "Sire, I am too much confused to answer your Majesty in a way."

"Compose yourself, Cardinal, and go into my cabinet; you will there find paper, pens, and ink,— write what you have to say to me."

The Cardinal went into the King's cabinet, and returned a quarter of an hour afterwards with a document as confused as his verbal answers had been. The King then said, "Withdraw, monsieur." The Cardinal left the King's chamber, with the Baron de Breteuil, who gave him in custody to a lieutenant of the Body Guard, with orders to take him to his apartment. M. d'Agoult, aide-major of the Body Guard, afterwards took him into custody, and conducted him to his hôtel, and thence to the Bastille. But while the Cardinal had with him only the young lieutenant of the Body Guard, who was much embarrassed at having such an order to execute, his Eminence met his *heyduc* at the door of the Salon of Hercules; he spoke to him in German, and then asked the lieutenant if he could lend him a pencil; the officer gave him that which he carried about him, and the Cardinal wrote to the Abbé Georgel, his grand vicar and friend, instantly to burn all Madame de Lamotte's correspondence, and all his other letters. This commission was executed before M. de Crosne, lieutenant of police, had received an order from the

Baron de Breteuil to put seals upon the Cardinal's papers. The destruction of all his Eminence's correspondence, and particularly that with Madame de Lamotte, threw an impenetrable cloud over the whole affair.

From that moment all proofs of this intrigue disappeared. Madame de Lamotte was apprehended at Bar-sur-Aube; her husband had already gone to England. From the beginning of this fatal affair all the proceedings of the Court appear to have been prompted by imprudence and want of foresight; the obscurity resulting left free scope for the fables of which the voluminous memorials written on one side and the other consisted. The Queen so little imagined what could have given rise to the intrigue, of which she was about to become the victim, that, at the moment when the King was interrogating the Cardinal, a terrific idea entered her mind. With that rapidity of thought caused by personal interest and extreme agitation, she fancied that, if a design to ruin her in the eyes of the King and the French people were the concealed motive of this intrigue, the Cardinal would, perhaps, affirm that she had the necklace; that he had been honoured with her confidence for this purchase, made without the King's knowledge; and point out some secret place in her apartment, where he might have got some villain to hide it. Want of money and the meanest swindling were the sole motives for this criminal affair. The necklace had already been taken to pieces and sold, partly in London, partly in Holland, and the rest in Paris.

The moment the Cardinal's arrest was known a universal clamour arose. Every memorial that appeared during the trial increased the outcry. On this occasion the clergy took that course which a little wisdom and the least

knowledge of the spirit of such a body ought to have foreseen. The Rohans and the House of Condé, as well as the
clergy, made their complaints heard everywhere. The King
consented to having a legal judgment, and early in September he addressed letters-patent to the Parliament, in which
he said that he was "filled with the most just indignation on
seeing the means which, by the confession of his Eminence
the Cardinal, had been employed in order to inculpate his
most dear spouse and companion."

Fatal moment! in which the Queen found herself, in
consequence of this highly impolitic step, on trial with a
subject, who ought to have been dealt with by the power of
the King alone. The Princes and Princesses of the House
of Condé, and of the Houses of Rohan, Soubise, and Guéménée, put on mourning, and were seen ranged in the way
of the members of the Grand Chamber to salute them as
they proceeded to the palace, on the days of the Cardinal's
trial; and Princes of the blood openly canvassed against the
Queen of France.

The Pope wished to claim, on behalf of the Cardinal
de Rohan, the right belonging to his ecclesiastical rank, and
demanded that he should be judged at Rome. The Cardinal de Bernis, ambassador from France to his Holiness,
formerly Minister for Foreign Affairs, blending the wisdom of an old diplomatist with the principles of a Prince
of the Church, wished that this scandalous affair should
be hushed up. The King's aunts, who were on very intimate
terms with the ambassador, adopted his opinion, and the
conduct of the King and Queen was equally and loudly
censured in the apartments of Versailles and in the hôtels
and coffee-houses of Paris.

Madame, the King's sister-in-law, had been the sole protectress of De Lamotte, and had confined her patronage to granting her a pension of twelve to fifteen hundred francs. Her brother was in the navy, but the Marquis de Chabert, to whom he had been recommended, could never train a good officer. The Queen in vain endeavoured to call to mind the features of this person, of whom she had often heard as an intriguing woman, who came frequently on Sundays to the gallery of Versailles. At the time when all France was engrossed by the persecution against the Cardinal, the portrait of the Comtesse de Lamotte-Valois was publicly sold. Her Majesty desired me one day, when I was going to Paris, to buy her the engraving, which was said to be a tolerable likeness, that she might ascertain whether she could recognise in it any person whom she might have seen in the gallery.[1]

The woman De Lamotte's father was a peasant at Auteuil, though he called himself Valois. Madame de Boulainvilliers once saw from her terrace two pretty little peasant girls, each labouring under a heavy bundle of sticks. The priest of the village, who was walking with her, told her that the children possessed some curious papers, and that he had no doubt they were descendants of a Valois, an illegitimate son of one of the princes of that name.

The family of Valois had long ceased to appear in the world. Hereditary vices had gradually plunged them into the deepest misery. I have heard that the last Valois then known occupied the estate called Gros Bois; that as he

---

1. The public, as the reader knows, with the exception of persons dressed in the style of the lowest of the people, were admitted into the gallery and larger apartments of Versailles, as they were into the park.

seldom came to Court, Louis XIII asked him what he was about that he remained so constantly in the country; and that this M. de Valois merely answered, "Sire, I only do there what I ought." It was shortly afterwards discovered that he was *coining*.

Neither the Queen herself nor any one near her ever had the slightest connection with the woman De Lamotte; and during her prosecution she could point out but one of the Queen's servants, named Desclos, a valet of the Queen's bedchamber, to whom she pretended she had delivered Bœhmer's necklace. This Desclos was a very honest man; upon being confronted with the woman De Lamotte, it was proved that she had never seen him but once, which was at the house of the wife of a surgeon-accoucheur at Versailles, the only person she visited at Court; and that she had not given him the necklace. Madame de Lamotte married a private in Monsieur's body-guard; she lodged at Versailles at the Belle Image, a very inferior furnished house; and it is inconceivable how so obscure a person could succeed in making herself believed to be a friend of the Queen, who, though so extremely affable, seldom granted audiences, and only to titled persons.

The trial of the Cardinal is too generally known to require me to repeat its details here. The point most embarrassing to him was the interview he had in February, 1785, with M. de Saint-James, to whom he confided the particulars of the Queen's pretended commission, and showed the contract approved and signed *Marie Antoinette de France*. The memorandum found in a drawer of the Cardinal's bureau, in which he had himself written what Bœhmer told him after having seen me at my country house, was likewise an unfortunate document for his Eminence.

I offered to the King to go and declare that Bœhmer had told me that the Cardinal assured him he had received from the Queen's own hand the thirty thousand francs given on account upon the bargain being concluded, and that his Eminence had seen her Majesty take that sum in bills from the porcelain *secrétaire* in her boudoir. The King declined my offer, and said to me, "Were you alone when Bœhmer told you this?" I answered that I was alone with him in my garden. "Well," resumed he, "the man would deny the fact; he is now sure of being paid his sixteen hundred thousand francs, which the Cardinal's family will find it necessary to make good to him; we can no longer rely upon his sincerity; it would look as if you were sent by the Queen, and that would not be proper."

The *procureur-général's* information was severe on the Cardinal. The Houses of Condé and Rohan and the majority of the nobility saw in this affair only an attack on the Prince's rank, the clergy only a blow aimed at the privileges of a cardinal. The clergy demanded that the unfortunate business of the Prince Cardinal de Rohan should be submitted to ecclesiastical jurisdiction, and the Archbishop of Narbonne, then President of the Convocation, made representations upon the subject to the King; the bishops wrote to his Majesty to remind him that a private ecclesiastic implicated in the affair then pending would have a right to claim his constitutional judges, and that this right was refused to a cardinal, his superior in the hierarchical order. In short, the clergy and the greater part of the nobility were at that time outrageous against authority, and chiefly against the Queen.

The *procureur-général's* conclusions, and those of a part of the heads of the magistracy, were as severe towards the

Cardinal as the information had been; yet he was *fully ac-quitted* by a majority of three voices; the woman De Lamotte was condemned to be whipped, branded, and imprisoned; and her husband, for contumacy, was condemned to the galleys for life.

M. Pierre de Laurencel, the *procureur-général*'s substitute, sent the Queen a list of the names of the members of the Grand Chamber, with the means made use of by the friends of the Cardinal to gain their votes during the trial. I had this list to keep among the papers which the Queen deposited in the house of M. Campan, my father-in-law, and which, at his death, she ordered me to preserve. I burnt this statement, but I remember ladies performed a part not very creditable to their principles; it was by them, in consideration of large sums which they received, that some of the oldest and most respected members were won over. I did not see a single name amongst the whole Parliament that was gained directly.

The belief confirmed by time is, that the Cardinal was completely duped by the woman De Lamotte and Cagliostro. The King may have been in error in thinking him an accomplice in this miserable and criminal scheme, but I have faithfully repeated his Majesty's judgment about it.

However, the generally received opinion that the Baron de Breteuil's hatred for the Cardinal was the cause of the scandal and the unfortunate result of this affair contributed to the disgrace of the former still more than his refusal to give his granddaughter in marriage to the son of the Duc de Polignac. The Abbé de Vermond threw the whole blame of the imprudence and impolicy of the affair of the Cardinal de Rohan upon the minister, and ceased to be the friend and supporter of the Baron de Breteuil with the Queen.

In the early part of the year 1786, the Cardinal as has been said, was fully acquitted, and came out of the Bastille, while Madame de Lamotte was condemned to be whipped, branded, and imprisoned. The Court, persisting in the erroneous views which had hitherto guided its measures, conceived that the Cardinal and the woman De Lamotte were equally culpable and unequally punished, and sought to restore the balance of justice by exiling the Cardinal to La Chaise-Dieu, and suffering Madame de Lamotte to escape a few days after she entered l'Hôpital. This new error confirmed the Parisians in the idea that the wretch De Lamotte, who had never been able to make her way so far as to the room appropriated to the Queen's women, had really interested the Queen herself.

XIV

THE Abbé de Vermond could not repress his exultation when he succeeded in getting the Archbishop of Sens appointed head of the council of finance. I have more than once heard him say that seventeen years of patience were not too long a term for success in a Court; that he spent all that time in gaining the end he had in view; but that at length the Archbishop was where he ought to be for the good of the State. The Abbé, from this time, in the Queen's private circle no longer concealed his credit and influence; nothing could equal the confidence with which he displayed the extent of his pretensions. He requested the Queen to order that the apartments appropriated to him should be enlarged, telling her that, being obliged to give audiences to bishops, cardinals, and ministers, he required a residence suitable to his present circumstances. The Queen continued to treat him as she did before the Archbishop's arrival at Court; but the household showed him increased consideration: the word "Monsieur" preceded that of Abbé; and from that moment not only the livery servants, but also the people of the antechambers rose when Monsieur l'Abbé was passing, though there never was, to my knowledge, any order given to that effect.

The Queen was obliged, on account of the King's disposition and the very limited confidence he placed in the Archbishop of Sens, to take a part in public affairs. While M. de Maurepas lived she kept out of that danger, as may be seen by the censure which the Baron de Besenval passes on her in his memoirs for not availing herself of the conciliation he had promoted between the Queen and that minister, who counteracted the ascendency which the Queen and her intimate friends might otherwise have gained over the King's mind.

The Queen has often assured me that she never interfered respecting the interests of Austria but once; and that was only to claim the execution of the treaty of alliance at the time when Joseph II was at war with Prussia and Turkey; that she then demanded that an army of twenty-four thousand men should be sent to him instead of fifteen millions, an alternative which had been left to option in the treaty, in case the Emperor should have a just war to maintain; that she could not obtain her object, and M. de Vergennes, in an interview which she had with him upon the subject, put an end to her importunities by observing that he was answering the mother of the Dauphin and not the sister of the Emperor. The fifteen millions were sent. There was no want of money at Vienna, and the value of a French army was fully appreciated.

"But how," said the Queen, "could they be so wicked as to send off those fifteen millions from the general post-office, diligently publishing, even to the street porters, that they were loading carriages with money that I was sending to my brother!—whereas it is certain that the money would equally have been sent if I had belonged to another house; and, besides, it was sent contrary to my inclination."

When the Comte de Moustier set out on his mission to the United States, after having had his public audience of leave he came and asked me to procure him a private one. I could not succeed even with the strongest solicitations; the Queen desired me to wish him a good voyage, but added that none but ministers could have anything to say to him in private, since he was going to a country where the names of *King* and *Queen* must be detested.

Marie Antoinette had then no direct influence over State affairs until after the deaths of M. de Maurepas and M. de Vergennes, and the retirement of M. de Calonne. She frequently regretted her new situation, and looked upon it as a misfortune which she could not avoid. One day, while I was assisting her to tie up a number of memorials and reports, which some of the ministers had handed to her to be given to the King, "Ah!" said she, sighing, "there is an end of all happiness for me, since they have made an intriguer of me." I exclaimed at the word. "Yes," resumed the Queen, "that is the right term; every woman who meddles with affairs above her understanding or out of her line of duty is an intriguer and nothing else; you will remember, however, that it is not my own fault, and that it is with regret I give myself such a title; Queens of France are happy only so long as they meddle with nothing, and merely preserve influence sufficient to advance their friends and reward a few zealous servants. Do you know what happened to me lately? One day since I began to attend private committees at the King's, while crossing the *œil-de-boeuf*, I heard one of the musicians of the chapel say so loud that I lost not a single word, 'A Queen who does her duty will remain in her apartment to knit.' I said within myself, 'Poor wretch, thou art right; but thou knowest not my situation; I yield to necessity and my evil destiny.'"

This situation was the more painful to the Queen inasmuch as Louis XVI had long accustomed himself to say nothing to her respecting State affairs; and when, towards the close of his reign, she was obliged to interfere in the most important matters, the same habit in the King frequently kept from her particulars which it was necessary she should have known. Obtaining, therefore, only insufficient information, and guided by persons more ambitious than skilful, the Queen could not be useful in important affairs; yet, at the same time, her ostensible interference drew upon her, from all parties and all classes of society, an unpopularity the rapid progress of which alarmed all those who were sincerely attached to her.

Carried away by the eloquence of the Archbishop of Sens, and encouraged in the confidence she placed in that minister by the incessant eulogies of the Abbé de Vermond on his abilities, the Queen unfortunately followed up her first mistake of bringing him into office in 1787 by supporting him at the time of his disgrace, which was obtained by the despair of a whole nation. She thought it was due to her dignity to give him some marked proof of her regard at the moment of his departure; misled by her feelings, she sent him her portrait enriched with jewelry, and a brevet for the situation of lady of the palace for Madame de Canisy, his niece, observing that it was necessary to indemnify a minister sacrificed to the intrigues of the Court and a factious spirit of the nation; that otherwise none would be found willing to devote themselves to the interests of the sovereign.

On the day of the Archbishop's departure the public joy was universal, both at Court and at Paris; there were bonfires; the attorneys' clerks burnt the Archbishop in effigy, and on the evening of his disgrace more than a hundred couriers were sent out from Versailles to spread the happy tidings among the country seats. I have seen the Queen shed bitter tears at the recollection of the errors she committed at this period, when subsequently, a short time before her death, the Archbishop had the audacity to say, in a speech which was printed, that the sole object of one part of his operations, during his administration, was the salutary crisis which the Revolution had produced.

The benevolence and generosity shown by the King and Queen during the severe winter of 1788, when the Seine was frozen over and the cold was more intense than it had been for eighty years, procured them some fleeting popularity. The gratitude of the Parisians for the succour their Majesties poured forth was lively if not lasting. The snow was so abundant that since that period there has never been seen such a prodigious quantity in France. In different parts of Paris pyramids and obelisks of snow were erected with inscriptions expressive of the gratitude of the people. The pyramid in the Rue d'Angiviller was supported on a base six feet high by twelve broad; it rose to the height of fifteen feet, and was terminated by a globe. Four blocks of stone, placed at the angles, corresponded with the obelisk, and gave it an elegant appearance. Several inscriptions, in honour of the

King and Queen, were affixed to it. I went to see this singular monument, and recollect the following inscription:

TO MARIE ANTOINETTE.

"Lovely and good, to tender pity true,
Queen of a virtuous King, this trophy view;
Cold ice and snow sustain its fragile form.
But ev'ry grateful heart to thee is warm.
Oh, may this tribute in your hearts excite,
Illustrious pair, more pure and real delight,
Whilst thus your virtues are sincerely prais'd,
Than pompous domes by servile flatt'ry rais'd."

The theatres generally rang with praises of the beneficence of the sovereigns: "La Partie de Chasse de Henri IV" was represented for the benefit of the poor. The receipts were very considerable.

When the fruitless measure of the Assembly of the Notables, and the rebellious spirit in the parliaments, had created the necessity for States General, it was long discussed in council whether they should be assembled at Versailles or at forty or sixty leagues from the capital; the Queen was for the latter course, and insisted to the King that they ought to be far away from the immense population of Paris. She feared that the people would influence the deliberations of the deputies; several memorials were presented to the King upon that question; but M. Necker prevailed, and Versailles was the place fixed upon.

The day on which the King announced that he gave his consent to the convocation of the States General, the Queen left the public dinner, and placed herself in the recess of the first window of her bedchamber, with her face towards the garden. Her chief butler followed her, to present her coffee, which she usually took standing, as she was about to leave the table. She beckoned to me to come close to her. The King was engaged in conversation with some one in his room. When the attendant had served her he retired; and she addressed me, with the cup still in her hand: "Great Heavens! what fatal news goes forth this day! The King assents to the convocation of the States General." Then she added, raising her eyes to heaven, "I dread it; this important event is a first fatal signal of discord in France." She cast her eyes down, they were filled with tears. She could not take the remainder of her coffee, but handed me the cup, and went to join the King. In the evening, when she was alone with me, she spoke only of this momentous decision. "It is the Parliament," said she, "that has compelled the King to have recourse to a measure long considered fatal to the repose of the kingdom. these gentlemen wish to restrain the power of the King; but they give a great shock to the authority of which they make so bad a use, and they will bring on their own destruction."

The double representation granted to the *Tiers Etat* was now the chief topic of conversation. The Queen favoured this plan, to which the King had agreed; she thought the hope of obtaining ecclesiastical favours would secure the clergy of the second order, and that M. Necker was sure to have the same degree of influence over the lawyers, and other people of that class comprised in the *Tiers Etat*. The Comte d'Artois, holding the contrary opinion, presented a memorial in the names of himself and several princes of the blood to the King against the double representation. The Queen was displeased with him for this; her confidential advisers infused into her apprehensions that the Prince was made the tool of a party; but his conduct was approved of by Madame de Polignac's circle, which the Queen thenceforward only frequented to avoid the appearance of a change in her habits. She almost always returned unhappy; she was treated with the profound respect due to a queen, but the devotion of friendship had vanished, to make way for the coldness of etiquette, which wounded her deeply. The alienation between her and the Comte d'Artois was also very painful to her, for she had loved him almost as tenderly as if he had been her own brother.

The opening of the States General took place on the 4th of May, 1789. The Queen on that occasion appeared for the last time in her life in regal magnificence. During the procession some low women, seeing the Queen pass, cried out *"Vive le Duc d'Orléans!"* in so threatening a manner that she nearly fainted. She was obliged to be supported, and those about her were afraid it would be necessary to stop the procession. The Queen, however, recovered herself, and much regretted that she had not been able to command more presence of mind.

The rapidly increasing distrust of the King and Queen shown by the populace was greatly attributable to incessant corruption by English gold, and the projects, either of revenge or of ambition, of the Duc d'Orléans. Let it not be thought that this accusation is founded on what has been so often repeated by the heads of the French Government since the Revolution. Twice between the 14th of July and the 6th of October, 1789, the day on which the Court was dragged to Paris, the Queen prevented me from making little excursions thither of business or pleasure, saying to me, "Do not go on such a day to Paris; the English have been scattering gold, we shall have some disturbance." The repeated visits of the Duc d'Orléans to England had excited the Anglomania to such a pitch that Paris was no longer distinguishable from London. The French, formerly imitated by the whole of Europe, became on a sudden a nation of imitators, without considering the evils that arts and manufactures must suffer in consequence of the change. Since the treaty of commerce made with England at the peace of 1783, not merely equipages, but everything, even to ribands and common earthenware, were of English make. If this predominance of English fashions had been confined to filling our drawing-rooms with young men in English frock-coats, instead of the French dress, good taste and commerce might alone have suffered; but the principles of English government had taken possession of these young heads. *Constitution, Upper House, Lower House, national guarantee, balance of power, Magna Charta, Law of Habeas Corpus,*—all these words were incessantly repeated, and seldom understood; but they were of fundamental importance to a party which was then forming.

The first sitting of the States took place on the following day. The King delivered his speech with firmness and dignity; the Queen told me that he had taken great pains about it, and had repeated it frequently. His Majesty gave public marks of attachment and respect for the Queen, who was applauded; but it was easy to see that this applause was in fact rendered to the King alone.

It was evident, during the first sittings, that Mirabeau would be very dangerous to the Government. It is affirmed that at this period he communicated to the King, and still more fully to the Queen, part of his schemes for abandoning them. He brandished the weapons afforded him by his eloquence and audacity, in order to make terms with the party he meant to attack. This man played the game of revolution to make his own fortune. The Queen told me that he asked for an embassy, and, if my memory does not deceive me, it was that of Constantinople. He was refused with well-deserved contempt, though policy would doubtless have concealed it, could the future have been foreseen.

The enthusiasm prevailing at the opening of this assembly, and the debates between the *Tiers Etat*, the nobility, and even the clergy, daily increased the alarm of their Majesties, and all who were attached to the cause of monarchy. The Queen went to bed late, or rather she began to be unable to rest. One evening, about the end of May, she was sitting in her room, relating several remarkable occurrences of the day; four wax candles were placed upon her toilet-table; the first went out of itself; I relighted it; shortly afterwards the second, and then the third went out also; upon which the Queen, squeezing my hand in terror, said to me: "Misfortune makes us superstitious; if the fourth taper should go out like the rest, nothing can prevent my looking upon it as a sinister omen." The fourth taper went out. It was remarked to the Queen that the four tapers had probably been run in the same mould, and that a defect in the wick had naturally occurred at the same point in each, since the candles had all gone out in the order in which they had been lighted.

The deputies of the *Tiers Etat* arrived at Versailles full of the strongest prejudices against the Court. They believed that the King indulged in the pleasures of the table to a shameful excess; and that the Queen was draining the treasury of the State in order to satisfy the most unbridled luxury. They almost all determined to see Petit Trianon. The extreme plainness of the retreat in question not answering the ideas they had formed, some of them insisted upon seeing the very smallest closets, saying that the richly furnished apartments were concealed from them. They particularised one which, according to them, was ornamented with diamonds, and with wreathed columns studded with sapphires and rubies. The Queen could not get these foolish ideas out of her mind, and spoke to the King on the subject. From the description given of this room by the deputies to the keepers of Trianon, the King concluded that they were looking for the scene enriched with paste ornaments, made in the reign of Louis XV for the theatre of Fontainebleau.

The King supposed that his Body Guards, on their return to the country, after their quarterly duty at Court, related what they had seen, and that their exaggerated accounts, being repeated, became at last totally perverted. This idea of the King, after the search for the diamond chamber, suggested to the Queen that the report of the King's propensity for drinking also sprang from the guards who accompanied his carriage when he hunted at Rambouillet. The King, who disliked sleeping out of his usual bed, was accustomed to leave that hunting-seat after supper; he generally slept soundly in his carriage, and awoke only on his arrival at the courtyard of his palace; he used to get down from his carriage in the midst of his Body Guards, staggering, as a man half awake will do, which was mistaken for intoxication.

The majority of the deputies who came imbued with prejudices produced by error or malevolence, went to lodge with the most humble private individuals of Versailles, whose inconsiderate conversation contributed not a little to nourish such mistakes. Everything, in short, tended to render the deputies subservient to the schemes of the leaders of the rebellion.

Shortly after the opening of the States General the first Dauphin died. That young Prince suffered from the rickets, which in a few months curved his spine, and rendered his legs so weak that he could not walk without being supported like a feeble old man. How many maternal tears did his condition draw from the Queen, already overwhelmed with apprehensions respecting the state of the kingdom! Her grief was enhanced by petty intrigues, which, when frequently renewed, became intolerable. An open quarrel between the families and friends of the Duc d'Harcourt, the Dauphin's governor, and those of the Duchesse de Polignac, his governess, added greatly to the Queen's affliction. The young Prince showed a strong dislike to the Duchesse de Polignac, who attributed it either to the Duc or the Duchesse d'Harcourt, and came to make her complaints respecting it to the Queen. The Dauphin twice sent her out of his room, saying to her, with that maturity of manner which long illness always gives to children: "Go out, Duchess; you are so fond of using perfumes, and they always make me ill;" and yet she never used any. The Queen perceived, also, that his prejudices against her friend extended to herself; her son would no longer speak in her presence. She knew that he had become fond of sweetmeats, and offered him some marshmallow and jujube lozenges. The under-governors and the first *valet de chambre* requested her not to give the Dauphin anything, as he was to receive no food of any kind without the consent of the faculty. I forbear to describe the wound this prohibition inflicted upon the Queen; she felt it the more deeply because she was aware it was unjustly believed she gave a decided preference to the Duc de Normandie, whose ruddy health and amiability did, in truth, form a striking contrast to the languid look and melancholy disposition of his elder brother. She even suspected that a plot had for some time existed to deprive her of the affection of a child whom she loved as a good and tender mother ought. Previous to the audience granted by the King on the 10th August, 1788, to the envoy of the Sultan Tippoo Saib, she had begged the Duc d'Harcourt to divert the Dauphin, whose deformity was already apparent, from his intention to be present at that ceremony, being unwilling to expose him to the gaze of the crowd of inquisitive Parisians who would be in the gallery. Notwithstanding this injunction, the Dauphin was suffered to write to his mother, requesting her permission to be present at the audience. The Queen was obliged to refuse him, and warmly reproached the governor, who merely answered that he could not oppose the wishes of a sick child. A year before the death of the Dauphin the Queen lost the Princess Sophie; this was, as the Queen said, the first of a series of misfortunes.

XV

THE ever-memorable oath of the States General, taken at the Tennis Court of Versailles, was followed by the royal sitting of the 23d of June. In this *séance* the King declared that the Orders must vote separately, and threatened, if further obstacles were met with, to himself act for the good of the people. The Queen looked on M. Necker's not accompanying the King as treachery or criminal cowardice: she said that he had converted a remedy into poison; that being in full popularity, his audacity, in openly disavowing the step taken by his sovereign, had emboldened the factious, and led away the whole Assembly; and that he was the more culpable inasmuch as he had the evening before given her his word to accompany the King. In vain did M. Necker endeavour to excuse himself by saying that his advice had not been followed.

Soon afterwards the insurrections of the 11th, 12th, and 14th of July opened the disastrous drama with which

France was threatened. The massacre of M. de Flesselles and M. de Launay drew bitter tears from the Queen, and the idea that the King had lost such devoted subjects wounded her to the heart.

The character of the movement was no longer merely that of a popular insurrection; cries of *"Vive la Nation! Vive le Roi! Vive la Liberté!"* threw the strongest light upon the views of the reformers. Still the people spoke of the King with affection, and appeared to think him favourable to the national desire for the reform of what were called abuses; but they imagined that he was restrained by the opinions and influence of the Comte d'Artois and the Queen; and those two august personages were therefore objects of hatred to the malcontents. The dangers incurred by the Comte d'Artois determined the King's first step with the States General. He attended their meeting on the morning of the 15th of July with his brothers, without pomp or escort; he spoke standing and uncovered, and pronounced these memorable words: "I trust myself to you; I only wish to be at one with my nation, and, counting on the affection and fidelity of my subjects, I have given orders to the troops to remove from Paris and Versailles." The King returned on foot from the chamber of the States General to his palace; the deputies crowded after him, and formed his escort, and that of the Princes who accompanied him. The rage of the populace was pointed against the Comte d'Artois, whose unfavourable opinion of the double representation was an odious crime in their eyes. They repeatedly cried out, "The King for ever, in spite of you and your opinions, Monseigneur!" One woman had the impudence to come up to the King and ask him whether what he had been doing was done sincerely, and whether he would not be forced to retract it.

The courtyards of the Château were thronged with an immense concourse of people; they demanded that the King and Queen, with their children, should make their appearance in the balcony. The Queen gave me the key of the inner doors, which led to the Dauphin's apartments, and desired me to go to the Duchesse de Polignac to tell her that she wanted her son, and had directed me to bring him myself into her room, where she waited to show him to the people. The Duchess said this order indicated that she was not to accompany the Prince. I did not answer; she squeezed my hand, saying, "Ah! Madame Campan, what a blow I receive!" She embraced the child and me with tears. She knew how much I loved and valued the goodness and the noble simplicity of her disposition. I endeavoured to reassure her by saying that I should bring back the Prince to her; but she persisted, and said she understood the order, and knew what it meant. She then retired to her private room, holding her handkerchief to her eyes. One of the under-governesses asked me whether she might go with the Dauphin; I told her the Queen had given no order to the contrary, and we hastened to her Majesty, who was waiting to lead the Prince to the balcony.

Having executed this sad commission, I went down into the courtyard, where I mingled with the crowd. I heard a thousand vociferations; it was easy to see, by the difference between the language and the dress of some persons among the mob, that they were in disguise. A woman, whose face was covered with a black lace veil, seized me by the arm with some violence, and said, calling me by my name, "I know you very well; tell your Queen not to meddle with government any longer; let her leave her husband and our good States General

to effect the happiness of the people." At the same moment a
man, dressed much in the style of a marketman, with his hat
pulled down over his eyes, seized me by the other arm, and
said, "Yes, yes; tell her over and over again that it will not be
with these States as with the others, which produced no good
to the people ; that the nation is too enlightened in 1789 not
to make something more of them; and that there will not now
be seen a deputy of the *Tiers Etat* making a speech with one
knee on the ground; tell her this, do you hear?" I was struck
with dread; the Queen then appeared in the balcony. "Ah!"
said the woman in the veil, "the Duchess is not with her."
"No," replied the man, "but she is still at Versailles; she is
working underground, mole-like; but we shall know how to
dig her out." The detestable pair moved away from me, and I
reentered the palace, scarcely able to support myself. I thought
it my duty to relate the dialogue of these two strangers to the
Queen; she made me repeat the particulars to the King.

About four in the afternoon I went across the terrace
to Madame Victoire's apartments; three men had stopped
under the windows of the throne-chamber. "Here is that
throne," said one of them aloud, "the vestiges of which will
soon be sought for." He added a thousand invectives against
their Majesties. I went in to the Princess, who was at work
alone in her closet behind a canvas blind, which prevented
her from being seen by those without. The three men were
still walking upon the terrace; I showed them to her, and
told her what they had said. She rose to take a nearer view of
them, and informed me that one of them was named Saint-
Huruge; that he was sold to the Duc d'Orléans, and was
furious against the Government, because he had been confined once under a *lettre de cachet* as a bad character.

The King was not ignorant of these popular threats; he also knew the days on which money was scattered about Paris, and once or twice the Queen prevented my going there, saying there would certainly be a riot the next day, because she knew that a quantity of crown pieces had been distributed in the faubourgs.[1]

On the evening of the 14th of July the King came to the Queen's apartments, where I was with her Majesty alone; he conversed with her respecting the scandalous report disseminated by the factious, that he had had the Chamber of the National Assembly undermined, in order to blow it up; but he added that it became him to treat such absurd assertions with contempt, as usual; I ventured to tell him that I had the evening before supped with M. Begouen, one of the deputies, who said that there were very respectable persons who thought that this horrible contrivance had been proposed without the King's knowledge. "Then," said his Majesty, "as the idea of such an atrocity was not revolting to so worthy a man as M. Begouen, I will order the chamber to be examined early to-morrow morning." In fact, it will be seen by the King's speech to the National Assembly, on the 15th of July, that the suspicions excited obtained his attention. "I know," said he in the speech in question, "that unworthy insinuations have been made; I know there are those who have dared to assert that your persons are not safe; can it be necessary to give you assurances upon the subject of reports so culpable, denied beforehand by my known character?"

1. I have seen a six-franc crown-piece which certainly served to pay some wretch on the night of the 12th of July; the words, "Midnight, 12th of July, three pistols," were rather deeply engraved on it. They no doubt communicated a signal for the first insurrection.

The proceedings of the 15th of July produced no mitigation of the disturbances. Successive deputations of *poissardes* came to request the King to visit Paris, where his presence alone would put an end to the insurrection.

On the 16th a committee was held in the King's apartments, at which a most important question was discussed: whether his Majesty should quit Versailles and set off with the troops whom he had recently ordered to withdraw, or go to Paris to tranquillise the minds of the people. The Queen was for the departure. On the evening of the 16th she made me take all her jewels out of their cases, to collect them in one small box, which she might carry off in her own carriage. With my assistance she burnt a large quantity of papers; for Versailles was then threatened with an early visit of armed men from Paris.

The Queen, on the morning of the 16th, before attending another committee at the King's, having got her jewels ready, and looked over all her papers, gave me one folded up but not sealed, and desired me not to read it until she should give me an order to do so from the King's room, and then I was to execute its contents; but she returned herself about ten in the morning; the affair was decided; the army was to go away without the King; all those who were in imminent danger were to go at the same time. "The King will go to the Hôtel de Ville to-morrow," said the Queen to me; "he did not choose this course for himself; there were long debates on the question; at last the King put an end to them by rising and saying, 'Well, gentlemen, we must decide; am I to go or to stay? I am ready to do either.' The majority were for the King staying; time will show whether the right choice has been made."

I returned the Queen the paper she had given me, which was now useless; she read it to me; it contained her orders for the departure; I was to go with her, as well on account of my office about her person as to serve as a teacher to Madame. The Queen tore the paper, and said, with tears in her eyes, "When I wrote this I thought it would be useful, but fate has ordered otherwise, to the misfortune of us all, as I much fear."

After the departure of the troops the new administration received thanks; M. Necker was recalled. The artillery soldiers were undoubtedly corrupted. "Wherefore all these guns?" exclaimed the crowds of women who filled the streets. "Will you kill your mothers, your wives, your children?" "Don't be afraid," answered the soldiers; "these guns shall rather be levelled against the tyrant's palace than against you!"

The Comte d'Artois, the Prince de Condé, and their children set off at the same time with the troops. The Duc and Duchesse de Polignac, their daughter, the Duchesse de Guiche, the Comtesse Diane de Polignac, sister of the Duke, and the Abbé de Balivière, also emigrated on the same night. Nothing could be more affecting than the parting of the Queen and her friend; extreme misfortune had banished from their minds the recollection of differences to which political opinions alone had given rise. The Queen several times wished to go and embrace her once more after their sorrowful adieu, but she was too closely watched. She desired M. Campan to be present at the departure of the Duchess, and gave him a purse of five hundred louis, desiring him to insist upon her allowing the Queen to lend her that sum to defray her expenses on the road. The Queen added that she knew her situation; that she had often calculated her income, and the expenses occasioned by her place at Court; that both husband and wife, having no other fortune than their official salaries, could not possibly have saved anything, however differently people might think at Paris.

M. Campan remained till midnight with the Duchess to see her enter her carriage. She was disguised as a *femme de chambre*, and got up in front of the berlin; she requested M. Campan to remember her frequently to the Queen, and then quitted for ever that palace, that favour, and that influence which had raised her up such cruel enemies. On their arrival at Sens the travellers found the people in a state of insurrection; they asked all those who came from Paris whether the Polignacs were still with the Queen. A group of inquisitive persons put that question to the Abbé de Balivière, who answered them in the firmest tone, and with the most cavalier air, that they were far enough from Versailles, and that we had got rid of all such bad people. At the following stage the postilion got on the doorstep and said to the Duchess, "Madame, there are some good people left in the world: I recognised you all at Sens." They gave the worthy fellow a handful of gold.

On the breaking out of these disturbances an old man above seventy years of age gave the Queen an extraordinary proof of attachment and fidelity. M. Péraque, a rich inhabitant of the colonies, father of M. d'Oudenarde, was coming from Brussels to Paris; while changing horses he was met by a young man who was leaving France, and who recommended him if he carried any letters from foreign countries to burn them immediately, especially if he had any for the Queen. M. Péraque had one from the Archduchess, the Gouvernante of the Low Countries, for her Majesty. He thanked the stranger, and carefully concealed his packet; but as he approached Paris the insurrection appeared to him so general and so violent, that he thought no means could be relied on for securing this letter from seizure. He took upon him to unseal it, and learned it by heart, which was a wonderful effort for a man at his time of life, as it contained four pages of writing. On his arrival at Paris he wrote it down, and then presented it to the Queen, telling her that the heart of an old and faithful subject had given him courage to form and execute such a resolution. The Queen received M. Péraque in her closet, and expressed her gratitude in an affecting manner most honourable to the worthy old man. Her Majesty thought the young stranger who had apprised him of the state of Paris was Prince George of Hesse-Darmstadt, who was very devoted to her, and who left Paris at that time.

The Marquise de Tourzel replaced the Duchesse de Polignac. She was selected by the Queen as being the mother of a family and a woman of irreproachable conduct, who had superintended the education of her own daughters with the greatest success.

The King went to Paris on the 17th of July, accompanied by the Maréchal de Beauvau, the Duc de Villeroi, and the Duc de Villequier; he also took the Comte d'Estaing[1], and the Marquis de Nesle, who were then very popular, in his carriage. Twelve Body Guards, and the town guard of Versailles, escorted him to the Pont du Jour, near Sèvres, where the Parisian guard was waiting for him. His departure caused equal grief and alarm to his friends, notwithstanding the calmness

1. The count used to dine with butchers at Versailles, and flattered the people by the meanest condescensions.

he exhibited. The Queen restrained her tears, and shut herself up in her private rooms with her family. She sent for several persons belonging to her Court; their doors were locked. Terror had driven them away. The silence of death reigned throughout the palace; they hardly dared hope that the King would return. The Queen had a robe prepared for her, and sent orders to her stables to have all her equipages ready. She wrote an address of a few lines for the Assembly, determining to go there with her family, the officers of her palace, and her servants, if the King should be detained prisoner at Paris. She got this address by heart; it began with these words: "Gentlemen, I come to place in your hands the wife and family of your sovereign; do not suffer those who have been united in heaven to be put asunder on earth." While she was repeating this address she was often interrupted by tears, and sorrowfully exclaimed: "They will not let him return!"

It was past four when the King, who had left Versailles at ten in the morning, entered the Hôtel de Ville. At length, at six in the evening, M. de Lastours, the King's first page, arrived; he was not half an hour in coming from the Barrière de la Conférence to Versailles. Everybody knows that the moment of calm in Paris was that in which the unfortunate sovereign received the tricoloured cockade from M. Bailly, and placed it in his hat. A shout of *"Vive le Roi!"* arose on all sides; it had not been once uttered before. The King breathed again, and with tears in his eyes exclaimed that his heart stood in need of such greetings from the people. One of his equerries (M. de Cubières) told him the people loved him, and that he could never have doubted it. The King replied in accents of profound sensibility: "Cubières, the French loved Henri IV, and what king ever better deserved to be beloved?"

His return to Versailles filled his family with inexpressible joy; in the arms of the Queen, his sister, and his children, he congratulated himself that no accident had happened; and he repeated several times. "Happily no blood has been shed, and I swear that never shall a drop of French blood be shed by my order," — a determination full of humanity, but too openly avowed in such factious times!

The King's last measure raised a hope in many that general tranquillity would soon enable the Assembly to resume its labours, and promptly bring its session to a close. The Queen never flattered herself so far; M. Bailly's speech to the King had equally wounded her pride and hurt her feelings. "Henri IV conquered his people, and here are the people conquering their King." The word "conquest" offended her; she never forgave M. Bailly for this fine academical phrase.

Five days after the King's visit to Paris, the departure of the troops, and the removal of the Princes and some of the nobility whose influence seemed to alarm the people, a horrible deed committed by hired assassins proved that the King had descended the steps of his throne without having effected a reconciliation with his people.

M. Foulon, *adjoint* to the administration while M. de Broglie was commanding the army assembled at Versailles, had concealed himself at Viry. He was there recognised, and the peasants seized him, and dragged him to the Hôtel de Ville. The cry for death was heard; the electors, the members of committee, and M. de La Fayette, at that time the idol of Paris, in vain endeavoured to save the unfortunate man. After tormenting him in a manner which makes humanity shudder, his body was dragged about the streets, and to the Palais Royal, and his heart was carried by *women* in the midst of a bunch of white carnations! M. Berthier, M. Foulon's son-in-law, intendant of Paris, was seized at Compiègne, at the same time that his father-in-law was seized at Viry, and treated with still more relentless cruelty.

The Queen was always persuaded that this horrible deed was occasioned by some indiscretion; and she informed me that M. Foulon had drawn up two memorials for the direction of the King's conduct at the time of his being called to Court on the removal of M. Necker; and that these memorials contained two schemes of totally different nature for extricating the King from the dreadful situation in which he was placed. In the first of these projects M. Foulon expressed himself without reserve respecting the criminal views of the Duc d'Orléans; said that he ought to be put under arrest, and that no time should be lost in commencing a prosecution against him, while the criminal tribunals were still in existence; he likewise pointed out such deputies as should be apprehended, and advised the King not to separate himself from his army until order was restored.

His other plan was that the King should make himself master of the revolution before its complete explosion; he advised his Majesty to go to the Assembly, and there, in person, to demand the *cahiers*, and to make the greatest sacrifices to satisfy the legitimate wishes of the people, and not to give the factious time to enlist them in aid of their criminal designs. Madame Adélaïde had M. Foulon's two memorials read to her in the presence of four or five persons. One of them, Comte Louis de Narbonne, was very intimate with Madame de Staël, and that intimacy gave the Queen reason to believe that the opposite party had gained information of M. Foulon's schemes.

It is known that young Barnave, during an aberration of mind, since expiated by sincere repentance, and even by death, uttered these atrocious words: *"Is then the blood now flowing so pure?"* when M. Berthier's son came to the Assembly to implore the eloquence of M. de Lally to entreat that body to save his father's life. I have since been informed that a son of M. Foulon, having returned to France after these first ebullitions of the Revolution, saw Barnave, and gave him one of those memorials in which M. Foulon advised Louis XVI to prevent the revolutionary explosion by voluntarily granting all that the Assembly required before the 14th of July. "Read this memorial," said he; "I have brought it to increase your remorse: it is the only revenge I wish to inflict on you." Barnave burst into tears, and said to him all that the profoundest grief could dictate.

XVI

A FTER the 14th of July, by a manœuvre for which the most skilful factions of any age might have envied the Assembly, the whole population of France was armed and organised into a National Guard. A report was spread throughout France on the same day, and almost at the same hour, that four thousand brigands were marching towards such towns or villages as it was wished to induce to take arms. Never was any plan better laid; terror spread at the same moment all over the kingdom. In 1791 a peasant showed me a steep rock in the mountains of the Mont d'Or on which his wife concealed herself on the day when the four thousand brigands were to attack their village, and told me they had been obliged to make use of ropes to let her down from the height which fear alone had enabled her to climb.

Versailles was certainly the place where the national military uniform appeared most offensive. All the King's valets, even of the lowest class, were metamorphosed into lieutenants or captains; almost all the musicians of the chapel ventured one day to make their appearance at the King's mass in a military costume; and an Italian soprano adopted the uniform of a grenadier captain. The King was very much offended at this conduct, and forbade his servants to appear in his presence in so unsuitable a dress.

The departure of the Duchesse de Polignac naturally left the Abbé de Vermond exposed to all the dangers of favouritism. He was already talked of as an adviser dangerous to the nation. The Queen was alarmed at it, and recommended him to remove to Valenciennes, where Count Esterhazy was in command. He was obliged to leave that place in a few days and set off for Vienna, where he remained.

On the night of the 17th of July the Queen, being unable to sleep, made me watch by her until three in the morning. I was extremely surprised to hear her say that it would be a very long time before the Abbé de Vermond would make his appearance at Court again, even if the existing ferment should subside, because he would not readily be forgiven for his attachment to the Archbishop of Sens; and that she had lost in him a very devoted servant. Then she suddenly remarked to me, that although he was not much prejudiced against me I could not have much regard for him, because he could not bear my father-in-law to hold the place of secretary of the closet. She went on to say that I must have studied the Abbé's character, and, as I had sometimes drawn her portraits of living characters, in imitation of those which were fashionable in the time of Louis XIV, she desired me to sketch that of the Abbé, without any reserve. My astonishment was extreme; the Queen spoke of the man who, the day before, had been in the greatest intimacy with her with the utmost coolness, and as a person whom, perhaps, she might never see again! I remained petrified; the Queen persisted, and told me that he had been the enemy of my family for more than twelve years, without having been able to injure it in her opinion; so that I had no occasion to dread his return, however severely I might depict him. I promptly summarised my ideas about the favourite; but I only remember that the portrait was drawn with sincerity, except that everything which could denote antipathy was kept out of it. I shall make but one extract from it; I said that he had been born talkative and indiscreet, and had assumed a character of singularity and abruptness in order to conceal those two failings. The Queen interrupted me by saying, "Ah! how true that is!" I have since discovered that, notwithstanding the high favour which the Abbé de Vermond enjoyed, the Queen took precautions to guard herself against an ascendency the consequences of which she could not calculate.

On the death of my father-in-law his executors placed in my hands a box containing a few jewels deposited by the Queen with M. Campan on the departure from Versailles of the 6th of October, and two sealed packets, each inscribed, *"Campan will take care of these papers for me."* I took the two packets to her Majesty, who kept the jewels and the larger packet, and, returning me the smaller, said, "Take care of that for me as your father-in-law did."

After the fatal 10th of August, 1792, when my house was about to be surrounded, I determined to burn the most interesting papers of which I was the depository; I thought it my duty, however, to open this packet, which it might perhaps be necessary for me to preserve at all hazards. I saw that it contained a letter from the Abbé de Vermond to the

Queen. I have already related that in the earlier days of Madame de Polignac's favour he determined to remove from Versailles, and that the Queen recalled him by means of the Comte de Mercy. This letter contained nothing but certain conditions for his return; it was the most whimsical of treaties; I confess I greatly regretted being under the necessity of destroying it. He reproached the Queen for her infatuation for the Comtesse Jules, her family, and society; and told her several truths about the possible consequences of a friendship which ranked that lady among the favourites of the Queens of France, a title always disliked by the nation. He complained that his advice was neglected, and then came to the conditions of his return to Versailles; after strong assurances that he would never, in all his life, aim at the higher church dignities, he said that he delighted in an unbounded confidence; and that he asked but two things of her Majesty as essential: the first was, not to give him her orders through any third person, and to write to him herself; he complained much that he had had no letter in her own hand since he had left Vienna; then he demanded of her an income of eighty thousand livres, in ecclesiastical benefices; and concluded by saying that, if she condescended to assure him herself that she would set about procuring him what he wished, her letter would be sufficient in itself to show him that her Majesty had accepted the two conditions he ventured to make respecting his return. No doubt the letter was written; at least it is very certain that the benefices were granted, and that his absence from Versailles lasted only a single week.

In the course of July, 1789, the regiment of French guards, which had been in a state of insurrection from the latter end of June, abandoned its colours. One single company of grenadiers remained faithful to its post at Versailles. M. le Baron de Leval was the captain of this company. He came every evening to request me to give the Queen an account of the disposition of his soldiers; but M. de La Fayette having sent them a note, they all deserted during the night and joined their comrades, who were enrolled in the Paris guard; so that Louis XVI on rising saw no guard whatever at the various posts entrusted to them.

The decrees of the 4th of August, by which all privileges were abolished, are well known. The King sanctioned all that tended to the diminution of his own personal gratifications, but refused his consent to the other decrees of that tumultuous night; this refusal was one of the chief causes of the ferments of the month of October.

In the early part of September meetings were held at the Palais Royal, and propositions made to go to Versailles; it was said to be necessary to separate the King from his evil counsellors, and keep him, as well as the Dauphin, at the Louvre. The proclamations by the officers of the commune for the restoration of tranquillity were ineffectual; but M. de La Fayette succeeded this time in dispersing the populace. The Assembly declared itself permanent; and during the whole of September, in which no doubt the preparations were made for the great insurrections of the following month, the Court was not disturbed.

The King had the Flanders regiment removed to Versailles; unfortunately the idea of the officers of that regiment fraternising with the Body Guards was conceived, and the latter invited the former to a dinner, which was given in the great theatre of Versailles, and not in the Salon of Hercules, as some chroniclers say. Boxes were appropriated to various persons who wished to be present at this entertainment. The Queen told me she had been advised to make her appearance on the occasion, but that under existing circumstances she thought such a step might do more harm than good; and that, moreover, neither she nor the King ought directly to have anything to do with such a festival. She ordered me to go, and desired me to observe everything closely, in order to give a faithful account of the whole affair.

The tables were set out upon the stage; at them were placed one of the Body Guard and an officer of the Flanders regiment alternately. There was a numerous orchestra in the room, and the boxes were filled with spectators. The air, "O Richard, ô mon Roi!" was played, and shouts of *"Vive le Roi!"* shook the roof for several minutes. I had with me one of my nieces, and a young person brought up with Madame by her Majesty. They were crying *"Vive le Roi!"* with all their might when a deputy of the Third Estate, who was in the next box to mine, and whom I had never seen, called to them, and reproached them for their exclamations; it hurt him, he said, to see young and handsome Frenchwomen brought up in such servile habits, screaming so outrageously for the life of one man, and with true fanaticism exalting him in their hearts above even their dearest relations; he told them what contempt worthy American women would feel on seeing Frenchwomen thus corrupted from their earliest infancy. My niece replied with tolerable spirit, and I requested the deputy to put an end to the subject, which could by no means afford him any satisfaction, inasmuch as the young persons who were with me lived, as well as myself, for the sole purpose of serving and loving the King. While I was speaking what was my astonishment at seeing the King, the Queen, and the Dauphin enter the chamber! It was M. de Luxembourg who had effected this change in the Queen's determination.

The enthusiasm became general; the moment their Majesties arrived the orchestra repeated the air I have just mentioned, and afterwards played a song in the "Deserter," "Can we grieve those whom we love?" which also made a powerful impression upon those present: on all sides were heard praises of their Majesties, exclamations of affection, expressions of regret for what they had suffered, clapping of hands, and shouts of *"Vive le Roi! Vive la Reine! Vive le Dauphin!"* It has been said that white cockades were worn on this occasion; that was not the case; the fact is, that a few young men belonging to the National Guard of Versailles, who were invited to the entertainment, turned the white lining of their national cockades outwards. All the military men quitted the hall, and reconducted the King and his family to their apartments. There was intoxication in these ebullitions of joy: a thousand extravagances were committed by the military, and many of them danced under the King's windows; a soldier belonging to the Flanders regiment climbed up to the balcony of the King's chamber in order to shout *"Vive le Roi!"* nearer his Majesty; this very soldier, as I have been told by several officers of the corps, was one of the first and most dangerous of their insurgents in the riots of the 5th and 6th of October. On the same evening another soldier of that regiment killed himself with a sword. One of my relations, chaplain to the Queen, who supped with me, saw him stretched out in a corner of the Place d'Armes; he went to him to give him spiritual assistance, and received his confession and his last sighs. He destroyed himself out of regret at having suffered himself to be corrupted by the enemies of his King, and said that, since he had seen him and the Queen and the Dauphin, remorse had turned his brain.

I returned home, delighted with all that I had seen. I found a great many people there. M. de Beaumetz, deputy for Arras, listened to my description with a chilling air, and, when I had finished, told me that all that had passed was terrific; that he knew the disposition of the Assembly, and that the greatest misfortunes would follow the drama of that night; and he begged my leave to withdraw that he might take time for deliberate reflection whether he should on the very next day emigrate, or pass over to the left side of the Assembly. He adopted the latter course, and never appeared again among my associates.

On the 2d of October the military entertainment was followed up by a breakfast given at the hôtel of the Body Guards. It is said that a discussion took place whether they should not march against the Assembly; but I am utterly ignorant of what passed at that breakfast. From that moment Paris was constantly in commotion; there were continual mobs, and the most virulent proposals were heard in all public places; the conversation was invariably about proceeding to Versailles. The King and Queen did not seem apprehensive of such a measure, and took no precaution against it; even when the army had actually left Paris, on the evening of the 5th of October, the King was shooting at Meudon, and the Queen was alone in her gardens at Trianon, which she then beheld for the last time in her life. She was sitting in her grotto absorbed in painful reflection, when she received a note from the Comte de Saint-Priest, entreating her to return to Versailles. M. de Cubières at the same time went off to request the King to leave his sport and return to the palace; the King did so on horseback, and very leisurely. A few minutes afterwards he was informed that a numerous body of women, which preceded the Parisian army, was at Chaville, at the entrance of the avenue from Paris.

The scarcity of bread and the entertainment of the Body Guards were the pretexts for the insurrection of the 5th and 6th of October, 1789; but it is clear to demonstration that this new movement of the people was a part of the original plan of the factious, insomuch as, ever since the beginning of September, a report had been industriously circulated that the King intended to withdraw, with his family and ministers, to some stronghold; and at all the popular assemblies there had been always a great deal said about going to Versailles to seize the King.

At first only women showed themselves; the latticed doors of the Château were closed, and the Body Guard and Flanders regiment were drawn up in the Place d'Armes. As the details of that dreadful day are given with precision in several works, I will only observe that general consternation and disorder reigned throughout the interior of the palace.

I was not in attendance on the Queen at this time. M. Campan remained with her till two in the morning. As he was leaving her she condescendingly, and with infinite kindness, desired him to make me easy as to the dangers of the moment, and to repeat to me M. de La Fayette's own words, which he had just used on soliciting the royal family to retire to bed, undertaking to answer for his army.

The Queen was far from relying upon M. de La Fayette's loyalty; but she has often told me that she believed on that day that La Fayette, having affirmed to the King, in the presence of a crowd of witnesses, that he would answer for the army of Paris, would not risk his honour as a commander, and was sure of being able to redeem his pledge. She also thought the Parisian army was devoted to him, and that all he said about his being forced to march upon Versailles was mere pretence.

On the first intimation of the march of the Parisians, the Comte de Saint-Priest prepared Rambouillet for the reception of the King, his family, and suite, and the carriages were even drawn out; but a few cries of *"Vive le Roi!"* when the women reported his Majesty's favourable answer, occasioned the intention of going away to be given up, and orders were given to the troops to withdraw. The Body Guards were, however, assailed with stones and musketry while they were passing from the Place d'Armes to their hôtel. Alarm revived; again it was thought necessary that the royal family should go away; some carriages still remained ready for travelling; they were called for; they were stopped by a wretched player belonging to the theatre of the town, seconded by "the mob" the opportunity for flight had been lost.

The insurrection was directed against the Queen in particular; I shudder even now at the recollection of the *poissardes*, or rather furies, who wore white aprons, which they screamed out were intended to receive the bowels of Marie Antoinette, and that they would make cockades of them, mixing the most obscene expressions with these horrible threats.

The Queen went to bed at two in the morning, and even slept, tired out with the events of so distressing a day. She had ordered her two women to bed, imagining there was nothing to dread, at least for that night; but the unfortunate Princess was indebted for her life to that feeling of attachment which prevented their obeying her. My sister, who was one of the ladies in question, informed me next day of all that I am about to relate.

On leaving the Queen's bedchamber, these ladies called their *femmes de chambre*, and all four remained sitting together against her Majesty's bedroom door. About half-past four in the morning they heard horrible yells and discharges of firearms; one ran to the Queen to awaken her and get her out of bed; my sister flew to the place from which the tumult seemed to proceed; she opened the door of the antechamber which leads to the great guard-room, and beheld one of the Body Guard holding his musket across the door, and attacked by a mob, who were striking at him; his face was covered with blood; he turned round and exclaimed: "Save the Queen, madame; they are come to assassinate her!" She hastily shut the door upon the unfortunate victim of duty, fastened it with the great bolt, and took the same precaution on leaving the next room. On reaching the Queen's chamber she cried out to her, "Get up Madame! Don't stay to dress yourself; fly to the King's apartment!" The terrified Queen threw herself out of bed; they put a petticoat upon her without tying it, and the two ladies conducted her towards the *œil-de-bœuf*. A door, which led from the Queen's dressing-room to that apartment, had never before been fastened but on her side. What a dreadful moment! It was found to be secured on the other side. They knocked repeatedly with all their strength; a servant of one of the King's *valets de chambre* came and opened it; the Queen entered the King's chamber, but he was not there. Alarmed for the Queen's life, he had gone clown the staircases and through the corridors under the *œil-de-bœuf*, by means of which he was accustomed to go to the Queen's apartments without being under the necessity of crossing that room. He entered her Majesty's room and found no one there but some Body Guards, who had taken refuge in it. The King, unwilling to expose their lives, told them to wait a few minutes, and afterwards sent to desire them to go to the *œil-de-bœuf*. Madame de Tourzel, at that time governess of the children of France, had just taken Madame and the Dauphin to the King's apartments. The Queen saw her children again. The reader must imagine this scene of tenderness and despair.

It is not true that the assassins penetrated to the Queen's chamber and pierced the bed with their swords. The fugitive Body Guards were the only persons who entered it; and if the crowd had reached so far they would all have been massacred. Besides, when the rebels had forced the doors of the antechamber, the footmen and officers on duty, knowing that the Queen was no longer in her apartments, told them so with that air of truth which always carries conviction. The ferocious horde instantly rushed towards the *œil-de-bœuf*, hoping, no doubt, to intercept her on her way.

Many have asserted that they recognised the Duc d'Orléans in a greatcoat and slouched hat, at half-past four in the morning, at the top of the marble staircase, pointing out with his hand the guard-room, which led to the Queen's apartments. This fact was deposed to at the Châtelet by several individuals in the course of the inquiry instituted respecting the transactions of the 5th and 6th of October.

The prudence and honourable feeling of several officers of the Parisian guards, and the judicious conduct of M. de Vaudreuil, lieutenant-general of marine, and of

M. de Chevanne, one of the King's Guards, brought about an understanding between the grenadiers of the National Guard of Paris and the King's Guard. The doors of the *œil-de-bœuf* were closed, and the antechamber which precedes that room was filled with grenadiers who wanted to get in to massacre the Guards. M. de Chevanne offered himself to them as a victim if they wished for one, and demanded what they would have. A report had been spread through their ranks that the Body Guards set them at defiance, and that they all wore black cockades. M. de Chevanne showed them that he wore, as did the corps, the cockade of their uniform; and promised that the Guards should exchange it for that of the nation. This was done; they even went so far as to exchange their grenadiers' caps for the hats of the Body Guards; those who were on guard took off their shoulder-belts; embraces and transports of fraternisation instantly succeeded to the savage eagerness to murder the band which had shown so much fidelity to its sovereign. The cry was now *"Vivent le Roi, la Nation, et les Gardes-du-corps!"*

The army occupied the Place d'Armes, all the court-yards of the Château, and the entrance to the avenue. They called for the Queen to appear in the balcony: she came forward with Madame and the Dauphin. There was a cry of "No children!" Was this with a view to deprive her of the interest she inspired accompanied as she was by her young family, or did the leaders of the democrats hope that some madman would venture to aim a mortal blow at her person? The unfortunate Princess certainly was impressed with the latter idea, for she sent away her children and with her hands and eyes raised towards heaven advanced upon the balcony like a self-devoted victim!

A few voices shouted "To Paris!" The exclamation soon became general. Before the King agreed to this removal he wished to consult the National Assembly, and caused that body to be invited to sit at the Château. Mirabeau opposed this measure. While these discussions were going forward it became more and more difficult to restrain the immense disorderly multitude. The King, without consulting any one, now said to the people: "You wish, my children, that I should follow you to Paris: I consent, but on condition that I shall not be separated from my wife and family." The King added that he required safety also for his Guards; he was answered by shouts of *"Vive le Roi! Vivent les Gardes-du-corps!"* The Guards, with their hats in the air, turned so as to exhibit the cockade, shouted *"Vive le Roi! Vive la Nation!"* Shortly afterwards a general discharge of all the muskets took place, in token of joy. The King and Queen set off from Versailles at one o'clock. The Dauphin, Madame the King's daughter, Monsieur, Madame, Madame Elisabeth, and Madame de Tourzel, were in the carriage; the Princesse de Chimay and the ladies of the bedchamber for the week, the King's suite and servants, followed in Court carriages; a hundred deputies in carriages, and the bulk of the Parisian army, closed the procession.

The *poissardes* went before and around the carriage of their Majesties, crying, "We shall no longer want bread! We have the baker, the baker's wife, and the baker's boy with us!" In the midst of this troop of cannibals the heads of two murdered Body Guards were carried on poles. The monsters, who made trophies of them, conceived the horrid idea of forcing a wigmaker of Sèvres to dress them up and powder their bloody locks. The unfortunate man who was forced to perform this dreadful work died in consequence of the shock it gave him.

The progress of the procession was so slow that it was near six in the evening when this august family, made prisoners by their own people, arrived at the Hôtel de Ville. Bailly received them there; they were placed upon a throne, just when that of their ancestors had been overthrown. The King spoke in a firm yet gracious manner; he said that he always came with pleasure and confidence among the inhabitants of his good city of Paris. M. Bailly repeated this observation to the representatives of the commune, who came to address the King; but he forgot the word *confidence*. The Queen instantly and loudly reminded him of the omission. The King and Queen, their children, and Madame Elisabeth, retired to the Tuileries. Nothing was ready for their reception there. All the living-rooms had been long given up to persons belonging to the Court; they hastily quitted them on that day, leaving their furniture, which was purchased by the Court. The Comtesse de la Marck, sister to the Maréchaux de Noailles and de Mouchy, had occupied the apartments now appropriated to the Queen. Monsieur and Madame retired to the Luxembourg.

The Queen had sent for me on the morning of the 6th of October, to leave me and my father-in-law in charge of her most valuable property. She took away only her casket of diamonds. Comte Gouvernet de la Tour-du-Pin, to whom the military government of Versailles was entrusted *pro tempore*, came and gave orders to the National Guard, which had taken possession of the apartments, to allow us to remove everything that we should deem necessary for the Queen's accommodation.

I saw her Majesty alone in her private apartments a moment before her departure for Paris; she could hardly speak; tears bedewed her face, to which all the blood in her body seemed to have rushed; she condescended to embrace me, gave her hand to M. Campan[1] to kiss, and said to us, "Come immediately and settle at Paris; I will lodge you at the Tuileries; come, and do not leave me henceforward; faithful servants at moments like these become useful friends; we are lost, dragged away, perhaps to death; when kings become prisoners they are very near it."

I had frequent opportunities during the course of our misfortunes of observing that the people never entirely give their allegiance to factious leaders, but easily escape their control when some cause reminds them of their duty. As soon as the most violent Jacobins had an opportunity of seeing the Queen near at hand, of speaking to her, and of hearing her voice, they became her most zealous partisans; and even when she was in the prison of the Temple several of those who had contributed to place her there perished for having attempted to get her out again.

On the morning of the 7th of October the same women who the day before surrounded the carriage of the august prisoners, riding on cannons and uttering the most abusive language, assembled under the Queen's windows, upon the terrace of the Château, and desired to see her. Her Majesty appeared. There are always among mobs of this description orators, that is to say, beings who have more assurance than

---

1. Let me here pay a well-merited tribute to the memory of my father-in-law. In the course of that one night he declined from the highest pitch of health into a languishing condition, which brought him to the grave in September, 1791.

the rest; a woman of this description told the Queen that she must now remove far from her all such courtiers as ruin kings, and that she must love the inhabitants of her good city. The Queen answered that she had loved them at Versailles, and would likewise love them at Paris. "Yes, yes," said another; "but on the 14th of July you wanted to besiege the city and have it bombarded; and on the 6th of October you wanted to fly to the frontiers." The Queen replied, affably, that they had been told so, and had believed it; that there lay the cause of the unhappiness of the people and of the best of kings. A third addressed a few words to her in German: the Queen told her she did not understand it; that she had become so entirely French as even to have forgotten her mother tongue. This declaration was answered with "Bravo!" and clapping of hands; they then desired her to make a compact with them. "Ah," said she, "how can I make a compact with you, since you have no faith in that which my duty points out to me, and which I ought for my own happiness to respect?" They asked her for the ribbons and flowers out of her hat; her Majesty herself unfastened them and gave them; they were divided among the party, which for above half an hour cried out, without ceasing, "Marie Antoinette for ever! Our good Queen for ever!"

Two days after the King's arrival at Paris, the city and the National Guard sent to request the Queen to appear at the theatre, and prove by her presence and the King's that it was with pleasure they resided in their capital. I introduced the deputation which came to make this request. Her Majesty replied that she would have infinite pleasure in acceding to the invitation of the city of Paris; but that time must be allowed her to soften the recollection of the distressing events which had just occurred, and from which she had suffered too much. She added, that having come into Paris preceded by the heads of the faithful Guards who had perished before the door of their sovereign, she could not think that such an entry into the capital ought to be followed by rejoicings; but that the happiness she had always felt in appearing I in the midst of the inhabitants of Paris was not effaced from her memory, and that she should enjoy it again as soon as she found herself able to do so.

Their Majesties found some consolation in their private life: from Madame's gentle manners and filial affection, from the accomplishments and vivacity of the little Dauphin, and the attention and tenderness of the pious Princess Elisabeth, they still derived moments of happiness. The young Prince daily gave proofs of sensibility and penetration; he was not yet beyond female care, but a private tutor, the Abbé Davout, gave him all the instruction suitable to his age; his memory was highly cultivated, and he recited verses with much grace and feeling.

The day after the arrival of the Court at Paris, terrified at hearing some noise in the gardens of the Tuileries, he threw himself into the arms of the Queen, crying out, "*Grand Dieu*, mamma! Will it be yesterday over again?" A few days after this affecting exclamation, he went up to the King, and looked at him with a pensive air. The King asked him what he wanted; he answered, that he had something very serious to say to him. The King having prevailed on him to explain himself, the young Prince asked why his people, who formerly loved him so well, were all at once angry with him; and what he had done to irritate them so much. His father took him upon his knees, and spoke to him nearly as follows: "I wished, child, to render the people still happier than they were; I wanted money to pay the expenses occasioned by wars. I asked my people for money, as my predecessors have always done; magistrates, composing the Parliament, opposed it, and said that my people alone had a right to consent to it. I assembled the principal inhabitants of every town, whether distinguished by birth, fortune, or talents, at Versailles ; that is what is called the States General. When they were assembled they required concessions of me which I could not make, either with due respect for myself or with justice to you, who will be my successor; wicked men inducing the people to rise have occasioned the excesses of the last few days; the people must not be blamed for them."

The Queen made the young Prince clearly comprehend that he ought to treat the commanders of battalions, the officers of the National Guard, and all the Parisians who were about him, with affability; the child took great pains to please all those people, and when he had had an opportunity of replying obligingly to the mayor or members of the commune he came and whispered in his mother's ear, "Was that right?"

He requested M. Bailly to show him the shield of Scipio, which is in the royal library; and M. Bailly asking him which he preferred, Scipio or Hannibal, the young Prince replied, without hesitation, that he preferred him who had defended his own country. He gave frequent proofs of ready wit. One day while the Queen was hearing Madame repeat her exercises in ancient history, the young Princess could not at the moment recollect the name of the Queen of Carthage; the Dauphin was vexed at his sister's want of memory, and though he never spoke to her in the second person singular, he bethought himself of the expedient of saying to her, "But *dis donc* the name of the Queen, to mamma; *dis donc* what her name was."

Shortly after the arrival of the King and his family at Paris the Duchesse de Luynes came, in pursuance of the advice of a committee of the Constitutional Assembly, to propose to the Queen a temporary retirement from France, in order to leave the constitution to perfect itself, so that the patriots should not accuse her of influencing the King to oppose it. The Duchess knew how far the schemes of the conspirers extended, and her attachment to the Queen was the principal cause of the advice she gave her. The Queen perfectly comprehended the Duchesse de Luynes's motive ; but replied that she would never leave either the King or her son; that if she thought herself alone obnoxious to public hatred she would instantly offer her life as a sacrifice; but that it was the throne which was aimed at, and that, in abandoning the King, she should be merely committing an act of cowardice, since she saw no other advantage in it than that of saving her own life.

One evening, in the month of November, 1790, I returned home rather late; I there found the Prince de Poix; he told me he came to request me to assist him in regaining his peace of mind; that at the commencement of the sittings of the National Assembly he had suffered himself to be seduced into the hope of a better order of things; that he blushed for his error, and that he abhorred plans which had already produced such fatal results; that he broke with the reformers for the rest of his life; that he had given in his resignation as a deputy of the National Assembly; and, finally, that he was anxious that the Queen should not sleep in ignorance of his sentiments. I undertook his commission, and acquitted myself of it in the best way I could; but I was totally unsuccessful. The Prince de Poix remained at Court; he there suffered many mortifications, never ceasing to serve the King in the most dangerous commissions with that zeal for which his house has always been distinguished.

When the King, the Queen, and the children were suitably established at the Tuileries, as well as Madame Elisabeth and the Princesse de Lamballe, the Queen resumed her usual habits; she employed her mornings in superintending the education of Madame, who received all her lessons in her presence, and she herself began to work large pieces of tapestry. Her mind was too much occupied with passing events and surrounding dangers to admit of her applying herself to reading; the needle was the only employment which could divert her.[1] She received the Court twice a week before going to mass, and on those days dined in public with the King; she spent the rest of the time with her family and children; she had no concert, and did not go to the play until 1791, after the acceptation of the constitution. The Princesse de Lamballe, however, had some evening parties in her apartments at the Tuileries, which were tolerably brilliant in consequence of the great number of persons who attended them. The Queen was present at a few of these assemblies; but being soon convinced that her present situation forbade her appearing much in public, she remained at home, and conversed

1. There is still at Paris, at the house of Mademoiselle Dubuquois, tapestry worker, a carpet worked by the Queen and Madame Elisabeth for the large room of her Majesty's ground-floor apartments at the Tuileries. The Empress Josephine saw and admired this carpet, and desired it might be preserved, in the hope of one day sending it to Madame.

as she sat at work.[1] The sole topic of her discourse was, as may well be supposed, the Revolution. She sought to discover the real opinions of the Parisians respecting her, and how she could have so completely lost the affections of the people, and even of many persons in the higher ranks. She well knew that she ought to impute the whole to the spirit of party, to the hatred of the Duc d'Orléans, and the folly of the French, who desired to have a total change in the constitution; but she was not the less desirous of ascertaining the private feelings of all the people in power.

From the very commencement of the Revolution Général Luckner indulged in violent sallies against her. Her Majesty, knowing that I was acquainted with a lady who had been long connected with the General, desired me to discover through that channel what was the private motive on which Luckner's hatred against her was founded. On being questioned upon this point, he answered that Maréchal de Ségur had assured him he had proposed him for the command of a camp of observation, but that the Queen had made a bar against his name; and that this *par*, as he called it, in his German accent, he could not forget.

The Queen ordered me to repeat this reply to the King myself, and said to him: "See, Sire, whether I was not right in telling you that your ministers, in order to give themselves full scope in the distribution of favours, persuaded the French that I interfered in everything; there was not a single license given out in the country for the sale

1. The Queen returned one evening from one of these assemblies very much affected; an English nobleman, who was playing at the same table with her Majesty, ostentatiously displayed an enormous ring, in which was a lock of Oliver Cromwell's hair.

of salt or tobacco but the people believed it was given to one of my favourites."

"That is very true," replied the King; "but I find it very difficult to believe that Maréchal de Ségur ever said any such thing to Luckner; he knew too well that you never interfered in the distribution of favours. That Luckner is a good-for-nothing fellow, and Ségur is a brave and honourable man who never uttered such a falsehood; however, you are right; and because you provided for a few dependents, you are most unjustly reported to have disposed of all offices, civil and military."

All the nobility who had not left Paris made a point of presenting themselves assiduously to the King, and there was a considerable influx to the Tuileries. Marks of attachment were exhibited even in external symbols; the women wore enormous bouquets of lilies in their bosoms and upon their heads, and sometimes even bunches of white ribbon. At the play there were often disputes between the pit and the boxes about removing these ornaments, which the people thought dangerous emblems. National cockades were sold in every corner of Paris; the sentinels stopped all who did not wear them; the young men piqued themselves upon breaking through this regulation, which was in some degree sanctioned by the acquiescence of Louis XVI. Frays took place, which were to be regretted, because they excited a spirit of lawlessness. The King adopted conciliatory measures with the Assembly in order to promote tranquillity; the revolutionists were but little disposed to think him sincere; unfortunately the royalists encouraged this incredulity by incessantly repeating that the King was not free, and that all that he did was completely null, and in no way bound him for the time to come. Such was the heat and violence of party spirit that persons the most sincerely attached to the King were not even permitted to use the language of reason, and recommend greater reserve in conversation. People would talk and argue at table without considering that all the servants belonged to the hostile army; and it may truly be said there was as much imprudence and levity in the party assailed as there was cunning, boldness, and perseverance in that which made the attack.

XVII

I N February, 1790, another matter gave the Court much uneasiness; a zealous individual of the name of Favras had conceived the scheme of carrying off the King, and effecting a counter-revolution. Monsieur, probably out of mere benevolence, gave him some money, and thence arose a report that he thereby wished to favour the execution of the enterprise. The step taken by Monsieur in going to the Hôtel de Ville to explain himself on this matter was unknown to the Queen; it is more than probable that the King was acquainted with it. When judgment was pronounced upon M. de Favras the Queen did not conceal from me her fears about the confessions of the unfortunate man in his last moments.

I sent a confidential person to the Hôtel de Ville; she came to inform the Queen that the condemned had demanded to be taken from Notre-Dame to the Hôtel de Ville to make a final declaration, and give some particulars verifying it. These particulars compromised nobody; Favras corrected his last will after writing it, and went to the scaffold with heroic courage and coolness. The judge who read his condemnation to him told him that his life was a sacrifice which he owed to public tranquillity. It was asserted at the time that Favras was given up as a victim in order to satisfy the people and save the Baron de Besenval, who was a prisoner in the Abbaye.

On the morning of the Sunday following this execution M. de la Villeurnoy[1] came to my house to tell me that he was going that day to the public dinner of the King and Queen to present Madame de Favras and her son, both of them in mourning for the brave Frenchman who fell a sacrifice for his King; and that all the royalists expected to see the Queen load the unfortunate family with favours. I did all that lay in my power to prevent this proceeding. I foresaw the effect it would have upon the Queen's feeling heart, and the painful constraint she would experience, having the horrible Santerre, the commandant of a battalion of the Parisian guard, behind her chair during dinner-time. I could not make M. de la Villeurnoy comprehend my argument; the Queen was gone to mass, surrounded by her whole Court, and I had not even means of apprising her of his intention.

When dinner was over I heard a knocking at the door of my apartment, which opened into the corridor next that of the Queen; it was herself. She asked me whether there was anybody with me; I was alone; she threw herself into an armchair, and told me she came to weep with me over the foolish conduct of the ultras of the King's party. "We must fall," said she, "attacked as we are by men who possess every

---

1. M. de la Villeurnoy, Master of the Requests, was deported to Sinamary, on the 18th Fructidor, by the Executive Directory, and there died.

talent and shrink from no crime, while we are defended only by those who are no doubt very estimable, but have no adequate idea of our situation. They have exposed me to the animosity of both parties by presenting the widow and son of Favras to me. Were I free to act as I wish, I should take the child of the man who has just sacrificed himself for us and place him at table between the King and myself; but surrounded by the assassins who have destroyed his father, I did not dare even to cast my eyes upon him. The royalists will blame me for not having appeared interested in this poor child; the revolutionists will be enraged at the idea that his presentation should have been thought agreeable to me." However, the Queen added that she knew Madame de Favras was in want, and that she desired me to send her next day, through a person who could be relied on, a few rouleaus of fifty louis and to direct that she should be assured her Majesty would always watch over the fortunes of herself and her son.

In the month of March following I had an opportunity of ascertaining the King's sentiments respecting the schemes which were continually proposed to him for making his escape. One night about ten o'clock Comte d'Inisdal, who was deputed by the nobility, came to request that I would see him in private, as he had an important matter to communicate to me. He told me that on that very night the King was to be carried off; that the section of the National Guard, that day commanded by M. d'Aumont,[1] was gained over, and that sets of horses, furnished by some good royalists, were placed in

---

1. A brother of the Duc de Villequier, who had joined the revolutionary party; a man of no weight or respectability, who desired he might be called "James Aumont;" a far different man from his brave brother, who always proved himself entirely devoted to the cause of his King.

relays at suitable distances; that he had just left a number of the nobility assembled for the execution of this scheme, and that he had been sent to me that I might, through the medium of the Queen, obtain the King's positive consent to it before midnight; that the King was aware of their plan, but that his Majesty never would speak decidedly, and that it was necessary he should consent to the undertaking. I greatly displeased Comte d'Inisdal by expressing my astonishment that the nobility at the moment of the execution of so important a project should send to me, the Queen's first woman, to obtain a consent which ought to have been the basis of any well-concerted scheme. I told him, also, that it would be impossible for me to go at that time to the Queen's apartments without exciting the attention of the people in the antechambers; that the King was at cards with the Queen and his family, and that I never broke in upon their privacy unless I was called for. I added, however, that M. Campan could enter without being called; and if the Count chose to give him his confidence he might rely upon him.

My father-in-law, to whom Comte d'Inisdal repeated what he had said to me, took the commission upon himself, and went to the Queen's apartments. The King was playing at whist with the Queen, Monsieur, and Madame; Madame Elisabeth was kneeling on a stool near the table. M. Campan informed the Queen of what had been communicated to me; nobody uttered a word. The Queen broke silence and said to the King, "Do you hear, Sire, what Campan says to us?" "Yes, I hear," said the King, and continued his game. Monsieur, who was in the habit of introducing passages from plays into his conversation, said to my father-in-law, "M. Campan, that pretty little couplet again, if you please;"

and pressed the King to reply. At length the Queen said, "But something must be said to Campan." The King then spoke to my father-in-law in these words; "Tell M. d'Inisdal that I cannot consent to be carried off!" The Queen enjoined M. Campan to take care and report this answer faithfully. "You understand," added she, "the King cannot consent to be carried off."

Comte d'Inisdal was very much dissatisfied with the King's answer, and went out, saying, "I understand; he wishes to throw all the blame, beforehand, upon those who are to devote themselves for him." He went away, and I thought the enterprise would be abandoned. However, the Queen remained alone with me till midnight, preparing her cases of valuables, and ordered me not to go to bed. She imagined the King's answer would be understood as a tacit consent, and merely a refusal to participate in the design. I do not know what passed in the King's apartments during the night; but I occasionally looked out at the windows: I saw the garden clear; I heard no noise in the palace, and day at length confirmed my opinion that the project had been given up. "We must, however, fly," said the Queen to me, shortly afterwards; "who knows how far the factious may go? The danger increases every day." This Princess received advice and memorials from all quarters. Rivarol addressed several to her, which I read to her. They were full of ingenious observations; but the Queen did not find that they contained anything of essential service under the circumstances in which the royal family was placed. Comte du Moustier also sent memorials and plans of conduct. I remember that in one of his writings he said to the King, "Read 'Telemachus' again, Sire; in that book which delighted your Majesty in infancy you will find the first seeds of those principles which, erroneously followed up by men of ardent imaginations, are bringing on the explosion we expect every moment." I read so many of these memorials that I could hardly give a faithful account of them, and I am determined to note in this work no other events than such as I witnessed; no other words than such as (notwithstanding the lapse of time) still in some measure vibrate in my ears.

Comte de Ségur, on his return from Russia, was employed some time by the Queen, and had a certain degree of influence over her; but that did not last long. Comte Augustus de la Marck likewise endeavoured to negotiate for the King's advantage with the leaders of the factious. M. de Fontanges, Archbishop of Toulouse, possessed also the Queen's confidence; but none of the endeavours which were made on the spot produced any beneficial result. The Empress Catherine II also conveyed her opinion upon the situation of Louis XVI to the Queen, and her Majesty made me read a few lines in the Empress's own handwriting, which concluded with these words: "Kings ought to proceed in their career undisturbed by the cries of the people, even as the moon pursues her course unimpeded by the baying of dogs." This maxim of the despotic sovereign of Russia was very inapplicable to the situation of a captive king.

Meanwhile the revolutionary party followed up its audacious enterprise in a determined manner, without meeting any opposition. The advice from without, as well from Coblentz as from Vienna, made various impressions upon the members of the royal family, and those cabinets were not in accordance with each other. I often had reason to infer from what the Queen said to me that she thought the King, by leaving all the honour of restoring order to the Coblentz party, would, on the return of the emigrants, be put under a kind of guardianship which would increase his own misfortunes. She frequently said to me, "If the emigrants succeed, they will rule the roost for a long time; it will be impossible to refuse them anything; to owe the crown to them would be contracting too great an obligation." It always appeared to me that she wished her own family to counterbalance the claims of the emigrants by disinterested services. She was fearful of M. de Calonne, and with good reason. She had proof that this minister was her bitterest enemy, and that he made use of the most criminal means in order to blacken her reputation. I can testify that I have seen in the hands of the Queen a manuscript copy of the infamous memoirs of the woman De Lamotte, which had been brought to her from London, and in which all those passages where a total ignorance of the customs of Courts had occasioned that wretched woman to make blunders which would have been too palpable were corrected in M. de Calonne's own handwriting.

The two King's Guards who were wounded at her Majesty's door on the 6th of October were M. du Repaire and M. de Miomandre de Sainte-Marie; on the dreadful night, of the 6th of October the latter took the post of the former the moment he became incapable of maintaining it.

A considerable number of the Body Guards, who were wounded on the 6th of October, betook themselves to the infirmary at Versailles. The brigands wanted to make their way into the infirmary in order to massacre them. M. Viosin, head surgeon of that infirmary, ran to the entrance hall, invited the assailants to refresh themselves, ordered wine to be brought, and found means to direct the Sister Superior to remove the Guards into a ward appropriated to the poor, and dress them in the caps and greatcoats furnished by the institution. The good sisters executed this order so promptly that the Guards were removed, dressed as paupers, and their beds made, while the assassins were drinking. They searched all the wards, and fancied they saw no persons there but the sick poor; thus the Guards were saved.

M. de Miomandre was at Paris, living on terms of friendship with another of the Guards, who, on the same day, received a gunshot wound from the brigands in another part of the Château. These two officers, who were attended and cured together at the infirmary of Versailles, were almost constant companions; they were recognised at the Palais Royal, and insulted. The Queen thought it necessary for them to quit Paris. She desired me to write to M. de Miomandre de Sainte-Marie, and tell him to come to me at eight o'clock in the evening; and then to communicate to him her wish to hear of his being in safety; and ordered me, when he had made up his mind to go, to tell him in her name that gold could not repay such a service as he had rendered; that she hoped some day to be in sufficiently happy circumstances to recompense him as she ought; but that for the present her offer of money was only that of a sister to a brother situated as he then was, and that she requested he would take whatever might be necessary to discharge his debts at Paris and defray the expenses of his journey. She told me also to desire he would bring his friend Bertrand with him, and to make him the same offer.

The two Guards came at the appointed hour, and accepted, I think, each one or two hundred louis. A moment afterwards the Queen opened my door; she was accompanied by the King and Madame Elisabeth; the King stood with his back against the fireplace; the Queen sat down upon a sofa and Madame Elisabeth sat near her; I placed myself behind the Queen, and the two Guards stood facing the King. The Queen told them that the King wished to see before they went away two of the brave men who had afforded him the strongest proofs of courage and attachment. Miomandre said all that the Queen's affecting observations were calculated to inspire. Madame Elisabeth spoke of the King's gratitude; the Queen resumed the subject of their speedy departure, urging the necessity of it; the King was silent; but his emotion was evident, and his eyes were suffused with tears. The Queen rose, the King went out, and Madame Elisabeth followed him; the Queen stopped and said to me, in the recess of a window, "I am sorry I brought the King here! I am sure Elisabeth thinks with me; if the King had but given utterance to a fourth part of what he thinks of those brave men they would have been in ecstasies; but he cannot overcome his diffidence."

The Emperor Joseph died about this time. The Queen's grief was not excessive; that brother of whom she had been so proud, and whom she had loved so tenderly, had probably suffered greatly in her opinion; she reproached him sometimes, though with moderation, for having adopted several of the principles of the new philosophy, and perhaps she knew that he looked upon our troubles with the eye of the sovereign of Germany rather than that of the brother of the Queen of France.

The Emperor on one occasion sent the Queen an engraving which represented unfrocked nuns and monks. The first were trying on fashionable dresses, the latter were having their hair arranged; the picture was always left in the closet, and never hung up. The Queen told me to have it taken away; for she was hurt to see how much influence the philosophers had over her brother's mind and actions.

Mirabeau had not lost the hope of becoming the last resource of the oppressed Court; and at this time some communications passed between the Queen and him. The question was about an office to be conferred upon him. This transpired, and it must have been about this period that the Assembly decreed that no deputy could hold an office as a minister of the King until the expiration of two years after the cessation of his legislative functions. I know that the Queen was much hurt at this decision, and considered that the Court had lost a promising opening.

The palace of the Tuileries was a very disagreeable residence during the summer, which made the Queen wish to go to St. Cloud. The removal was decided on without any opposition; the National Guard of Paris followed the Court thither. At this period new opportunities of escape were presented; nothing would have been more easy than to execute them. The King had obtained leave (!) to go out without guards, and to be accompanied only by an aide-de-camp of M. de La Fayette. The Queen also had one on duty with her, and so had the Dauphin. The King and Queen often went out at four in the afternoon, and did not return until eight or nine.

I will relate one of the plans of emigration which the Queen communicated to me, the success of which seemed infallible. The royal family were to meet in a wood four leagues from St. Cloud; some persons who could be fully relied on were to accompany the King, who was always followed by his equerries and pages; the Queen was to join him with her daughter and Madame Elisabeth. These Princesses, as well as the Queen, had equerries and pages, of whose fidelity no doubt could be entertained. The Dauphin likewise was to be at the place of rendezvous with Madame de Tourzel; a large berlin and a chaise for the attendants were sufficient for the whole family; the aides-de-camp were to have been gained over or mastered. The King was to leave a letter for the President of the National Assembly on his bureau at St. Cloud. The people in the service of the King and Queen would have waited until nine in the evening without anxiety, because the family sometimes did not return until that hour. The letter could not be forwarded to Paris until ten o'clock at the earliest. The Assembly would not then be sitting; the President must have been sought for at his own house or elsewhere; it would have been midnight before the Assembly could have been summoned and couriers sent off to have the royal family stopped; but the latter would have been six or seven hours in advance, as they would have started at six leagues' distance from Paris; and at this period travelling was not yet impeded in France.

The Queen approved of this plan; but I did not venture to interrogate her, and I even thought if it were put in execution she would leave me in ignorance of it. One evening in the month of June the people of the Château, finding the King did not return by nine o'clock, were walking about the courtyards in a state of great anxiety. I thought the family was gone, and I could scarcely breathe amidst the confusion of my good wishes, when I heard the sound of the carriages. I confessed to the Queen that I thought she had set off; she told me she must wait until Mesdames the King's aunts had quitted France, and afterwards see whether the plan agreed with those formed abroad.

XVIII

THERE was a meeting at Paris for the first federation on the 14th of July, 1790, the anniversary of the taking of the Bastille. What an astonishing assemblage of four hundred thousand men of whom there were not perhaps two hundred who did not believe that the King found happiness and glory in the order of things then being established. The love which was borne him by all, with the exception of those who meditated his ruin, still reigned in the hearts of the French in the departments; but if I may judge from those whom I had an opportunity of seeing, it was totally impossible to enlighten them; they were as much attached to the King as to the constitution, and to the constitution as to the King; and it was impossible to separate the one from the other in their hearts and minds.

The Court returned to St. Cloud after the federation. A wretch, named Rotondo, made his way into the palace with the intention of assassinating the Queen. It is known that he penetrated to the inner gardens: the rain prevented her Majesty from going out that day. M. de La Fayette, who was aware of this plot, gave all the sentinels the strictest orders, and a description of the monster was distributed throughout the palace by order of the General. I do not know how he was saved from punishment. The police belonging to the King discovered that there was likewise a scheme on foot for poisoning the Queen. She spoke to me, as well as to her head physician, M. Vicq-d'Azyr, about it, without the slightest emotion, but both he and I consulted what precautions it would be proper to take. He relied much upon the Queen's temperance; yet he recommended me always to have a bottle of oil of sweet almonds within reach, and to renew it occasionally, that oil and milk being, as is known, the most certain antidotes to the divellication of corrosive poisons.

The Queen had a habit which rendered M. Vicq-d'Azyr particularly uneasy: there was always some pounded sugar upon the table in her Majesty's bedchamber; and she frequently, without calling anybody, put spoonfuls of it into a glass of water when she wished to drink. It was agreed that I should get a considerable quantity of sugar powdered; that I should always have some papers of it in my bag, and that three or four times a day, when alone in the Queen's room, I should substitute it for that in her sugar basin. We knew that the Queen would have prevented all such precautions, but we were not aware of her reason. One day she caught me alone making this exchange, and told me she supposed it was agreed on between myself and M. Vicq-d'Azyr, but that I gave myself very unnecessary trouble. "Remember," added she, "that not a grain of poison will be put in use against me.

The Brinvilliers do not belong to this century: this age possesses calumny, which is a much more convenient instrument of death; and it is by that I shall perish."

Even while melancholy presentiments afflicted this unfortunate Princess, manifestations of attachment to her person, and to the King's cause, would frequently raise agreeable illusions in her mind, or present to her the affecting spectacle of tears shed for her sorrows. I was one day, during this same visit to St. Cloud, witness of a very touching scene, which we took great care to keep secret. It was four in the afternoon; the guard was not set; there was scarcely anybody at St. Cloud that day, and I was reading to he Queen, who was at work in a room the balcony of which hung over the courtyard. The windows were closed, yet we heard a sort of inarticulate murmur from a great number of voices. The Queen desired me to go and see what it was; I raised the muslin curtain, and perceived more than fifty persons beneath the balcony: this group consisted of women, young and old, perfectly well dressed in the country costume, old chevaliers of St. Louis, young knights of Malta, and a few ecclesiastics. I told the Queen it was probably an assemblage of persons residing in the neighbourhood who wished to see her. She rose, opened the window, and appeared in the balcony; immediately all these worthy people said to her, in an undertone: "Courage, Madame; good Frenchmen suffer for you, and with you; they pray for you. Heaven will hear their prayers; we love you, we respect you, we will continue to venerate our virtuous King." The Queen burst into tears, and held her handkerchief to her eyes. "Poor Queen! she weeps!" said the women and young girls; but the dread of exposing her Majesty, and even the persons who showed so much affection for her to observation, prompted me to take her hand, and prevail upon her to retire into her room; and, raising my eyes, I gave the excellent people to understand that my conduct was dictated by prudence. They comprehended me, for I heard, "That lady is right;" and afterwards, "Farewell, Madame!" from several of them; and all this in accents of feeling so true and so mournful, that I am affected at the recollection of them even after a lapse of twenty years.

A few days afterwards the insurrection of Nancy took place. Only the ostensible cause is known; there was another, of which I might have been in full possession, if the great confusion I was in upon the subject had not deprived me of the power of paying attention to it. I will endeavour to make myself understood. In the early part of September the Queen, as she was going to bed, desired me to let all her people go, and to remain with her myself; when we were alone she said to me, "The King will come here at midnight. You know that he has always shown you marks of distinction; he now proves his confidence in you by selecting you to write down the whole affair of Nancy from his dictation. He must have several copies of it." At midnight the King came to the Queen's apartments, and said to me, smiling, "You did not expect to become my secretary, and that, too, during the night." I followed the King into the council chamber. I found there sheets of paper, an inkstand, and pens all ready prepared. He sat down by my side and dictated to me the report of the Marquis de Bouillé, which he himself copied at the same time. My hand trembled; I wrote with difficulty; my reflections scarcely left me sufficient power of attention to listen to the King. The large table, the velvet cloth, seats which ought to have been filled by none but the King's chief councillors; what that chamber had been, and what it was at that moment, when the King was employing a woman in an office which had so little affinity with her ordinary functions; the misfortunes which had brought him to the necessity of doing so,—all these ideas made such an impression upon me that when I had returned to the Queen's apartments I could not sleep for the remainder of the night, nor could I remember what I had written.

The more I saw that I had the happiness to be of some use to my employers, the more scrupulously careful was I to live entirely with my family; and I never indulged in any conversation which could betray the intimacy to which I was admitted; but nothing at Court remains long concealed, and I soon saw I had many enemies. The means of injuring others in the minds of sovereigns are but too easily obtained, and they had become still more so since the mere suspicion of communication with partisans of the Revolution was sufficient to forfeit the esteem and confidence of the King and Queen; happily, my conduct protected me, with them, against calumny. I had left St. Cloud two days, when I received at Paris a note from the Queen, containing these words; "Come to St. Cloud immediately; I have something concerning you to communicate." I set off without loss of time. Her Majesty told me she had a sacrifice to request of me; I answered that it was made. She said it went so far as the renunciation of a friend's society; that such a renunciation was always painful, but that it must be particularly so to me; that, for her own part, it might have been very useful that a deputy, a man of talent, should be constantly received at my house; but at this moment she thought only of my welfare. The Queen then informed me that the ladies of the bedchamber had, the preceding evening, assured her that M. de Beaumetz, deputy from the nobility of Artois, who had taken his seat on the left of the Assembly, spent his whole time at my house. Perceiving on what false grounds the attempt to injure me was based, I replied respectfully, but at the same time smiling, that it was impossible for me to make the sacrifice exacted by her Majesty; that M. de Beaumetz, a man of great judgment, had not determined to cross over to the left of the Assembly with the intention of afterwards making himself unpopular by spending his time with the Queen's first woman; and that, ever since the 1st of October, 1789, I had seen him nowhere but at the play, or in the public walks, and even then without his ever coming to speak to me; that this line of conduct had appeared to me perfectly consistent: for whether he was desirous to please the popular party, or to be sought after by the Court, he could not act in any other way towards me. The Queen closed this explanation by saying, "Oh! it is clear, as clear as the day! this opportunity for trying to do you an injury is very ill chosen; but be cautious in your slightest actions; you perceive that the confidence placed in you by the King and myself raises you up powerful enemies."

The private communications which were still kept up between the Court and Mirabeau at length procured him an interview with the Queen, in the gardens of St. Cloud.[1] He left Paris on horseback, on pretence of going

---

1. It was not in her apartments, as is asserted by M. de Lacretelle, that the Queen received Mirabeau; his person was too generally known; she went alone into her garden, to a round tuft of ground, which is still upon the heights of the private garden of St. Cloud.

into the country, to M. de Clavières, one of his friends; but he stopped at one of the gates of the gardens of St. Cloud, and was led to a spot situated in the highest part of the private garden, where the Queen was waiting for him. She told me she accosted him by saying, "With a common enemy, with a man who had sworn to destroy monarchy without appreciating its utility among a great people, I should at this moment be guilty of a most ill-advised step; but in speaking to a Mirabeau," etc. The poor Queen was delighted at having discovered this method of exalting him above all others of his principles; and in imparting the particulars of this interview to me she said, "Do you know that those words, 'a Mirabeau,' appeared to flatter him exceedingly." On leaving the Queen he said to her with warmth, "Madame, the monarchy is saved!" It must have been soon afterwards that Mirabeau received considerable sums of money. He showed it too plainly by the increase of his expenditure. Already did some of his remarks upon the necessity of arresting the progress of the democrats circulate in society. Being once invited to meet a person at dinner who was very much attached to the Queen, he learned that that person withdrew on hearing that he was one of the guests; the party who invited him told him this with some degree of satisfaction; but all were very much astonished when they heard Mirabeau eulogise the absent guest, and declare that in his place he would have done the same; but, he added, they had only to invite that person again in a few months, and he would then dine with the restorer of the monarchy. Mirabeau forgot that it was more easy to do harm than good, and thought himself the political Atlas of the whole world.

Outrages and mockery were incessantly mingled with the audacious proceedings of the revolutionists. It was customary to give serenades under the King's windows on New Year's Day. The band of the National Guard repaired thither on that festival in 1791; in allusion to the liquidation of the debts of the State, decreed by the Assembly, they played solely, and repeatedly, that air from the comic opera of the "Debts," the burden of which is, "But our creditors are paid, and that makes us easy."

On the same day some "conquerors of the Bastille," grenadiers of the Parisian guard, preceded by military music, came to present to the young Dauphin, as a New Year's gift, a box of dominoes, made of some of the stone and marble of which that state prison was built. The Queen gave me this inauspicious curiosity, desiring me to preserve it, as it would be a curious illustration of the history of the Revolution. Upon the lid were engraved some bad verses, the purport of which was as follows: "Stones from those walls, which enclosed the innocent victims of arbitrary power, have been converted into a toy, to be presented to you, Monseigneur, as a mark of the people's love; and to teach you their power."

The Queen said that M. de La Fayette's thirst for popularity induced him to lend himself, without discrimination, to all popular follies. Her distrust of the General increased daily, and grew so powerful that when, towards the end of the Revolution, he seemed willing to support the tottering throne, she could never bring herself to incur so great an obligation to him.

M. de J——, a colonel attached to the staff of the army, was fortunate enough to render several services to the

Queen, and acquitted himself with discretion and dignity of various important missions.[1] Their Majesties had the highest confidence in him, although it frequently happened that his prudence, when inconsiderate projects were under discussion, brought upon him the charge of adopting the principles of the constitutionals. Being sent to Turin, he had some difficulty in dissuading the Princes from a scheme they had formed at that period of reëntering France, with a very weak army, by way of Lyons; and when, in a council which lasted till three o'clock in the morning, he showed his instructions, and demonstrated that the measure would endanger the King, the Comte d'Artois alone declared against the plan, which emanated from the Prince de Condé.

Among the persons employed in subordinate situations, whom the critical circumstances of the times involved in affairs of importance, was M. de Goguelat, a geographical engineer at Versailles, and an excellent draughtsman. He made plans of St. Cloud and Trianon for the Queen; she was very much pleased with them, and had the engineer admitted into the staff of the army. At the commencement of the Revolution he was sent to Count Esterhazy, at Valenciennes, in the capacity of aide-de-camp. The latter rank was given him solely to get him away from Versailles, where his rashness endangered the Queen during the earlier months of the Assembly of the States General. Making a parade of his devotion to the King's interests, he went repeatedly to the tribunes of the Assembly, and there openly railed at

1. During the Queen's detention in the Temple he introduced himself into that prison in the dirty dress of a lamp-lighter, and there discharged his duty unrecognised. This act of attachment is still known only to his family, and a few very intimate friends.

all the motions of the deputies, and then returned to the Queen's antechamber, where he repeated all that he had just heard, or had had the imprudence to say. Unfortunately, at the same time that the Queen sent away M. de Goguelat, she still believed that, in a dangerous predicament, requiring great self-devotion, the man might be employed advantageously. In 1791 he was commissioned to act in concert with the Marquis de Bouillé in furtherance of the King's intended escape.

Projectors in great numbers endeavoured to introduce themselves not only to the Queen, but to Madame Elisabeth, who had communications with many individuals who took upon themselves to make plans for the conduct of the Court. The Baron de Gilliers and M. de Vanoise were of this description; they went to the Baronne de Mackau's, where the Princess spent almost all her evenings. The Queen did not like these meetings, where Madame Elisabeth might adopt views in opposition to the King's intentions or her own.

The Queen gave frequent audiences to M. de La Fayette. One day, when he was in her inner closet, his aides-de-camp, who waited for him, were walking up and down the great room where the persons in attendance remained. Some imprudent young women were thoughtless enough to say, with the intention of being overheard by those officers, that it was very alarming to see the Queen alone with a rebel and a brigand. I was annoyed at their indiscretion, and imposed silence on them. One of them persisted in the appellation "brigand." I told her that M. de La Fayette well deserved the name of rebel, but that the title of leader of a party was given by history to every man commanding forty thousand men, a capital, and forty leagues of country; that kings had frequently treated with such leaders, and if it was convenient

THE PRIVATE LIFE OF MARIE ANTOINETTE

to the Queen to do the same, it remained for us only to be silent and respect her actions. On the morrow the Queen, with a serious air, but with the greatest kindness, asked what I had said respecting M. de La Fayette on the preceding day; adding that she had been assured I had enjoined her women silence, because they did not like him, and that I had taken his part. I repeated what had passed to the Queen, word for word. She condescended to tell me that I had done perfectly right.

Whenever any false reports respecting me were conveyed to her she was kind enough to inform me of them; and they had no effect on the confidence with which she continued to honour me, and which I am happy to think I have justified even at the risk of my life.

Mesdames, the King's aunts, set out from Bellevue in the beginning of the year 1791. Alexandre Berthier, afterwards Prince de Neufchâtel, then a colonel on the staff of the army, and commandant of the National Guard of Versailles, facilitated the departure of Mesdames. The Jacobins of that town procured his dismissal, and he ran the greatest risk, on account of having rendered this service to these Princesses. I went to take leave of Madame Victoire. I little thought that I was then seeing her for the last time. She received me alone in her closet, and assured me that she hoped, as well as wished, soon to return to France; that the French would be much to be pitied if the excesses of the Revolution should arrive at such a pitch as to force her to prolong her absence. I knew from the Queen that the departure of Mesdames was deemed necessary, in order to leave the King free to act when he should be compelled to go away with his family. It being impossible that the constitution of the clergy should be otherwise than in direct opposition to the religious principles of Mesdames, they thought their journey to Rome would be attributed to piety alone. It was, however, difficult to deceive an Assembly which weighed the slightest actions of the royal family, and from that moment they were more than ever alive to what was passing at the Tuileries.

Mesdames were desirous of taking Madame Elisabeth to Rome. The free exercise of religion, the happiness of taking refuge with the head of the Church, and the prospect of living in safety with her aunts, whom she tenderly loved, were sacrificed by that virtuous Princess to her attachment to the King.

The oath required of priests by the civil constitution of the clergy introduced into France a division which added to the dangers by which the King was already surrounded. Mirabeau spent a whole night with the curé of St. Eustache, confessor of the King and Queen, to persuade him to take the oath required by that constitution. Their Majesties chose another confessor, who remained unknown.

A few months afterwards (2d April, 1791), the too celebrated Mirabeau, the mercenary democrat and venal royalist, terminated his career. The Queen regretted him, and was astonished at her own regret; but she had hoped that he who had possessed adroitness and weight enough to throw everything into confusion would have been able by the same means to repair the mischief he had caused. Much has been said respecting the cause of Mirabeau's death. M. Cabanis, his friend and physician, denied that he was poisoned. M. Vicq-d'Azyr assured the Queen that the *procès-verbal* drawn up on the state of the intestines would apply just as well to a case of death produced by violent remedies as to one produced by poison. He said, also, that the report had been faithful; but that it was prudent to conclude it by a declaration of natural death, since, in the critical state in which France then was, if a suspicion of foul play were admitted, a person innocent of any such crime might be sacrificed to public vengeance.

XIX

IN the beginning of the spring of 1791, the King, tired of remaining at the Tuileries, wished to return to St. Cloud. His whole household had already gone, and his dinner was prepared there. He got into his carriage at one; the guard mutinied, shut the gates, and declared they would not let him pass. This event certainly proceeded from some suspicion of a plan to escape. Two persons who drew near the King's carriage were very ill treated. My father-in-law was violently laid hold of by the guards, who took his sword from him. The King and his family were obliged to alight and return to their apartments. They did not much regret this outrage in their hearts; they saw in it a justification, even in the eyes of the people, of their intention to leave Paris.

So early as the month of March in the same year, the Queen began to busy herself in preparing for her departure. I spent that month with her, and executed a great number of secret orders which she gave me respecting the intended event. It was with uneasiness that I saw her occupied with cares which seemed to me useless, and even dangerous, and I remarked to her that the Queen of France would find linen and gowns everywhere. My observations were made in vain; she determined to have a complete wardrobe with her at Brussels, as well for her children as her self. I went out alone and almost disguised to purchase the articles necessary and have them made up.

I ordered six chemises at the shop of one seamstress, six at that of another, gowns, combing cloths, etc. My sister had a complete set of clothes made for Madame, by the measure of her eldest daughter, and I ordered clothes for the Dauphin from those of my son. I filled a trunk with these things, and addressed them, by the Queen's orders, to one of her women, my aunt, Madame Cardon,—a widow living at Arras, by virtue of an unlimited leave of absence, —in order that she might be ready to start for Brussels, or any other place, as soon as she should be directed to do so. This lady had landed property in Austrian Flanders, and could at any time quit Arras unobserved.

The Queen was to take only her first woman in attendance with her from Paris. She apprised me that if I should not be on duty at the moment of departure, she would make arrangements for my joining her. She determined also to take her travelling dressing-case. She consulted me on her idea of sending it off, under pretence of making a present of it to the Archduchess Christina, Gouvernante of the Netherlands. I ventured to oppose this plan strongly, and observed that, amidst so many people who watched her slightest actions, there would be found a sufficient number sharp-sighted enough to discover that it was only a pretext for sending away the property in question before her own departure; she persisted in her intention, and all I could arrange was that the dressing-case should not be removed from her apartment, and that M. de —, *chargé d'affaires* from the Court of Vienna during the absence of the Comte de Mercy, should come and ask her, at her toilet, before all her people, to order one exactly like her own for Madame the Gouvernante of the Netherlands. The Queen, therefore, commanded me before the *chargé d'affaires* to order the article in question. This occasioned only an expense of five hundred louis, and appeared calculated to lull suspicion completely.

About the middle of May, 1791, a month after the Queen had ordered me to bespeak the dressing-case, she asked me whether it would soon be finished. I sent for the ivory-turner who had it in hand. He could not complete it for six weeks. I informed the Queen of this, and she told me she should not be able to wait for it, as she was to set out in the course of June. She added that, as she had ordered her sister's dressing-case in the presence of all her attendants, she had taken a sufficient precaution, especially by saying that her sister was out of patience at not receiving it, and that therefore her own must be emptied and cleaned, and taken to the *chargé d'affaires*, who would send it off. I executed this order without any appearance of mystery. I desired the wardrobe woman to take out of the dressing-case all that it contained, because that intended for the Archduchess could not be finished for some time; and to take great care to leave no remains of the perfumes which might not suit that Princess.

The woman in question executed her commission punctually; but, on the evening of that very day, the 15th of May, 1791, she informed M. Bailly, the Mayor of Paris, that preparations were making at the Queen's residence for a departure; and that the dressing-case was already sent off, under pretence of its being presented to the Archduchess Christina.

It was necessary, likewise, to send off all the diamonds belonging to the Queen. Her Majesty shut herself up with me in a closet in the *entresol*, looking into the garden of the Tuileries, and we packed all the diamonds, rubies, and pearls she possessed in a small chest. The cases containing these ornaments, being altogether of considerable bulk, had been deposited, ever since the 6th of October, 1789, with the *valet de chambre* who had the care of the Queen's jewels. That faithful servant, himself detecting the use that was to be made of the valuables, destroyed all the boxes, which were, as usual, covered with red morocco, marked with the cipher and arms of France. It would have been impossible for him to hide them from the eyes of the popular inquisitors during the domiciliary visits in January, 1793, and the discovery might have formed a ground of accusation against the Queen.

I had but a few articles to place in the box when the Queen was compelled to desist from packing it, being obliged to go down to cards, which began at seven precisely. She therefore desired me to leave all the diamonds upon the sofa, persuaded that, as she took the key of her closet herself, and there was a sentinel under the window, no danger was to be apprehended for that night, and she reckoned upon returning very early next day to finish the work.

The same woman who had given information of the sending away of the dressing-case was also deputed by the Queen to take care of her more private rooms. No other servant was permitted to enter them; she renewed the flowers, swept the carpets, etc. The Queen received back the key, when the woman had finished putting them in order, from her own hands; but, desirous of doing her duty well, and sometimes having the key in her possession for a few minutes only, she had probably on that account ordered one without the Queen's knowledge. It is impossible not to believe this, since the despatch of the diamonds was the subject of a second accusation which the Queen heard of after the return from Varennes. She made a formal declaration that her Majesty, with the assistance of Madame Campan, had packed up all her jewelry some time before the departure; that she was certain of it, as she had found the diamonds, and the cotton which served to wrap them, scattered upon the sofa in the Queen's closet in the *entresol*; and most assuredly she could only have seen these preparations in the interval between seven in the evening and seven in the morning. The Queen having met me next day at the time appointed, the box was handed over to Léonard, her Majesty's hair dresser, who left the country with the Duc de Choiseul. The box remained a long time at Brussels, and at length got into the hands of Madame la Duchesse d'Angoulême, being delivered to her by the Emperor on her arrival at Vienna.

In order not to leave out any of the Queen's diamonds, I requested the first tirewoman to give me the body of the full dress, and all the assortment which served for the stomacher of the full dress on days of state, articles which always remained at the wardrobe.

The superintendent and the *dame d'honneur* being absent, the first tirewoman required me to sign a receipt, the terms of which she dictated, and which acquitted her of all responsibility for these diamonds. She had the prudence to burn this document on the 10th of August, 1792. The

Queen having determined, upon the arrest at Varennes, not to have her diamonds brought back to France, was often anxious about them during the year which elapsed between that period and the 10th of August, and dreaded above all things that such a secret should be discovered.

In consequence of a decree of the Assembly, which deprived the King of the custody of the Crown diamonds, the Queen had at this time already given up those which she generally used.

She preferred the twelve brilliants called *Mazarins*, from the name of the Cardinal who had enriched the treasury with them, a few rose-cut diamonds, and the *Sanci*. She determined to deliver, with her own hands, the box containing them to the commissioner nominated by the National Assembly to place them with the Crown diamonds. After giving them to him, she offered him a row of pearls of great beauty, saying to him that it had been brought into France by Anne of Austria; that it was invaluable, on account of its rarity; that, having been appropriated by that Princess to the use of the Queens and Dauphinesses, Louis XV had placed it in her hands on her arrival in France; but that she considered it national property. "That is an open question, Madame," said the commissary. "Monsieur," replied the Queen, "it is one for me to decide, and is now settled."

My father-in-law, who was dying of the grief he felt for the misfortunes of his master and mistress, strongly interested and occupied the thoughts of the Queen. He had been saved from the fury of the populace in the courtyard of the Tuileries.

On the day on which the King was compelled by an insurrection to give up a journey to St. Cloud, her Majesty looked upon this trusty servant as inevitably lost, if, on going away, she should leave him in the apartment he occupied in the Tuileries. Prompted by her apprehensions, she ordered M. Vicq-d'Azyr, her physician, to recommend him the waters of Mont d'Or in Auvergne, and to persuade him to set off at the latter end of May. At the moment of my going away the Queen assured me that the grand project would be executed between the 15th and the 20th of June; that as it was not my month to be on duty, Madame Thibaut would take the journey; but that she had many directions to give me before I went. She then desired me to write to my aunt, Madame Cardon, who was by that time in possession of the clothes which I had ordered, that as soon as she should receive a letter from M. Auguié, the date of which should be accompanied with a B, an L. or an M. she was to proceed with her property to Brussels, Luxembourg, or Montmédy. She desired me to explain the meaning of these three letters clearly to my sister, and to leave them with her in writing, in order that at the moment of my going away she might be able to take my place in writing to Arras.

The Queen had a more delicate commission for me: it was to select from among my acquaintance a prudent person of obscure rank, wholly devoted to the interests of the Court, who would be willing to receive a portfolio which she was to give up only to me, or some one furnished with a note from the Queen. She added that she would not travel with this portfolio, and that it was of the utmost importance that my opinion of the fidelity of the person to whom it was to be entrusted should be well founded. I proposed to her Madame Vallayer Coster, a painter of the Academy, and an amiable and worthy artist, whom I had known from my infancy.

She lived in the galleries of the Louvre. The choice seemed a good one. The Queen remembered that she had made her marriage possible by giving her a place in the financial offices, and added that gratitude ought sometimes to be reckoned on. She then pointed out to me the valet belonging to her toilet, whom I was to take with me, to show him the residence of Madame Coster, so that he might not mistake it when he should take the portfolio to her. The day before her departure the Queen particularly recommended me to proceed to Lyons and the frontiers as soon as she should have started. She advised me to take with me a confidential person, fit to remain with M. Campan when I should leave him, and assured me that she would give orders to M.—to set off as soon as she should be known to be at the frontiers in order to protect me in going out. She condescended to add that, having a long journey to make in foreign countries, she determined to give me three hundred louis.

I bathed the Queen's hands with tears at the moment of this sorrowful separation; and, having money at my disposal, I declined accepting her gold. I did not dread the road I had to travel in order to rejoin her; all my apprehension was that by treachery or miscalculation a scheme, the safety of which was not sufficiently clear to me, should fail. I could answer for all those who belonged to the service immediately about the Queen's person, and I was right; but her wardrobe woman gave me well-founded reason for alarm. I mentioned to the Queen many revolutionary remarks which this woman had made to me a few days before. Her office was directly under the control of the first *femme de chambre*, yet she had refused to obey the directions I gave her, talking insolently to me about "hierarchy overturned, equality among men," of course more especially among persons holding offices at Court; and this jargon, at that time in the mouths of all the partisans of the Revolution, was terminated by an observation which frightened me. "You know many important secrets, madame," said this woman to me, "and I have guessed quite as many. I am not a fool; I see all that is going forward here in consequence of the bad advice given to the King and Queen; I could frustrate it all if I chose." This argument, in which I had been promptly silenced, left me pale and trembling. Unfortunately, as I began my narrative to the Queen with particulars of this woman's refusal to obey me,— and sovereigns are all their lives importuned with complaints upon the rights of places,—she believed that my own dissatisfaction had much to do with the step I was taking; and she did not sufficiently fear the woman. Her office, although a very inferior one, brought her in nearly fifteen thousand francs a year. Still young, tolerably handsome, with comfortable apartments in the *entresols* of the Tuileries, she saw a great deal of company, and in the evening had assemblies, consisting of deputies of the revolutionary party. M. de Gouvion, major-general of the National Guard, passed almost every day with her; and it is to be presumed that she had long worked for the party in opposition to the Court. The Queen asked her for the key of a door which led to the principal vestibule of the Tuileries, telling her she wished to have a similar one, that she might not be under the necessity of going out through the pavilion of Flora. M. de Gouvion and M. de La Fayette would, of course, be apprised of this circumstance, and well-informed persons have assured me that on the very night of the Queen's departure this wretched woman had a spy with her, who saw the royal family set off.

As soon as I had executed all the Queen's orders, on the 30th of May, 1791, I set out for Auvergne, and was settled in the gloomy narrow valley of Mont d'Or, when, about four in the afternoon of the 25th of June, I heard the beat of a drum to call the inhabitants of the hamlet together. When it had ceased I heard a hairdresser from Bresse proclaim in the provincial dialect of Auvergne: "The King and Queen were taking flight in order to ruin France, but I come to tell you that they are stopped, and are well guarded by a hundred thousand men under arms." I still ventured to hope that he was repeating only a false report, but he went on: "The Queen, with her well known haughtiness, lifted up the veil which covered her face, and said to the citizens who were upbraiding the King, 'Well, since you recognise your sovereign, respect him.'" Upon hearing these expressions, which the Jacobin club of Clermont could not have invented, I exclaimed, "The news is true!"

I immediately learnt that, a courier being come from Paris to Clermont, the *procureur* of the commune had sent off messengers to the chief places of the canton; these again sent couriers to the districts, and the districts in like manner informed the villages and hamlets which they contained. It was through this ramification, arising from the establishment of clubs, that the afflicting intelligence of the misfortune of my sovereigns reached me in the wildest part of France, and in the midst of the snows by which we were environed.

On the 28th I received a note written in a hand which I recognised as that of M. Diet[1], usher of the Queen's chamber,

---

1. This officer was massacred in the Queen's chamber on the 10th of August, 1792.

but dictated by her Majesty. It contained these words: "I am this moment arrived; I have just got into my bath; I and my family exist, that is all. I have suffered much. Do not return to Paris until I desire you. Take good care of my poor Campan, soothe his sorrow. Look for happier times." This note was for greater safety addressed to my father-in-law's *valet de chambre*. What were my feelings on perceiving that after the most distressing crisis we were among the first objects of the kindness of that unfortunate Princess!

M. Campan having been unable to benefit by the waters of Mont d'Or, and the first popular effervescence having subsided, I thought I might return to Clermont. The committee of surveillance, or that of general safety, had resolved to arrest me there; but the Abbé Louis, formerly a parliamentary counsellor and then a member of the Constituent Assembly, was kind enough to affirm that I was in Auvergne solely for the purpose of attending my father-in-law, who was extremely ill. The precautions relative to my absence from Paris were limited to placing us under the surveillance of the *procureur* of the commune, who was at the same time president of the Jacobin club; but he was also a physician of repute, and without having any doubt that he had received secret orders relative to me, I thought it would favour the chances of our safety if I selected him to attend my patient. I paid him according to the rate given to the best Paris physicians, and I requested him to visit us every morning and every evening. I took the precaution to subscribe to no other newspaper than the *Moniteur*. Doctor Monestier (for that was the physician's name) frequently took upon himself to read it to us. Whenever he thought proper to speak of the King and Queen in the insulting and brutal terms at that time unfortunately adopted throughout France, I used to stop him and say, coolly, "Monsieur, you are here in company with the servants of Louis XVI and Marie Antoinette. Whatever may be the wrongs with which the nation believes it has to reproach them, our principles forbid our losing sight of the respect due to them from us." Notwithstanding that he was an inveterate patriot, he felt the force of this remark, and even procured the revocation of a second order for our arrest, becoming responsible for us to the committee of the Assembly, and to the Jacobin society.

The two chief women about the Dauphin, who had accompanied the Queen to Varennes, Diet, her usher, and Camot, her *garçon de toilette*,—the women on account of the journey, and the men in consequence of the denunciation of the woman belonging to the wardrobe,—were sent to the prisons of the Abbaye. After my departure the *garçon de toilette* whom I had taken to Madame Vallayer Coster's was sent there with the portfolio she had agreed to receive. This commission could not escape the detestable spy upon the Queen. She gave information that a portfolio had been carried out on the evening of the departure, adding that the King had placed it upon the Queen's easy-chair, that the *garçon de toilette* wrapped it up in a napkin and took it under his arm, and that she did not know where he had carried it. The man, who was remarkable for his fidelity, underwent three examinations without making the slightest disclosure. M. Diet, a man of good family, a servant on whom the Queen placed particular reliance, likewise experienced the severest treatment. At length, after a lapse of three weeks, the Queen succeeded in obtaining the release of her servants.

The Queen, about the 15th of August, had me informed by letter that I might come back to Paris without being under any apprehension of arrest there, and that she greatly desired my return. I brought my father-in-law back in a dying state, and on the day preceding that of the acceptation of the constitutional act, I informed the Queen that he was no more. "The loss of Lassonne and Campan," said she, as she applied her handkerchief to her streaming eyes, "has taught me how valuable such subjects are to their masters. I shall never find their equals."

I resumed my functions about the Queen on the 1st of September, 1791. She was unable then to converse with me on all the lamentable events which had occurred since the time of my leaving her, having on guard near her an officer whom she dreaded more than all the others. She merely told me that I should have some secret services to perform for her, and that she would not create uneasiness by long conversations with me, my return being a subject of suspicion. But next day the Queen, well knowing the discretion of the officer who was to be on guard that night, had my bed placed very near hers, and having obtained the favour of having the door shut, when I was in bed she began the narrative of the journey, and the unfortunate arrest at Varennes. I asked her permission to put on my gown, and kneeling by her bedside I remained until three o'clock in the morning, listening with the liveliest and most sorrowful interest to the account I am about to repeat, and of which I have seen various details, of tolerable exactness, in papers of the time.

The King entrusted Count Fersen with all the preparations for departure. The carriage was ordered by him; the passport, in the name of Madame de Korf, was procured through his connection with that lady, who was a foreigner. And lastly, he himself drove the royal family, as their coachman, as far as Bondy, where the travellers got into their berlin. Madame Brunier and Madame Neuville, the first women of Madame and the Dauphin, there joined the principal carriage. They were in a cabriolet. Monsieur and Madame set out from the Luxembourg and took another road. They as well as the King were recognised by the master of the last post in France, but this man, devoting himself to the fortunes of the Prince, left the French territory, and drove them himself as postilion. Madame Thibaut, the Queen's first woman, reached Brussels without the slightest difficulty. Madame Cardon, from Arras, met with no hindrance; and Léonard, the Queen's hairdresser, passed through Varennes a few hours before the royal family. Fate had reserved all its obstacles for the unfortunate monarch.

Nothing worthy of notice occurred in the beginning of the journey. The travellers were detained a short time, about twelve leagues from Paris, by some repairs which the carriage required. The King chose to walk up one of the hills, and these two circumstances caused a delay of three hours, precisely at the time when it was intended that the berlin should have been met, just before reaching Varennes, by the detachment commanded by M. de Goguelat. This detachment was punctually stationed upon the spot fixed on, with orders to wait there for the arrival of certain treasure, which it was to escort; but the peasantry of the neighbourhood, alarmed at the sight of this body of troops, came armed with staves, and asked several questions, which manifested their anxiety. M. de Goguelat, fearful of causing a riot, and not finding the carriage arrive as he expected, divided his men into two companies, and unfortunately made them leave the highway in order to return to Varennes by two cross roads. The King looked out of the carriage at Ste. Menehould, and asked several questions concerning the road. Drouet, the postmaster, struck by the resemblance of Louis to the impression of his head upon the assignats, drew near the carriage, felt convinced that he recognised the Queen also, and that the remainder of the travellers consisted of the royal family and their suite, mounted his horse, reached Varennes by cross roads before the royal fugitives, and gave the alarm.

The Queen began to feel all the agonies of terror; they were augmented by the voice of a person unknown, who, passing close to the carriage in full gallop, cried out, bending towards the window without slackening his speed, "You are recognised!"[1] They arrived with beating hearts at the gates of Varennes without meeting one of the horsemen by whom they were to have been escorted into the place. They were ignorant where to find their relays, and some minutes were lost in waiting, to no purpose. The cabriolet had preceded them, and the two ladies in attendance found the bridge already blocked up with old carts and lumber. The town guards were all under arms. The King at last entered Varennes. M. de Goguelat had arrived there with his detachment. He came up to the King and asked him *if he chose to effect a passage by force!* What an unlucky question to put

1. The Queen informed me, while summing up all the events of that ill-omened journey, that at two leagues from Varennes, a stranger passed close to the King's carriage, full gallop, uttering aloud some words which the noise of the wheels upon the pavement prevented their hearing; but the subsequently to their arrest, the King and herself, recalling the sound of the stranger's words, were almost certain that he had said to them, "You are known;" or "You are discovered."

to Louis XVI, who from the very beginning of the Revolution had shown in every crisis the fear he entertained of giving the least order which might cause an effusion of blood! "Would it be a brisk action?" said the King. "It is impossible that it should be otherwise, Sire," replied the aide-de-camp. Louis XVI was unwilling to expose his family. They therefore went to the house of a grocer, Mayor of Varennes. The King began to speak, and gave a summary of his intentions in departing, analogous to the declaration he had made at Paris. He spoke with warmth and affability, and endeavoured to demonstrate to the people around him that he had only put himself, by the step he had taken, into a fit situation to treat with the Assembly, and to sanction with freedom the constitution which he would maintain, though many of its articles were incompatible with the dignity of the throne, and the force by which it was necessary that the sovereign should be surrounded. Nothing could be more affecting, added the Queen, than this moment, in which the King felt bound to communicate to the very humblest class of his subjects his principles, his wishes for the happiness of his people, and the motives which had determined him to depart.

Whilst the King was speaking to this mayor, whose name was Sauce, the Queen, seated at the farther end of the shop, among parcels of soap and candles, endeavoured to make Madame Sauce understand that if she would prevail upon her husband to make use of his municipal authority to cover the flight of the King and his family, she would have the glory of having contributed to restore tranquillity to France. This woman was moved; she could not, without streaming eyes, see herself thus solicited by her Queen; but she could not be got to say anything more than, "*Bon Dieu*, Madame, it would be the destruction of M. Sauce; I love my King, but I love my husband too, you must know, and he would be answerable, you see." Whilst this strange scene was passing in the shop, the people, hearing that the King was arrested, kept pouring in from all parts. M. de Goguelat, making a last effort, demanded of the dragoons whether they would protect the departure of the King; they replied only by murmurs, dropping the points of their swords. Some person unknown fired a pistol at M. de Goguelat; he was slightly wounded by the ball. M. Romeuf, aide-de-camp to M. de La Fayette, arrived at that moment. He had been chosen, after the 6th of October, 1789, by the commander of the Parisian guard to be in constant attendance about the Queen. She reproached him bitterly with the object of his mission. "If you wish to make your name remarkable, monsieur," said the Queen to him, "you have chosen strange and odious means, which will produce the most fatal consequences." This officer wished to hasten their departure. The Queen, still cherishing the hope of seeing M. de Bouillé arrive with a sufficient force to extricate the King from his critical situation, prolonged her stay at Varennes by every means in her power.

The Dauphin's first woman pretended to be taken ill with a violent colic, and threw herself upon a bed, in the hope of aiding the designs of her superiors; she went and implored for assistance. The Queen understood her perfectly well, and refused to leave one who had devoted herself to follow them in such a state of suffering. But no delay in departing was allowed. The three Body Guards (Valory, Du Moustier, and Maiden) were gagged and fastened upon the seat of the carriage. A horde of National Guards, animated with fury and the barbarous joy with which their fatal triumph inspired them, surrounded the carriage of the royal family.

The three commissioners sent by the Assembly to meet the King, MM. de Latour-Maubourg, Barnave, and Pétion, joined them in the environs of Epernay. The two last mentioned got into the King's carriage. The Queen astonished me by the favourable opinion she had formed of Barnave. When I quitted Paris a great many persons spoke of him only with horror. She told me he was much altered, that he was full of talent and noble feeling. "A feeling of pride which I cannot much blame in a young man belonging to the *Tiers Etat*," she said, "made him applaud everything which smoothed the road to rank and fame for that class in which he was born. And if we get the power in our own hands again, Barnave's pardon is already written on our hearts." The Queen added, that she had not the same feeling towards those nobles who had joined the revolutionary party, who had always received marks of favour, often to the injury of those beneath them in rank, and who, born to be the safeguard of the monarchy, could never be pardoned for having deserted it. She then told me that Barnave's conduct upon the road was perfectly correct, while Pétion's republican rudeness was disgusting; that the latter ate and drank in the King's berlin in a slovenly manner, throwing the bones of the fowls out through the window at the risk of sending them even into the King's face; lifting up his glass, when Madame Elisabeth poured him out wine, to show her that there was enough, without saying a word; that this offensive behaviour must have been intentional, because the man was not without education; and that Barnave was hurt at it. On being pressed by the Queen to take something, "Madame," replied Barnave, "on so solemn an occasion the deputies of the National Assembly ought to occupy your Majesties solely about their mission, and by no means about their wants." In short, his respectful delicacy, his considerate attentions, and all that he said, gained the esteem not only of the Queen, but of Madame Elisabeth also.

The King began to talk to Pétion about the situation of France, and the motives of his conduct, which were founded upon the necessity of giving to the executive power a strength necessary for its action, for the good even of the constitutional act, since France could not be a republic. "Not yet, 'tis true," replied Pétion, "because the French are not ripe enough for that." This audacious and cruel answer silenced the King, who said no more until his arrival at Paris. Pétion held the little Dauphin upon his knees, and amused himself with curling the beautiful light hair of the interesting child round his fingers; and, as he spoke with much gesticulation, he pulled his locks hard enough to make the Dauphin cry out. "Give me my son," said the Queen to him; "he is accustomed to tenderness and delicacy, which render him little fit for such familiarity."

The Chevalier de Dampierre was killed near the King's carriage upon leaving Varennes. A poor village curé, some leagues from the place where the crime was committed, was imprudent enough to draw near to speak to the King; the cannibals who surrounded the carriage rushed upon him. "Tigers," exclaimed Barnave, "have you ceased to be Frenchmen? Nation of brave men, are you become a set of assassins?" These words alone saved the curé, who was already upon the ground, from certain death. Barnave, as he spoke to them, threw himself almost out of the coach window, and

Madame Elisabeth, affected by this noble burst of feeling, held him by the skirt of his coat. The Queen, while speaking of this event, said that on the most momentous occasions whimsical contrasts always struck her, and that even at such a moment the pious Elisabeth holding Barnave by the flap of his coat was a ludicrous sight.

The deputy was astonished in another way. Madame Elisabeth's comments upon the state of France, her mild and persuasive eloquence, and the ease and simplicity with which she talked to him, yet without sacrificing her dignity in the slightest degree, appeared to him unique, and his heart, which was doubtless inclined to right principles though he had followed the wrong path, was overcome by admiration. The conduct of the two deputies convinced the Queen of the total separation between the republican and constitutional parties. At the inns where she alighted she had some private conversation with Barnave. The latter said a great deal about the errors committed by the royalists during the Revolution, adding that he had found the interest of the Court so feebly and so badly defended that he had been frequently tempted to go and offer it, in himself, an aspiring champion, who knew the spirit of the age and nation. The Queen asked him what was the weapon he would have recommended her to use.

"Popularity, Madame."

"And how could I use that," replied her Majesty, "of which I have been deprived?"

"Ah! Madame, it was much more easy for you to regain it, than for me to acquire it."

The Queen mainly attributed the arrest at Varennes to M. de Goguelat; she said he calculated the time that would be spent in the journey erroneously. He performed that from Montmédy to Paris before taking the King's last orders, alone in a post-chaise, and he founded all his calculations upon the time he spent thus. The trial has been made since, and it was found that a light carriage without any courier was nearly three hours less in running the distance than a heavy carriage preceded by a courier.

The Queen also blamed him for having quitted the high-road at Pont-de-Sommevelle, where the carriage was to meet the forty hussars commanded by him. She thought that he ought to have dispersed the very small number of people at Varennes, and not have asked the hussars whether they were for the King or the nation; that, particularly, he ought to have avoided taking the King's orders, as he was previously aware of the reply M. d'Inisdal had received when it was proposed to carry off the King.

After all that the Queen had said to me respecting the mistakes made by M. de Goguelat, I thought him of course disgraced. What was my surprise when, having been set at liberty after the amnesty which followed the acceptance of the constitution, he presented himself to the Queen, and was received with the greatest kindness! She said he had done what he could, and that his zeal ought to form an excuse for all the rest.

When the royal family was brought back from Varennes to the Tuileries, the Queen's attendants found the greatest difficulty in making their way to her apartments; everything had been arranged so that the wardrobe woman, who had acted as spy, should have the service; and she was to be assisted in it only by her sister and her sister's daughter.

M. de Gouvion, M. de La Fayette's aide-de-camp, had this woman's portrait placed at the foot of the staircase which led to the Queen's apartments, in order that the sentinel should not permit any other women to make their way in. As soon as the Queen was informed of this contemptible precaution, she told the King of it, who sent to ascertain the fact. His Majesty then called for M. de La Fayette, claimed freedom in his household, and particularly in that of the Queen, and ordered him to send a woman in whom no one but himself could confide out of the palace. M. de La Fayette was obliged to comply.[1]

On the day when the return of the royal family was expected, there were no carriages in motion in the streets of Paris. Five or six of the Queen's women, after being refused admittance at all the other gates, went with one of my sisters to that of the Feuillans, insisting that the sentinel should admit them. The *poissardes* attacked them for their boldness in resisting the order excluding them. One of them seized my sister by the arm, calling her the slave of the Austrian. "Hear me," said my sister to her, "I have been attached to the Queen ever since I was fifteen years of age; she gave me my marriage portion; I served her when she was powerful and happy. She is now unfortunate. Ought I to abandon her?" "She is right," cried the *poissardes*; "she ought not to abandon her mistress; let us make an entry for them." They instantly surrounded the sentinel, forced the passage, and introduced the Queen's women, accompanying them to the terrace of the Feuillans.

1. The orders by which all the women attached to the Queen's service were kept out were broken by the people, in a manner which shows that sudden change which striking circumstances never fail to effect in mobs.

One of these furies, whom the slightest impulse would have driven to tear my sister to pieces, then taking her under her protection, gave her some advice by which she might reach the palace in safety. "But of all things, my dear friend," said she to her, "pull off that green ribbon sash; it is the sash of that d'Artois, whom we will never forgive."

The measures adopted for guarding the King were rigorous with respect to the entrance into the palace, and insulting as to his private apartments. The commandants of battalion, stationed in the *salon* called the *grand cabinet*, and which led to the Queen's bedchamber, were ordered to keep the door of it always open, in order that they might have their eyes upon the royal family. The King shut this door one day; the officer of the guard opened it, and told him such were his orders, and that he would always open it; so that his Majesty in shutting it gave himself useless trouble. It remained open even during the night, when the Queen was in bed; and the officer placed himself in an armchair between the two doors, with his head turned towards her Majesty. They only obtained permission to have the inner door shut when the Queen was rising. The Queen had the bed of her first *femme de chambre* placed very near her own; this bed, which ran on casters, and was furnished with curtains, hid her from the officer's sight.

Madame de Jarjaye, my companion, who continued her functions during the whole period of my absence, told me that one night the commandant of battalion, who slept between the two doors, seeing that she was sleeping soundly, and that the Queen was awake, quitted his post and went close to her Majesty, to advise her as to the line of conduct she should pursue. Although she had the kindness to desire him to speak lower in order that he might not disturb Madame de Jarjaye's rest, the latter awoke, and nearly died with fright at seeing a man in the uniform of the Parisian guard so near the Queen's bed. Her Majesty comforted her, and told her not to rise; that the person she saw was a good Frenchman, who was deceived respecting the intentions and situation of his sovereign and herself, but whose conversation showed sincere attachment to the King.

There was a sentinel in the corridor which runs behind the apartments in question, where there is a staircase, which was at that time an inner one, and enabled the King and Queen to communicate freely. This post, which was very onerous, because it was to be kept four and twenty hours, was often claimed by Saint Prix, an actor belonging to the Théâtre Français. He took it upon himself sometimes to contrive brief interviews between the King and Queen in this corridor. He left them at a distance, and gave them warning if he heard the slightest noise. M. Collot, commandant of battalion of the National Guard, who was charged with the military duty of the Queen's household, in like manner softened down, so far as he could with prudence, all the revolting orders he received; for instance, one to follow the Queen to the very door of her wardrobe was never executed. An officer of the Parisian guard dared to speak insolently of the Queen in her own apartment. M. Collot wished to make a complaint to M. de La Fayette against him, and have him dismissed. The Queen opposed it, and condescended to say a few words of explanation and kindness to the man; he instantly became one of her most devoted partisans.

The first time I saw her Majesty after the unfortunate catastrophe of the Varennes journey, I found her getting out of bed; her features were not very much altered; but after the first kind words she uttered to me she took off her cap and desired me to observe the effect which grief had produced upon her hair. It had become, in one single night, as white as that of a woman of seventy. Her Majesty showed me a ring she had just had mounted for the Princesse de Lamballe; it contained a lock of her whitened hair, with the inscription, "*Blanched by sorrow.*" At the period of the acceptance of the constitution the Princess wished to return to France. The Queen, who had no expectation that tranquillity would be restored, opposed this; but the attachment of Madame de Lamballe to the royal family impelled her to come and seek death.

When I returned to Paris most of the hard precautions were abandoned; the doors were not kept open; greater respect was paid to the sovereign; it was known that the constitution soon to be completed would be accepted, and a better order of things was hoped for.

ON my arrival at Paris on the 25th of August I found the state of feeling there much more temperate than I had dared to hope. The conversation generally ran upon the acceptance of the constitution, and the fêtes which would be given in consequence. The struggle between the Jacobins and the constitutionals on the 17th of July, 1791, nevertheless had thrown the Queen into great terror for some moments; and the firing of the cannon from the Champ de Mars upon a party which called for a trial of the King, and the leaders of which were in the very bosom of the Assembly, left the most gloomy impressions upon her mind.

The constitutionals, the Queen's connection with whom was not slackened by the intervention of the three members already mentioned, had faithfully served the royal family during their detention.

"We still hold the wire by which this popular mass is moved," said Barnave to M. de J — one day, at the same time showing him a large volume, in which the names of all those who were influenced with the power of gold alone were registered. It was at that time proposed to hire a considerable number of persons in order to secure loud acclamations when the King and his family should make their appearance at the play upon the acceptance of the constitution. That day, which afforded a glimmering hope of tranquillity, was the 14th of September; the fêtes were brilliant; but already fresh anxieties forbade the royal family to encourage much hope.

The Legislative Assembly, which had just succeeded the Constituent Assembly (October, 1791), founded its conduct upon the wildest republican principles; created from the midst of popular assemblies, it was wholly inspired by the spirit which animated them. The constitution, as I have said, was presented to the King on the 3d of September, 1791. The ministers, with the exception of M. de Montmorin, insisted upon the necessity of accepting the constitutional act in its entirety. The Prince de Kaunitz was of the same opinion. Malouet wished the King to express himself candidly respecting any errors or dangers that he might observe in the constitution. But Duport and Barnave, alarmed at the spirit prevailing in the Jacobin Club, and even in the Assembly, where Robespierre had already denounced them as traitors to the country, and dreading still greater evils, added their opinions to those of the majority of the ministers and M. de Kaunitz; those who really desired that the constitution should be maintained advised that it should not be accepted thus literally. The King seemed inclined to this advice; and this is one of the strongest proofs of his sincerity.

Alexandre Lameth, Duport, and Barnave, still relying on the resources of their party, hoped to have credit for directing the King through the influence they believed they had acquired over the mind of the Queen. They also consulted people of acknowledged talent, but belonging to no council nor to any assembly. Among these was M. Dubucq, formerly intendant of the marine and of the colonies. He answered laconically in one phrase: "Prevent disorder from organising itself."

The letter written by the King to the Assembly, claiming to accept the constitution in the very place where it had been created, and where he announced he would be on the 14th September at mid-day, was received with transport, and the reading was repeatedly interrupted by plaudits. The sitting terminated amidst the greatest enthusiasm, and M. de La Fayette obtained the release of all those who were detained on account of the King's journey [to Varennes], the abandonment of all proceedings relative to the events of the Revolution, and the discontinuance of the use of passports and of temporary restraints upon free travelling, as well in the interior as without. The whole was conceded by acclamation. Sixty members were deputed to go to the King and express to him fully the satisfaction his Majesty's letter had given. The Keeper of the Seals quitted the chamber, in the midst of applause, to precede the deputation to the King.

The King answered the speech addressed to him, and concluded by saying to the Assembly that a decree of that morning, which had abolished the order of the Holy Ghost, had left him and his son alone permission to be decorated with it; but that an order having no value in his eyes, save for the power of conferring it, he would not use it.

The Queen, her son, and Madame, were at the door of the chamber into which the deputation was admitted. The

King said to the deputies, "You see there my wife and children, who participate in my sentiments;" and the Queen herself confirmed the King's assurance. These apparent marks of confidence were very inconsistent with the agitated state of her mind. "These people want no sovereigns," said she. "We shall fall before their treacherous though well-planned tactics; they are demolishing the monarchy stone by stone."

Next day the particulars of the reception of the deputies by the King were reported to the Assembly, and excited warm approbation. But the President having put the question whether the Assembly ought not to remain seated while the King took the oath— "Certainly," was repeated by many voices; "*and the King, standing, uncovered.*" M. Malouet observed that there was no occasion on which the nation, assembled in the presence of the King, did not acknowledge him as its head; that the omission to treat the head of the State with the respect due to him would be an offence to the nation, as well as to the monarch. He moved that the King should take the oath standing, and that the Assembly should also stand while he was doing so. M. Malouet's observations would have carried the decree, but a deputy from Brittany exclaimed, with a shrill voice, that he had an amendment to propose which would render all unanimous. "Let us decree," said he, "that M. Malouet, and whoever else shall so please, may have leave to receive the King upon their knees; but let us stick to the decree."

The King repaired to the chamber at mid-day. His speech was followed by plaudits which lasted several minutes. After the signing of the constitutional act all sat down. The President rose to deliver his speech; but after he had begun, perceiving that the King did not rise to hear him, he sat down again. His speech made a powerful impression; the sentence with which it concluded excited fresh acclamations, cries of "Bravo!" and "*Vive le Roi!*" "Sire," said he, "how important in our eyes, and how dear to our hearts—how sublime a feature in our history—must be the epoch of that regeneration which gives citizens to France, and a country to Frenchmen,—to you, as a king, a new title of greatness and glory, and, as a man, a source of new enjoyment." The whole Assembly accompanied the King on his return, amidst the people's cries of happiness, military music, and salvoes of artillery.

At length I hoped to see a return of that tranquillity which had so long vanished from the countenances of my august master and mistress. Their suite left them in the *salon*; the Queen hastily saluted the ladies, and returned much affected; the King followed her, and, throwing himself into an armchair, put his handkerchief to his eyes. "Ah! Madame," cried he, his voice choked by tears, "why were you present at this sitting? to witness—" these words were interrupted by sobs. The Queen threw herself upon her knees before him, and pressed him in her arms. I remained with them, not from any blamable curiosity, but from a stupefaction which rendered me incapable of determining what I ought to do. The Queen said to me, "Oh! go, go!" with an accent which expressed, "Do not remain to see the dejection and despair of your sovereign!" I withdrew, struck with the contrast between the shouts of joy without the palace and the profound grief which oppressed the sovereigns within. Half an hour afterwards the Queen sent for me. She desired to see M. de Goguelat, to announce to him his departure on that very night for Vienna. The renewed attacks upon the dignity of the throne which had been made during the sitting; the spirit of an Assembly worse than the former; the monarch put upon a level with the President, without any deference to the throne,—all this proclaimed but too loudly that the sovereignty itself was aimed at. The Queen no longer saw any ground for hope from the Provinces. The King wrote to the Emperor; she told me that she would herself, at midnight, bring the letter which M. de Goguelat was to bear to the Emperor, to my room.

During all the remainder of the day the Château and the Tuileries were crowded; the illuminations were magnificent. The King and Queen were requested to take an airing in their carriage in the Champs-Elyséés, escorted by the aides-de-camp, and leaders of the Parisian army, the Constitutional Guard not being at the time organised. Many shouts of "*Vive le Roi!*" were heard; but as often as they ceased, one of the mob, who never quitted the door of the King's carriage for a single instant, exclaimed with a stentorian voice, "No, don't believe them! *Vive la Nation!*" This ill-omened cry struck terror into the Queen.

A few days afterwards M. de Montmorin sent to say he wanted to speak to me; that he would come to me, if he were not apprehensive his doing so would attract observation; and that he thought it would appear less conspicuous if he should see me in the Queen's great closet at a time which he specified, and when nobody would be there. I went. After having made some polite observations upon the services I had already performed, and those I might yet perform, for my master and mistress, he spoke to me of the King's imminent danger, of the plots which were hatching, and of the lamentable composition of the Legislative Assembly; and he particularly dwelt upon the necessity of appearing, by prudent remarks, determined as much as possible to abide by the act the King had just recognised. I told him that could not be done without committing ourselves in the eyes of the royalist party, with which moderation was a crime; that it was painful to hear ourselves taxed with being constitution-alists, at the same time that it was our opinion that the only constitution which was consistent with the King's honour, and the happiness and tranquillity of his people, was the ab-solute power of the sovereign; that this was my creed, and it would pain me to give any room for suspicion that I was wavering in it.

"Could you ever believe," said he, "that I should desire any other order of things? Have you any doubt of my at-tachment to the King's person, and the maintenance of his rights?"

"I know it, Count," replied I; "but you are not ignorant that you lie under the imputation of having adopted revolu-tionary ideas."

"Well, madame, have resolution enough to dissemble and to conceal your real sentiments; dissimulation was nev-er more necessary. Endeavours are being made to paralyse the evil intentions of the factious as much as possible; but we must not be counteracted here by certain dangerous ex-pressions which are circulated in Paris as coming from the King and Queen."

I told him that I had been already struck with appre-hension of the evil which might be done by the intemperate observations of persons who had no power to act; and that I had felt ill consequences from having repeatedly enjoined silence on those in the Queen's service.

"I know that," said the Count; "the Queen informed me of it, and that determined me to come and request you to increase and keep alive, as much as you can, that spirit of discretion which is so necessary."

While the household of the King and Queen were a prey to all these fears, the festivities in celebration of the acceptance of the constitution proceeded. Their Majesties went to the Opéra; the audience consisted entirely of persons who sided with the King, and on that day the happiness of seeing him for a short time surrounded by faithful subjects might be enjoyed. The acclamations were then sincere.

"La Coquette Corrigée" had been selected for representation at the Théâtre Français solely because it was the piece in which Mademoiselle Contat shone most. Yet the notions propagated by the Queen's enemies coinciding in my mind with the name of the play, I thought the choice very ill-judged. I was at a loss, however, how to tell her Majesty so; but sincere attachment gives courage. I explained myself; she was obliged to me, and desired that another play might be performed. They accordingly selected "La Gouvernante," almost equally unfortunate in title.

The Queen, Madame the King's daughter, and Madame Elisabeth were all well received on this occasion. It is true that the opinions and feelings of the spectators in the boxes could not be otherwise than favourable, and great pains had been taken, previously to these two performances, to fill the pit with proper persons. But, on the other hand, the Jacobins took the same precautions on their side at the Théâtre Italien, and the tumult was excessive there. The play was Grétry's "Les Evénements Imprévus." Unfortunately, Madame Dugazon thought proper to bow to the Queen as she sang the words, "Ah, how I love my mistress!" in a duet. About twenty voices immediately exclaimed from the pit,

"No mistress! no master! liberty!" A few replied from the boxes and slips, "*Vive le Roi! vive la Reine!*" Those in the pit answered, "No master! no Queen!" The quarrel increased; the pit formed into parties; they began fighting, and the Jacobins were beaten; tufts of their black hair flew about the theatre.[1] A military guard arrived. The Faubourg St. Antoine, hearing of what was going on at the Théâtre Italien, flocked together, and began to talk of marching towards the scene of action. The Queen preserved the calmest demeanour; the commandants of the guard surrounded and encouraged her; they conducted themselves promptly and discreetly. No accident happened. The Queen was highly applauded as she quitted the theatre; it was the last time she was ever in one!

While couriers were bearing confidential letters from the King to the Princes, his brothers, and to the foreign sovereigns, the Assembly invited him to write to the Princes in order to induce them to return to France. The King desired the Abbé de Montesquiou to write the letter he was to send; this letter, which was admirably composed in a simple and affecting style, suited to the character of Louis XVI, and filled with very powerful arguments in favour of the advantages to be derived from adopting the principles of the constitution, was confided to me by the King, who desired me to make him a copy of it.

At this period M. M—, one of the intendants of Monsieur's household, obtained a passport from the Assembly to join that Prince on business relative to his domestic concerns. The Queen selected him to be the bearer of this letter. She determined to give it to him herself, and to inform

---

1. At this time none but the Jacobins had discontinued the use of hair-powder.

him of its object. I was astonished at her choice of this courier. The Queen assured me he was exactly the man for her purpose, that she relied even upon his indiscretion, and that it was merely necessary that the letter from the King to his brothers should be known to exist. The Princes were doubtless informed beforehand on the subject by the private correspondence. Monsieur nevertheless manifested some degree of surprise, and the messenger returned more grieved than pleased at this mark of confidence, which nearly cost him his life during the Reign of Terror.

Among the causes of uneasiness to the Queen there was one which was but too well founded— the thoughtlessness of the French whom she sent to foreign Courts. She used to say that they had no sooner passed the frontiers than they disclosed the most secret matters relative to the King's private sentiments, and that the leaders of the Revolution were informed of them through their agents, many of whom were Frenchmen who passed themselves off as emigrants in the cause of their King.

After the acceptance of the constitution, the formation of the King's household, as well military as civil, formed a subject of attention. The Duc de Brissac had the command of the Constitutional Guard, which was composed of officers and men selected from the regiments, and of several officers drawn from the National Guard of Paris. The King was satisfied with the feelings and conduct of this band, which, as is well known, existed but a very short time.

The new constitution abolished what were called honours, and the prerogatives belonging to them. The Duchesse de Duras resigned her place of lady of the bedchamber, not choosing to lose her right to the tabouret at Court. This step hurt the Queen, who saw herself forsaken through the loss of a petty privilege at a time when her own rights and even life were so hotly attacked. Many ladies of rank left the Court for the same reason. However, the King and Queen did not dare to form the civil part of their household, lest by giving the new names of the posts they should acknowledge the abolition of the old ones, and also lest they should admit into the highest positions persons not calculated to fill them well. Some time was spent in discussing the question, whether the household should be formed without chevaliers and without ladies of honour. The Queen's constitutional advisers were of opinion that the Assembly, having decreed a civil list adequate to uphold the splendour of the throne, would be dissatisfied at seeing the King adopting only a military household, and not forming his civil household upon the new constitutional plan. "How is it, Madame," wrote Barnave to the Queen, "that you will persist in giving these people even the smallest doubt as to your sentiments? When they decree you a civil and a military household, you, like young Achilles among the daughters of Lycomedes, eagerly seize the sword and scorn the mere ornaments." The Queen persisted in her determination to have no civil household. "If," said she, "this constitutional household be formed, not a single person of rank will remain with us, and upon a change of affairs we should be obliged to discharge the persons received into their place."

"Perhaps," added she, "perhaps I might find one day that I had saved the nobility, if I now had resolution enough to afflict them for a time; I have it not. When any measure which injures them is wrested from us they sulk with me; nobody comes to my card party; the King goes unattended to bed. No allowance is made for political necessity; we are punished for our very misfortunes."

The Queen wrote almost all day, and spent part of the night in reading: her courage supported her physical strength; her disposition was not at all soured by misfortunes, and she was never seen in an ill-humour for a moment. She was, however, held up to the people as a woman absolutely furious and mad whenever the rights of the Crown were in any way attacked.

I was with her one day at one of her windows. We saw a man plainly dressed, like an ecclesiastic, surrounded by an immense crowd. The Queen imagined it was some abbé whom they were about to throw into the basin of the Tuileries; she hastily opened her window and sent a *valet de chambre* to know what was going forward in the garden. It was Abbé Grégoire, whom the men and women of the tribunes were bringing back in triumph, on account of a motion he had just made in the National Assembly against the royal authority. On the following day the democratic journalists described the Queen as witnessing this, triumph, and showing, by expressive gestures at her window, how highly she was exasperated by the honours conferred upon the patriot.

The correspondence between the Queen and the foreign powers was carried on in cipher. That to which she gave the preference can never be detected but the greatest patience is requisite for its use! Each correspondent must have a copy of the same edition of some work. She selected "Paul and Virginia." The page and line in which the letters required, and occasionally a monosyllable, are to be found are pointed out in ciphers agreed upon. I assisted her in finding the letters, and frequently I made an exact copy for her of all that she had ciphered, without knowing a single word of its meaning.

There were always several secret committees in Paris occupied in collecting information for the King respecting the measures of the factions, and in influencing some of the committees of the Assembly. M. Bertrand de Molleville was in close correspondence with the Queen. The King employed M. Talon and others; much money was expended through the latter channel for the secret measures. The Queen had no confidence in them. M. de Laporte, minister of the civil list and of the household, also attempted to give a bias to public opinion by means of hireling publications; but these papers influenced none but the royalist party, which did not need influencing. M. de Laporte had a private police which gave him some useful information.

I determined to sacrifice myself to my duty, but by no means to any intrigue, and I thought that, circumstanced as I was, I ought to confine myself to obeying the Queen's orders. I frequently sent off couriers to foreign countries, and they were never discovered, so many precautions did I take. I am indebted for the preservation of my own existence to the care I took never to admit any deputy to my abode, and to refuse all interviews which even people of the highest importance often requested of me; but this line of conduct exposed me to every species of ill-will, and on the same day I saw myself denounced by Prud'homme, in his *Gazette Révolutionnaire*, as capable of making an aristocrat of the mother of the Gracchi, if a person so dangerous as myself could have got into her household; and by Gauthier's *Gazette Royaliste*, as a monarchist, a constitutionalist, more dangerous to the Queen's interests than a Jacobin.

At this period an event with which I had nothing to do placed me in a still more critical situation. My brother, M. Genet, began his diplomatic career, successfully. At eighteen he was attached to the embassy to Vienna; at twenty he was appointed chief secretary of Legation in England, on occasion of the peace of 1783. A memorial which he presented to M. de Vergennes upon the dangers of the treaty of commerce then entered into with England gave offence to M. de Calonne, a patron of that treaty, and particularly to M. Gérard de Rayneval, chief clerk for foreign affairs. So long as M. de Vergennes lived, having upon my father's death declared himself the protector of my brother, he supported him against the enemies his views had created. But on his death M. de Montmorin, being much in need of the long experience in business which he found in M. de Rayneval, was guided solely by the latter. The office of which my brother was the head was suppressed. He then went to St. Petersburg, strongly recommended to the Comte de Ségur, minister from France to that Court, who appointed him secretary of Legation. Some time afterwards the Comte de Ségur left him at St. Petersburg, charged with the affairs of France. After his return from Russia, M. Genet was appointed ambassador to the United States by the party called Girondists, the deputies who headed it being from the department of the Gironde. He was recalled by the Robespierre party, which overthrew the former faction, on the 31st of May, 1793, and condemned to appear before the Convention. Vice-President Clinton, at that time Governor of New York, offered him an asylum in his house and the hand of his daughter, and M. Genet established himself prosperously in America.

When my brother quitted Versailles he was much hurt at being deprived of a considerable income for having penned a memorial which his zeal alone had dictated, and the importance of which was afterwards but too well understood. I perceived from his correspondence that he inclined to some of the new notions. He told me it was right he should no longer conceal from me that he sided with the constitutional party; that the King had in fact commanded it, having himself accepted the constitution; that he would proceed firmly in that course, because in this case disingenuousness would be fatal, and that he took that side of the question because he had had it proved to him that the foreign powers would not serve the King's cause without advancing pretensions prompted by long-standing interests, which always would influence their councils; that he saw no salvation for the King and Queen but from within France, and that he would serve the constitutional King as he served him before the Revolution. And lastly, he requested me to impart to the Queen the real sentiments of one of his Majesty's agents at a foreign Court. I immediately went to the Queen and gave her my brother's letter; she read it attentively, and said, "This is the letter of a young man led astray by discontent and ambition; I know you do not think as he does; do not fear that you will lose the confidence of the King and myself." I offered to discontinue all correspondence with my brother; she opposed that, saying it would be dangerous. I then entreated she would permit me in future to show her my own and my brother's letters, to which she consented. I wrote warmly to my brother against the course he had adopted. I sent my letters by sure channels; he answered me by the post, and no longer touched upon anything but family affairs. Once only he informed me that if I should write to him respecting the affairs of the day he would give me no answer. "Serve your august mistress with the unbounded devotion which is due from you," said he, "and let us each do our duty. I will only observe to you that at Paris the fogs of the Seine often prevent people from seeing that immense capital, even from the Pavilion of Flora, and I see it more clearly from St. Petersburg." The Queen said, as she read this letter, "Perhaps he speaks but too truly; who can decide upon so disastrous a position as ours has become?"

The day on which I gave the Queen my brother's first letter to read she had several audiences to give to ladies and other persons belonging to the Court, who came on purpose to inform her that my brother was an avowed constitutionalist and revolutionist. The Queen replied, "I know it; Madame Campan has told me so." Persons jealous of my situation having subjected me to mortifications, and these unpleasant circumstances recurring daily, I requested the Queen's permission to withdraw from Court. She exclaimed against the very idea, represented it to me as extremely dangerous for my own reputation, and had the kindness to add that, for my sake as well as for her own, she never would consent to it. After this conversation I retired to my apartment. A few minutes later a footman brought me this note from the Queen: "I have never ceased to give you and yours proofs of my attachment; I wish to tell you in writing that I have full faith in your honour and fidelity, as well as in your other good qualities; and that I ever rely on the zeal and address you exert to serve me."[1]

At the moment that I was going to express my gratitude to the Queen I heard a tapping at the door of my room, which opened upon the Queen's inner corridor. I opened it; it was the King. I was confused; he perceived it, and said to me, kindly: "I alarm you, Madame Campan; I come, however, to comfort you; the Queen has told me how much she is hurt at the injustice of several persons towards you. But how is it that you complain of injustice and calumny when you see that we are victims of them? In some of your companions it is jealousy; in the people belonging to the Court it is anxiety. Our situation is so disastrous, and we have met with so much ingratitude and treachery, that the apprehensions of those who love us are excusable! I could quiet them by telling them all the secret services you perform for us daily; but

---

1. I had just received this letter from the Queen, when M. de la Chapelle, commissary general of the King's household and head of the offices of M. de Laporte, minister of the civil list, came to see me. The palace having been already forced by the brigands on the 20th of June, he proposed that I should entrust the paper to him, that he might place it in a safer situation than the apartments of the unfortunate Queen would be. When he returned into his offices, he placed the letter she had condescended to write to me behind a large picture in his closet, but on the 10th of August M. de la Chapelle was thrown into the prisons of the Abbaye, and the committee of public safety established themselves in his offices, whence they issued all their decrees of death. There it was that a villainous servant belonging to M. de Laporte went to declare that in the minister's apartment, under a board in the floor, a number of papers would be found. They were brought forth, and M. de Laporte was sent, the first of all, to the scaffold, where he suffered "for having betrayed the State by serving his master and sovereign." M. de la Chapelle was saved, as if by a miracle, from the massacres of the 2nd of September. The committee of public safety having abolished his employments in order to seat itself in the King's apartments at the Tuileries, M. de la Chapelle had permission to return to his closet to take away some property belonging to him. Turning up the picture, behind which he had hidden the Queen's letter, he found it in the place into which he had slipped it, and, delighted to see that I was safe from the ill consequences the discovery of this paper might have brought upon me, he burnt it instantly. In troublesome times a mere nothing may save life, or destroy it.

I will not do it. Out of good-will to you they would repeat all I should say, and you would be lost with the Assembly. It is much better, both for you and for us, that you should be thought a constitutionalist. It has been mentioned to me a hundred times already; I have never contradicted it; but I come to give you my word that if we are fortunate enough to see an end of all this, I will, at the Queen's residence, and in the presence of my brothers, relate the important services you have rendered us, and I will recompense you and your son for them." I threw myself at the King's feet and kissed his hand. He raised me up, saying, "Come, come, do not grieve; the Queen, who loves you, confides in you as I do."

Down to the day of the acceptance it was impossible to introduce Barnave into the interior of the palace; but when the Queen was free from the inner guard she said she would see him. The very great precautions which it was necessary for the deputy to take in order to conceal his connection with the King and Queen compelled them to spend two hours waiting for him in one of the corridors of the Tuileries, and all in vain. The first day that he was to be admitted, a man whom Barnave knew to be dangerous having met him in the courtyard of the palace, he determined to cross it without stopping, and walked in the gardens in order to lull suspicion. I was desired to wait for Barnave at a little door belonging to the *entresols* of the palace, with my hand upon the open lock. I was in that position for an hour. The King came to me frequently, and always to speak to me of the uneasiness which a servant belonging to the Château, who was a patriot, gave him. He came again to ask me whether I had heard the door called *de Decret* opened. I assured him nobody had been in the corridor, and he became easy. He was dreadfully apprehensive that his connection with Barnave would be discovered. "It would," said the King, "be a ground for grave accusations, and the unfortunate man would be lost." I then ventured to remind his Majesty that as Barnave was not the only one in the secret of the business which brought him in contact with their Majesties, one of his colleagues might be induced to speak of the association with which they were honoured, and that in letting them know by my presence that I also was informed of it, a risk was incurred of removing from those gentlemen part of the responsibility of the secret. Upon this observation the King quitted me hastily and returned a moment afterwards with the Queen. "Give me your place," said she; "I will wait for him in my turn. You have convinced the King. We must not increase in their eyes the number of persons informed of their communications with us."

The police of M. de Laporte, intendant of the civil list, apprised him, as early as the latter end of 1791, that a man belonging to the King's offices who had set up as a pastrycook at the Palais Royal was about to resume the duties of his situation, which had devolved upon him again on the death of one who held it for life; that he was so furious a Jacobin that he had dared to say it would be a good thing for France if the King's days were shortened. His duty was confined to making the pastry; he was closely watched by the head officers of the kitchen, who were devoted to his Majesty; but it is so easy to introduce a subtle poison into made dishes that it was determined the King and Queen should eat only plain roast meat in future; that their bread should be brought to them by M. Thierry de Ville-d'Avray, intendant of the smaller apartments, and that he should likewise take upon himself to supply the wine. The King was fond of pastry; I was directed to order some, as if for myself, sometimes of one pastry-cook, and sometimes of another. The pounded sugar, too, was kept in my room. The King, the Queen, and Madame Elisabeth ate together, and nobody remained to wait on them. Each had a dumb waiter and a little bell to call the servants when they were wanted. M. Thierry used himself to bring me their Majesties' bread and wine, and I locked them up in a private cupboard in the King's closet on the ground floor. As soon as the King sat down to table I took in the pastry and bread. All was hidden under the table lest it might be necessary to have the servants in. The King thought it dangerous as well as distressing to show any apprehension of attempts against his person, or any mistrust of his officers of the kitchen. As he never drank a whole bottle of wine at his meals (the Princesses drank nothing but water), he filled up that out of which he had drunk about half from the bottle served up by the officers of his butlery. I took it away after dinner. Although he never ate any other pastry than that which I brought, he took care in the same manner that it should seem that he had eaten of that served at table. The lady who succeeded me found this duty all regulated, and she executed it in the same manner; the public never was in possession of these particulars, nor of the apprehensions which gave rise to them. At the end of three or four months the police of M. de Laporte gave notice that nothing more was to be dreaded from that sort of plot against the King's life; that the plan was entirely changed; and that all the blows now to be struck would be directed as much against the throne as against the person of the sovereign.

There are others besides myself who know that at this time one of the things about which the Queen most desired to be satisfied was the opinion of the famous Pitt. She would sometimes say to me, "I never pronounce the name of Pitt without feeling a chill like that of death." (I repeat here her very expressions.) "That man is the mortal enemy of France; and he takes a dreadful revenge for the impolitic support given by the Cabinet of Versailles to the American insurgents. He wishes by our destruction to guarantee the maritime power of his country forever against the efforts made by the King to improve his marine power and their happy results during the last war. He knows that it is not only the King's policy but his private inclination to be solicitous about his fleets, and that the most active step he has taken during his whole reign was to visit the port of Cherbourg. Pitt had served the cause of the French Revolution from the first disturbances; he will perhaps serve it until its annihilation. I will endeavour to learn to what point lie intends to lead us, and I am sending M.—[1] to London for that purpose. He has been intimately connected with Pitt, and they have often had political conversations respecting the French Government. I will get him to make him speak out, at least so far as such a man can speak out."

Some time afterwards the Queen told me that her secret envoy was returned from London, and that all he had been able to wring from Pitt, whom he found alarmingly

---

1. I thought, for some time, that this secret agent was M. Crawford. His Memoirs, which I read very eagerly, have altered my opinion, because he certainly would have mentioned this mission. I have forgotten the name of the person whom the Queen sent to London, though she condescended to entrust me with it.

reserved, was that *he would not suffer the French monarchy to perish*; that to suffer the revolutionary spirit to erect an organised republic in France would be a great error, affecting the tranquillity of Europe. "Whenever," said she, "Pitt expressed himself upon the necessity of supporting *monarchy* in France, he maintained the most profound silence upon what concerns the monarch. The result of these conversations is anything but encouraging; but, even as to that monarchy which he wishes to save, will he have means and strength to save it if he suffers us to fall?"

The death of the Emperor Leopold took place or the 1st of March 1792. When the news of this event reached the Tuileries, the Queen was gone out. Upon her return I put the letter containing it into her hands. She exclaimed that the Emperor had been poisoned; that she had remarked and preserved a newspaper, in which, in an article upon the sitting of the Jacobins, at the time when the Emperor Leopold declared for the coalition, it was said, speaking of him, that a *pie-crust* would settle that matter. At this period Barnave obtained the Queen's consent that he should read all the letters she should write. He was fearful of private correspondences that might hamper the plan marked out for her; he mistrusted her Majesty's sincerity on this point; and the diversity of counsels, and the necessity of yielding, on the one hand, to some of the views of the constitutionalists, and on the other, to those of the French Princes, and even of foreign Courts, were unfortunately the circumstances which most rapidly impelled the Court towards its ruin.

However, the emigrants showed great apprehensions of the consequences which might follow in the interior from a connection with the constitutionalists, whom they described as a party existing only in idea, and totally without means of repairing their errors. The Jacobins were preferred to them, because, said they, there would be no treaty to be made with any one at the moment of extricating the King and his family from the abyss in which they were plunged.

XXI

IN the beginning of the year 1792, a worthy priest requested a private interview with me. He had learned the existence of a new libel by Madame de Lamotte. He told me that the people who came from London to get it printed in Paris only desired gain, and that they were ready to deliver the manuscript to him for a thousand louis, if he could find any friend of the Queen disposed to make that sacrifice for her peace; that he had thought of me, and if her Majesty would give him the twenty-four thousand francs, he would hand the manuscript to me.

I communicated this proposal to the Queen, who rejected it, and desired me to answer that at the time when she had power to punish the hawkers of these libels she deemed them so atrocious and incredible that she despised them too much to stop them; that if she were imprudent and weak enough to buy a single one of them, the Jacobins might possibly discover the circumstance through their espionage;

that were this libel bought up, it would be printed nevertheless, and would be much more dangerous when they apprised the public of the means she had used to suppress it.

Baron d'Aubier, gentleman-in-ordinary to the King, and my particular friend, had a good memory and a clear way of communicating the substance of the debates and decrees of the National Assembly. I went daily to the Queen's apartments to repeat all this to the King, who used to say, on seeing me, "Ah! here's the *Postilion par Calais*,"—a newspaper of the time.

M. d'Aubier one day said to me: "The Assembly has been much occupied with an information laid by the workmen of the Sévres manufactory. They brought to the President's office a bundle of pamphlets which they said were the life of Marie Antoinette. The director of the manufactory was ordered up to the bar, and declared he had received orders to burn the printed sheets in question in the furnaces used for baking his china."

While I was relating this business to the Queen the King coloured and held his head down over his plate. The Queen said to him, "Do you know anything about this, Sire?" The King made no answer. Madame Elisabeth requested him to explain what it meant. Louis was still silent. I withdrew hastily. A few minutes afterwards the Queen came to my room and informed me that the King, out of regard for her, had purchased the whole edition struck off from the manuscript which I had mentioned to her, and that M. de Laporte had not been able to devise any more secret way of destroying the work than that of having it burnt at Sévres, among two hundred workmen, one hundred and eighty of whom must, in all probability, be Jacobins! She told me she had concealed her vexation from the King; that he was in consternation, and that she could say nothing, since his good intentions and his affection for her had been the cause of the mistake.

Some time afterwards the Assembly received a denunciation against M. de Montmorin. The ex-minister was accused of having neglected forty dispatches from M. Genet, the *chargé d'affaires* from France in Russia, not having even unsealed them, because M. Genet acted on constitutional principles. M. de Montmorin appeared at the bar to answer this accusation. Whatever distress I might feel in obeying the order I had received from the King to go and give him an account of the sitting, I thought I ought not to fail in doing so. But instead of giving my brother his family name, I merely said "your Majesty's *chargé d'affaires* at St. Petersburg."

The King did me the favour to say that he noticed a reserve in my account, of which he approved. The Queen condescended to add a few obliging remarks to those of the King. However, my office of journalist gave me in this instance so much pain that I took an opportunity, when the King was expressing his satisfaction to me at the manner in which I gave him this daily account, to tell him that its merits belonged wholly to M. d'Aubier; and I ventured to request the King to suffer that excellent man to give him an account of the sittings himself. I assured the King that if he would permit it, that gentleman might proceed to the Queen's apartments through mine unseen; the King consented to the arrangement. Thenceforward M. d'Aubier gave the King repeated proofs of zeal and attachment.

The Curé of St. Eustache ceased to be the Queen's confessor when he took the constitutional oath. I do not remember the name of the ecclesiastic who succeeded him; I only know that he was conducted into her apartments with the greatest mystery. Their Majesties did not perform their Easter devotions in public, because they could neither declare for the constitutional clergy, nor act so as to show that they were against them.

The Queen did perform her Easter devotions in 1792; but she went to the chapel attended only by myself. She desired me beforehand to request one of my relations, who was her chaplain, to celebrate a mass for her at five o'clock in the morning. It was still dark; she gave me her arm, and I lighted her with a taper. I left her alone at the chapel door. She did not return to her room until the dawn of day.

Dangers increased daily. The Assembly were strengthened in the eyes of the people by the hostilities of the foreign armies and the army of the Princes. The communication with the latter party became more active; the Queen wrote almost every day. M. de Goguelat possessed her confidence for all correspondence with the foreign parties, and I was obliged to have him in my apartments; the Queen asked for him very frequently, and at times which she could not previously appoint.

All parties were exerting themselves either to ruin or to save the King. One day I found the Queen extremely agitated; she told me she no longer knew where she was; that the leaders of the Jacobins offered themselves to her through the medium of Dumouriez; or that Dumouriez, abandoning the Jacobins, had come and offered himself to her; that she had granted him an audience; that when alone with her, he had thrown himself at her feet, and told her that he had drawn the *bonnet rouge* over his head to the very ears; but that he neither was nor could be a Jacobin; that the Revolution had been suffered to extend even to that rabble of destroyers who, thinking of nothing but pillage, were ripe for anything, and might furnish the Assembly with a formidable army, ready to undermine the remains of a throne already but too much shaken. Whilst speaking with the utmost ardour he seized the Queen's hand and kissed it with transport, exclaiming, "Suffer yourself to be saved!" The Queen told me that the protestations of a traitor were not to be relied on; that the whole of his conduct was so well known that undoubtedly the wisest course was not to trust to it; that, moreover, the Princes particularly recommended that no confidence should be placed in any proposition emanating from within the kingdom; that the force without became imposing; and that it was better to rely upon their success, and upon the protection due from Heaven to a sovereign so virtuous as Louis XVI and to so just a cause.

The constitutionalists, on their part, saw that there had been nothing more than a pretence of listening to them. Barnave's last advice was as to the means of continuing, a few weeks longer, the Constitutional Guard, which had been denounced to the Assembly, and was to be disbanded. The denunciation against the Constitutional Guard affected only its staff, and the Duc de Brissac. Barnave wrote to the Queen that the staff of the guard was already attacked; that the Assembly was about to pass a decree to reduce it; and he entreated her to prevail on the King, the very instant the decree should appear, to form the staff afresh of persons whose names he sent her. Barnave said that all who were set down in it passed for decided Jacobins, but were not so in fact; that they, as well as himself, were in despair at seeing the monarchical government attacked; that they had learnt to dissemble their sentiments, and that it would be at least a fortnight before the Assembly could know them well, and certainly before it could succeed in making them unpopular; that it would be necessary to take advantage of that short space of time to get away from Paris, immediately after their nomination. The Queen was of opinion that she ought not to yield to this advice. The Duc de Brissac was sent to Orléans, and the guard was disbanded.

Barnave, seeing that the Queen did not follow his counsel in anything, and convinced that she placed all her reliance on assistance from abroad, determined to quit Paris. He obtained a last audience. "Your misfortunes, Madame," said he, "and those which I anticipate for France, determined me to sacrifice myself to serve you. I see, however, that my advice does not agree with the views of your Majesties. I augur but little advantage from the plan you are induced to pursue,—you are too remote from your succours; you will be lost before they reach you. Most ardently do I wish I may be mistaken in so lamentable a prediction; but I am sure to pay with my head for the interest your misfortunes have raised in me, and the services I have sought to render you. I request, for my sole reward, the honour of kissing your hand." The Queen, her eyes suffused with tears, granted him that favour, and remained impressed with a favourable idea of his sentiments. Madame Elisabeth participated in this opinion, and the two Princesses frequently spoke of Barnave. The Queen also received M. Duport several times, but with less mystery. Her connection with the constitutional deputies transpired. Alexandre de Lameth was the only one of the three who survived the vengeance of the Jacobins.

The National Guard, which succeeded the King's Guard, having occupied the gates of the Tuileries, all who came to see the Queen were insulted with impunity. Menacing cries were uttered aloud even in the Tuileries; they called for the destruction of the throne, and the murder of the sovereign; the grossest insults were offered by the very lowest of the mob.

About this time the King fell into a despondent state, which amounted almost to physical helplessness. He passed ten successive days without uttering a single word, even in the bosom of his family; except, indeed, when playing at backgammon after dinner with Madame Elisabeth. The Queen roused him from this state, so fatal at a critical period, by throwing herself at his feet, urging every alarming idea, and employing every affectionate expression. She represented also what he owed to his family; and told him that if they were doomed to fall they ought to fall honourably, and not wait to be smothered upon the floor of their apartment.

About the 15th of June, 1792, the King refused his sanction to the two decrees ordaining the deportation of priests and the formation of a camp of twenty thousand men under the walls of Paris. He himself wished to sanction them, and said that the general insurrection only waited for a pretence to burst forth. The Queen insisted upon the veto, and reproached herself bitterly when this last act of the constitutional authority had occasioned the day of the 20th of June.

A few days previously about twenty thousand men had gone to the Commune to announce that, on the 20th, they would plant the tree of liberty at the door of the National Assembly, and present a petition to the King respecting the veto which he had placed upon the decree for the deportation of the priests. This dreadful army crossed the garden of the Tuileries, and marched under the Queen's windows; it consisted of people who called themselves the citizens of the Faubourgs St. Antoine and St. Marceau. Clothed in filthy rags, they bore a most terrifying appearance, and even infected the air. People asked each other where such an army could come from; nothing so disgusting had ever before appeared in Paris.

On the 20th of June this mob thronged about the Tuileries in still greater numbers, armed with pikes, hatchets, and murderous instruments of all kind decorated with ribbons of the national colours, shouting, "The nation for ever! Down with the veto!" The King was without guards. Some of these desperadoes rushed up to his apartment; the door was about to be forced in, when the King commanded that it should be opened. Messieurs de Bougainville, d'Hervilly, de Parois, d'Aubier, Acloque,[1] Gentil, and other courageous men who were in the apartment of M. de Septeuil, the King's first *valet de chambre*, instantly ran to his Majesty's apartment. M. de Bougainville, seeing the torrent furiously advancing, cried out, "Put the King in the recess of the window, and place benches before him." Six royalist grenadiers of the battalion of the Filles Saint Thomas made their way by an inner staircase, and ranged themselves before the benches. The order given by M. de Bougainville saved the King from the blades of the assassins, among whom was a Pole named Lazousky, who was to strike the first blow. The King's brave defenders said, "Sire, fear nothing." The King's reply is well known: "Put your hand upon my heart, and you will perceive whether I am afraid." M. Vanot, commandant

---

1. A citizen of Paris, commandant of battalion, who during the whole of the Revolution was, both in virtue and conduct, in direct opposition to the regicide Santerre.

of battalion, warded off a blow aimed by a wretch against the King; a grenadier of the Filles Saint Thomas parried a sword-thrust made in the same direction. Madame Elisabeth ran to her brother's apartments; when she reached the door she heard loud threats of death against the Queen: they called for the head of the Austrian. "Ah ! let them think I am the Queen," she said to those around her, "that she may have time to escape."

The Queen could not join the King; she was in the council chamber, where she had been placed behind the great table to protect her, as much as possible, against the approach of the barbarians. Preserving a noble and becoming demeanour in this dreadful situation, she held the Dauphin before her, seated upon the table. Madame was at her side; the Princesse de Lamballe, the Princesse de Tarente, Madame de la Roche-Aymon, Madame de Turzel, and Madame de Mackau surrounded her. She had fixed a tri-coloured cockade, which one of the National Guard had given her, upon her head. The poor little Dauphin was, like the King, shrouded in an enormous red cap. The horde passed in files before the table; the sort of standards which they carried were symbols of the most atrocious barbarity. There was one representing a gibbet, to which a dirty doll was suspended; the words *Marie Antoinette à la lanterne*" were written beneath it. Another was a board, to which a bullock's heart was fastened, with "Heart of Louis XVI" written round it. And a third showed the horn of an ox, with an obscene inscription.

One of the most furious Jacobin women who marched with these wretches stopped to give vent to a thousand imprecations against the Queen. Her Majesty asked whether she had ever seen her. She replied that she had not. Whether she had done her any personal wrong? Her answer was the same; but she added:

"It is you who have caused the misery of the nation."

"You have been told so," answered the Queen; "you are deceived. As the wife of the King of France, and mother of the Dauphin, I am a Frenchwoman; I shall never see my own country again,— I can be happy or unhappy only in France; I was happy when you loved me."

The fury began to weep, asked her pardon, and said, "It was because I did not know you; I see that you are good."

Santerre, the monarch of the faubourgs, made his subjects file off as quickly as he could; and it was thought at the time that he was ignorant of the object of this insurrection, which was the murder of the royal family. However, it was eight o'clock in the evening before the palace was completely cleared. Twelve deputies, impelled by attachment to the King's person, ranged themselves near him at the commencement of the insurrection; but the deputation from the Assembly did not reach the Tuileries until six in the evening; all the doors of the apartments were broken. The Queen pointed out to the deputies the state of the King's palace, and the disgraceful manner in which his asylum had been violated under the very eyes of the Assembly; she saw that Merlin de Thionville was so much affected as to shed tears while she spoke.

"You weep, M. Merlin," said she to him, "at seeing the King and his family so cruelly treated by a people whom he always wished to make happy."

"True, Madame," replied Merlin; "I weep for the misfortunes of a beautiful and feeling woman, the mother of a family; but do not mistake, not one of my tears falls for either King or Queen; I hate kings and queens, it is my religion."

The Queen could not appreciate this madness, and saw all that was to be apprehended by persons who evinced it.

All hope was gone, and nothing was thought of but succour from abroad. The Queen appealed to her family and the King's brothers; her letters probably became more pressing, and expressed apprehensions upon the tardiness of relief. Her Majesty read me one to herself from the Archduchess Christina, Gouvernante of the Low Countries: she reproached the Queen for some of her expressions, and told her that those out of France were at least as much alarmed as herself at the King's situation and her own; but that the manner of attempting to assist her might either save her or endanger her safety; and that the members of the coalition were bound to act prudently, entrusted as they were with interests so dear to them.

The 14th of July, 1792, fixed by the constitution as the anniversary of the independence of the nation, drew near. The King and Queen were compelled to make their appearance on the occasion; aware that the plot of the 20th of June had their assassination for its object, they had no doubt but that their death was determined on for the day of this national festival. The Queen was recommended, in order to give the King's friends time to defend him if the attack should be made, to guard him against the first stroke of a dagger by making him wear a breastplate. I was directed to get one made in my apartments: it was composed of fifteen folds of Italian taffety, and formed into an under-waistcoat and a wide belt. This breastplate was tried; it resisted all thrusts of the dagger, and several balls were turned aside by it. When it was completed the difficulty was to let the King try it on without running the risk of being surprised. I wore the immense heavy waistcoat as an under-petticoat for three days without being able to find a favourable moment. At length the King found an opportunity one morning to pull off his coat in the Queen's chamber and try on the breastplate. [1]

The Queen was in bed; the King pulled me gently by the gown, and drew me as far as he could from the Queen's bed, and said to me, in a very low tone of voice: "It is to satisfy her that I submit to this inconvenience: they will not assassinate me; their scheme is changed; they will put me to death another way." The Queen heard the King whispering to me, and when he was gone out she asked me what he had said. I hesitated to answer; she insisted that I should, saying that nothing must be concealed from her, and that she was resigned upon every point When she was informed of the King's remark she told me she had guessed it, that he had long since observed to her that all which was going forward in France was an imitation of the revolution in England in the time of Charles I, and that he was incessantly reading the history of that unfortunate monarch in order that he might act better than Charles had done at a similar crisis. "I begin to be fearful of the King's being brought to trial," continued the Queen; "as to me, I am a foreigner; they will assassinate me. What will become of my poor children?" These sad ejaculations were followed by a torrent of tears. I wished to give her an antispasmodic; she refused it, saying that only happy

---

1. M. Genet, the first valet of the wardrobe, assisted me to try on this under-waistcoat, which the King wore on the 14th July, 1792; but M. de Parios had a second made a few days before the 10th of August.

women could feel nervous; that the cruel situation to which she was reduced rendered these remedies useless. In fact, the Queen, who during her happier days was frequently attacked by hysterical disorders, enjoyed more uniform health when all the faculties of her soul were called forth to support her physical strength.

I had prepared a corset for her, for the same purpose as the King's under-waistcoat, without her knowledge; but she would not make use of it; all my entreaties, all my tears, were in vain. " If the factions assassinate me," she replied, "it will be a fortunate event for me; they will deliver me from a most painful existence." A few days after the King had tried on his breastplate I met him on a back staircase. I drew back to let him pass. He stopped and took my hand; I wished to kiss his; he would not suffer it, but drew me towards him by the hand, and kissed both my cheeks without saying a single word.

The fear of another attack upon the Tuileries occasioned scrupulous search among the King's papers: I burnt almost all those belonging to the Queen. She put her family letters, a great deal of correspondence which she thought it necessary to preserve for the history of the era of the Revolution, and particularly Barnave's letters and her answers, of which she had copies, into a portfolio, which she entrusted to M. de J—. That gentleman was unable to save this deposit, and it was burnt. The Queen left a few papers in her *secrétaire*. Among them were instructions to Madame de Tourzel, respecting the dispositions of her children and the characters and abilities of the sub-governesses under that lady's orders. This paper, which the Queen drew up at the time of Madame de Tourzel's appointment, with several letters from Maria Theresa, filled with the best advice and

instructions, was printed after the 10th of August by order of the Assembly in the collection of papers found in
the *secrétaires* of the King and Queen.

Her Majesty had still, without reckoning the income
of the month, one hundred and forty thousand francs in
gold. She was desirous of depositing the whole of it with
me; but I advised her to retain fifteen hundred louis, as
a sum of rather considerable amount might be suddenly
necessary for her. The King had an immense quantity of
papers, and unfortunately conceived the idea of privately
making, with the assistance of a locksmith who had worked
with him above ten years, a place of concealment in an inner corridor of his apartments. The place of concealment,
but for the man's information, would have been long un-
discovered. The wall in which it was made was painted to
imitate large stones, and the opening was entirely concealed
among the brown grooves which formed the shaded part
of these painted stones. But even before this locksmith had
denounced what was afterwards called *the iron closet* to the
Assembly, the Queen was aware that he had talked of it to
some of his friends; and that this man, in whom the King
from long habit placed too much confidence, was a Jacobin.
She warned the King of it, and prevailed on him to fill a very
large portfolio with all the papers he was most interested in
preserving, and entrust it to me. She entreated him in my
presence to leave nothing in this closet; and the King, in
order to quiet her, told her that he had left nothing there.
I would have taken the portfolio and carried it to my apartment, but it was too heavy for me to lift. The King said he
would carry it himself; I went before to open the doors for
him. When he placed the portfolio in my inner closet he

merely said, "The Queen will tell you what it contains." Upon my return to the Queen I put the question to her, deeming, from what the King had said, that it was necessary I should know. "They are," the Queen answered me, "such documents as would be most dangerous to the King should they go so far as to proceed to a trial against him. But what he wishes me to tell you is, that the portfolio contains a *procès-verbal* of a cabinet council, in which the King gave his opinion against the war. He had it signed by all the ministers, and, in case of a trial, he trusts that this document will be very useful to him." I asked the Queen to whom she thought I ought to commit the portfolio. "To whom you please," answered she; "you alone are answerable for it. Do not quit the palace even during your vacation months: there may be circumstances under which it would be very desirable that we should be able to have it instantly."

At this period M. de La Fayette, who had probably given up the idea of establishing a republic in France similar to that of the United States, and was desirous to support the first constitution which he had sworn to defend, quitted his army and came to the Assembly for the purpose of supporting by his presence and by an energetic speech a petition signed by twenty thousand citizens against the late violation of the residence of the King and his family. The General found the constitutional party powerless, and saw that he himself had lost his popularity. The Assembly disapproved of the step he had taken; the King, for whom it was taken, showed no satisfaction at it, and he saw himself compelled to return to his army as quickly as he could. He thought he could rely on the National Guard; but on the day of his arrival those officers who were in the King's interest inquired of his Majesty whether they were to forward the views of Général de La Fayette by joining him in such measures as he should pursue during his stay at Paris. The King enjoined them not to do so. From this answer M. de La Fayette perceived that he was abandoned by the remainder of his party in the Paris guard.

On his arrival a plan was presented to the Queen, in which it was proposed by a junction between La Fayette's army and the King's party to rescue the royal family and convey them to Rouen. I did not learn the particulars of this plan; the Queen only said to me upon the subject that M. de La Fayette was offered to them as a resource; but that it would be better for them to perish than to owe their safety to the man who had done them the most mischief, or to place themselves under the necessity of treating with him.

I passed the whole month of July without going to bed; I was fearful of some attack by night. There was one plot against the Queen's life which has never been made known. I was alone by her bedside at one o'clock in the morning; we heard somebody walking softly down the corridor, which passes along the whole line of her apartments, and which was then locked at each end. I went out to fetch the *valet de chambre*; he entered the corridor, and the Queen and myself soon heard the noise of two men fighting. The unfortunate Princess held me locked in her arms, and said to me, "What a situation! insults by day and assassins by night!" The *valet de chambre* cried out to her from the corridor, "Madame, it is a wretch that I know; I have him!" "Let him go," said the Queen; "open the door to him; he came to murder me; the Jacobins would carry him about in triumph to-morrow." The man was a servant of the King's toilet, who had taken the key of the corridor out of his Majesty's pocket after he was in bed, no doubt with the intention of committing the crime suspected. The *valet de chambre*, who was a very strong man, held him by the wrists, and thrust him out at the door. The wretch did not speak a word. The *valet de chambre* said, in answer to the Queen, who spoke to him gratefully of the danger to which he had exposed himself, that he feared nothing, and that he had always a pair of excellent pistols about him for no other purpose than to defend her Majesty. The next day M. de Septeuil had all the locks of the King's inner apartments changed. I did the same by those of the Queen.

We were every moment told that the Faubourg St. Antoine was preparing to march against the palace. At four o'clock one morning towards the latter end of July a person came to give me information to that effect. I instantly sent off two men, on whom I could rely, with orders to proceed to the usual places for assembling, and to come back speedily, and give me an account of the state of the city. We knew that at least an hour must elapse before the populace or the faubourgs assembled on the site of the Bastille could reach the Tuileries. It seemed to me sufficient for the Queen's safety that all about her should be awakened. I went softly into her room; she was asleep; I did not awaken her. I found Général de W—in the great closet; he told me the meeting was, for this once, dispersing. The General had endeavoured to please the populace by the same means as M. de La Fayette had employed. He saluted the lowest *poissarde*, and lowered his hat down to his very stirrup. But the populace, who had been flattered for three years, required far different homage to its power, and the poor man was unnoticed. The King had been awakened, and so had Madame Elisabeth, who had gone to him. The Queen, yielding to the weight of her griefs, slept till nine o'clock on that day, which was very unusual with her. The King had already been to know whether she was awake; I told him what I had done, and the care I had taken not to disturb her. He thanked me, and said, "I was awake, and so was the whole palace; she ran no risk. I am very glad to see her take a little rest. Alas! her griefs double mine!" What was my chagrin when, upon awaking and learning what had passed, the Queen burst into tears from regret at not having been called, and began to upbraid me, on whose friendship she ought to have been able to rely, for having served her so ill under such circumstances! In vain did I reiterate that it had been only a false alarm, and that she required to have her strength recruited. "It is not diminished," said she; "misfortune gives us additional strength. Elisabeth was with the King, and I was asleep,—I who am determined to perish by his side! I am his wife; I will not suffer him to incur the smallest risk without my sharing it."

XXII

D URING July the correspondence of M. Bertrand
de Molleville with the King and Queen was most
active. M. de Marsilly, formerly a lieutenant of the
Cent-Suisses of the Guard, was the bearer of the letters. He
came to mo the first time with a note from the Queen directed to M. Bertrand himself. In this note the Queen said:
"Address yourself with full confidence to Madame Campan;
the conduct of her brother in Russia has not at all influenced
her sentiments; she is wholly devoted to us; and if, hereafter,
you should have anything to say to us verbally, you may rely
entirely upon her devotion and discretion."

The mobs which gathered almost nightly in the faubourgs alarmed the Queen's friends; they entreated her not
to sleep in her room on the ground floor of the Tuileries. She
removed to the first floor, to a room which was between the
King's apartments and those of the Dauphin. Being awake
always from daybreak, she ordered that neither the shutters

nor the window-blinds should be closed, that her long sleep-less nights might be the less weary. About the middle of one of these nights, when the moon was shining into her bedcham-ber, she gazed at it, and told me that in a month she should not see that moon unless freed from her chains, and beholding the King at liberty. She then imparted to me all that was con-curring to deliver them; but said that the opinions of their intimate advisers were alarmingly at variance; that some vouched for complete success, while others pointed out in-surmountable dangers. She added that she possessed the itinerary of the march of the Princes and the King of Prus-sia: that on such a day they would be at Verdun, on another day at such a place, that Lille was about to be besieged, but that M. de J—, whose prudence and intelligence the King, as well as herself, highly valued, alarmed them much respect-ing the success of that siege, and made them apprehensive that, even were the commandant devoted to them, the civil authority, which by the constitution gave great power to the mayors of towns, would overrule the military commandant. She was also very uneasy as to what would take place at Paris during the interval, and spoke to me of the King's want of energy, but always in terms expressive of her veneration for his virtues and her attachment to himself. "The King," said she, "is not a coward; he possesses abundance of passive courage, but he is overwhelmed by an awkward shyness, a mistrust of himself, which proceeds from his education as much as from his disposition. He is afraid to command, and, above all things, dreads speaking to assembled numbers. He lived like a child, and always ill at ease under the eyes of Louis XV, until the age of twenty-one. This constraint confirmed his timidity. Circumstanced as we are, a few well-delivered words addressed to the Parisians, who are devoted to him, would multiply the strength of our party a hundredfold: he will not utter them. What can we expect from those addresses to the people which he has been advised to post up? Nothing but fresh outrages. As for myself, I could do anything, and would appear on horseback, if necessary. But if I were really to begin to act, that would be furnishing arms to the King's enemies; the cry against the Austrian, and against the sway of a woman, would become general in France; and, moreover, by showing myself, I should render the King a mere nothing. A queen who is not regent ought, under these circumstances, to remain passive and prepare to die."

The garden of the Tuileries was full of maddened men, who insulted all who seemed to side with the Court. "The Life of Marie Antoinette" was cried under the Queen's windows, infamous plates were annexed to the book, the hawkers showed them to the passers-by. On all sides were heard the jubilant outcries of a people in a state of delirium almost as frightful as the explosion of their rage. The Queen and her children were unable to breathe the open air any longer. It was determined that the garden of the Tuileries should be closed; as soon as this step was taken the Assembly decreed that the whole length of the Terrace des Feuillans belonged to it, and fixed the boundary between what was called the *national ground* and the *Coblentz ground* by a tricoloured ribbon stretched from one end of the terrace to the other. All good citizens were ordered, by notices affixed to it, not to go down into the garden, under pain of being treated in the same manner as Foulon and Berthier. A young man who did not observe this written order went down into the garden; furious outcries, threats of *la lanterne*, and the crowd of people which collected upon the terrace warned him of his imprudence, and the danger which he ran. He immediately pulled off his shoes, took out his handkerchief, and wiped the dust from their soles. The people cried out, "Bravo! the good citizen for ever!" He was carried off in triumph. The shutting up of the Tuileries did not enable the Queen and her children to walk in the garden. The people on the terrace sent forth dreadful shouts, and she was twice compelled to return to her apartments.

In the early part of August many zealous persons offered the King money; he refused considerable sums, being unwilling to injure the fortunes of individuals. M. de la Ferté, intendant of the *menus plaisirs*, brought me a thousand louis, requesting me to lay them at the feet of the Queen. He thought she could not have too much money at so perilous a time, and that every good Frenchman should hasten to place all his ready money in her hands. She refused this sum, and others of much greater amount which were offered to her.[1] However, a few days afterwards., she told me she would accept M. de la Ferté's twenty-four thousand francs, because they would make up a sum which the King had to expend. She therefore directed me to go and receive those twenty-four thousand francs, to add them to the one hundred thousand francs she had placed in my hands, and to change the whole into assignats to increase their amount. Her orders were executed, and the assignats were delivered to the King.

1. M. Auguié, my brother-in-law, receiver-general of the finances, offered her, through the medium of his wife, a portfolio containing one hundred thousand crowns in paper money. On this occasion, the Queen said the most affecting things to my sister, expressive of her happiness at having contributed to the fortunes of such faithful subjects as herself and her husband, but declined accepting her offer.

The Queen informed me that Madame Elisabeth had found a well-meaning man who had engaged to gain over Pétion by the bribe of a large sum of money, and that deputy would, by a preconcerted signal, inform the King of the success of the project. His Majesty soon had an opportunity of seeing Pétion, and on the Queen asking him before me if he was satisfied with him, the King replied, "Neither more nor less satisfied than usual; he did not make the concerted signal, and I believe I have been cheated." The Queen then condescended to explain the whole of the enigma to me. "Pétion," said she, "was, while talking to the King, to have kept his finger fixed upon his right eye for at least two seconds." "He did not even put his hand up to his chin," said the King; "after all, it is but so much money stolen: the thief will not boast of it, and the affair will remain a secret. Let us talk of something else." He turned to me and said, "Your father was an intimate friend of Mandat, who now commands the National Guard; describe him to me; what ought I to expect from him?" I answered that he was one of his Majesty's most faithful subjects, but that with a great deal of loyalty he possessed very little sense, and that he was involved in the constitutional vortex. "I understand," said the King; "he is a man who would defend my palace and my person, because that is enjoined by the constitution which he has sworn to support, but who would fight against the party in favour of sovereign authority; it is well to know this with certainty."

On the next day the Princesse de Lamballe sent for me very early in the morning. I found her on a sofa facing a window that looked upon the Pont Royal. She then occupied that apartment of the Pavilion of Flora which was on a level with that of the Queen. She desired me to sit down by her. Her Highness had a writing-desk upon her knees. "You have had many enemies," said she; "attempts have been made to deprive you of the Queen's favour; they have been far from successful. Do you know that even I myself, not being so well acquainted with you as the Queen, was rendered suspicious of you; and that upon the arrival of the Court at the Tuileries I gave you a companion to be a spy upon you;[1] and that I had another belonging to the police placed at your door! I was assured that you received five or six of the most virulent deputies of the *Tiers Etat*; but it was that wardrobe woman whose rooms were above you. In short," said the Princess, "persons of integrity have nothing to fear from the evil-disposed when they belong to so upright a prince as the King. As to the Queen, she knows you, and has loved you ever since she came into France. You shall judge of the King's opinion of you: it was yesterday evening decided in the family circle that, at a time when the Tuileries is likely to be attacked, it was necessary to have the most faithful account of the opinions and conduct of all the individuals composing the Queen's service. The King takes the same precaution on his part respecting all who are about him. He said there was with him a person of great integrity, to whom he would commit this inquiry; and that, with regard to the Queen's household, you must be spoken to, that he had long studied your character, and that he esteemed your veracity."

The Princess had a list of the names of all who belonged to the Queen's chamber on her desk. She asked me

---

1. This was M. de P—, who afterwards owned it to me, telling me that though he did accept of this base employment, it was because he was sure that my acquaintance consisted only of royalists; and that, moreover, he did not doubt the sincerity of my sentiments.

for information respecting each individual. I was fortunate in having none but the most favourable information to give. I had to speak of my avowed enemy in the Queen's chamber; of her who most wished that I should be responsible for my brother's political opinions. The Princess, as the head of the chamber, could not be ignorant of this circumstance; but as the person in question, who idolised the King and Queen, would not have hesitated to sacrifice her life in order to save theirs, and as possibly her attachment to them, united to considerable narrowness of intellect and a limited education, contributed to her jealousy of me, I spoke of her in the highest terms.

The Princess wrote as I dictated, and occasionally looked at me with astonishment. When I had done I entreated her to write in the margin that the lady alluded to was my declared enemy. She embraced me, saying, "Ah! do not write it! we should not record an unhappy circumstance which ought to be forgotten." We came to a man of genius who was much attached to the Queen, and I described him as a man born solely to contradict, showing himself an aristocrat with democrats, and a democrat among aristocrats; but still a man of probity, and well disposed to his sovereign. The Princess said she knew many persons of that disposition, and that she was delighted I had nothing to say against this man, because she herself had placed him about the Queen.

The whole of her Majesty's chamber, which consisted entirely of persons of fidelity, gave throughout all the dreadful convulsions of the Revolution proofs of the greatest prudence and self-devotion. The same cannot be said of the antechambers. With the exception of three or four, all the servants of that class were outrageous Jacobins; and I saw on those occasions the necessity of composing the private household of princes of persons completely separated from the class of the people.

The situation of the royal family was so unbearable during the months which immediately preceded the 10th of August that the Queen longed for the crisis, whatever might be its issue. She frequently said that a long confinement in a tower by the seaside would seem to her less intolerable than those feuds in which the weakness of her party daily threatened an inevitable catastrophe.

Not only were their Majesties prevented from breathing the open air, but they were also insulted at the very foot of the altar. The Sunday before the last day of the monarchy, while the royal family went through the gallery to the chapel, half the soldiers of the National Guard exclaimed, "Long live the King!" and the other half, "No; no King! Down with the veto!" and on that day at vespers the choristers preconcerted to use loud and threatening emphasis when chanting the words, "*Deposuit potentes de sede,*" in the "Magnificat." Incensed at such an irreverent proceeding, the royalists in their turn thrice exclaimed, "*Et reginam,*" after the "*Domine salvum fac regem.*" The tumult during the whole time of divine service was excessive.

At length the terrible night of the 10th of August, 1792, arrived. On the preceding evening Pétion went to the Assembly and informed it that preparations were making for an insurrection on the following day; that the tocsin would sound at midnight; and that he feared he had not sufficient means for resisting the attack which was about to take place. Upon this information the Assembly passed to the order of the day. Pétion, however, gave an order for repelling force by force. M. Mandat was armed with this order; and, finding his fidelity to the King's person supported by what he considered the law of the State, he conducted himself in all his operations with the greatest energy. On the evening of the 9th I was present at the King's supper. While his Majesty was giving me various orders we heard a great noise at the door of the apartment. I went to see what was the cause of it, and found the two sentinels fighting. One said, speaking of the King, that he was hearty in the cause of the constitution, and would defend it at the peril of his life; the other maintained that he was an encumbrance to the only constitution suitable to a free people. They were almost ready to cut one another's throats. I returned with a countenance which betrayed my emotion. The King desired to know what was going forward at his door; I could not conceal it from him. The Queen said she was not at all surprised at it, and that more than half the guard belonged to the Jacobin party.

The toscin sounded at midnight. The Swiss were drawn up like walls; and in the midst of their soldier like silence, which formed a striking contrast with the perpetual din of the town guard, the King informed M. de J—, an officer of the staff, of The plan of defence laid down by Général Vioménil. M. de J—said to me, after this private conference, "Put your jewels and money into your pockets; our dangers are unavoidable; the means of defence are nil; safety might be obtained by some degree of energy in the King, but that is the only virtue in which he is deficient."

An hour after midnight the Queen and Madame Elisabeth said they would lie down on a sofa in a room in the *entresols*, the windows of which commanded the courtyard of the Tuileries.

The Queen told me the King had just refused to put on his quilted under-waiscoat; that he had consented to wear it on the 14th of July because he was merely going to a ceremony where the blade of an assassin was to be apprehended; but that on a day on which his party might fight against the revolutionists he thought there was something cowardly in preserving his life by such means.

During this time Madame Elisabeth disengaged herself from some of her clothing which encumbered her in order to lie down on the sofa: she took a cornelian pin out of her cape, and before she laid it down on the table she showed it to me, and desired me to read a motto engraved upon it round a stalk of lilies. The words were, "Oblivion of injuries; pardon for offences." "I much fear," added that virtuous Princess, "this maxim has but little influence among our enemies; but it ought not to be less dear to us on that account."[1]

The Queen desired me to sit down by her; the two Princesses could not sleep; they were conversing mournfully upon their situation when a musket was discharged in the courtyard. They both quitted the sofa, saying, "There is the first shot, unfortunately it will not be the last; let us go up to the King." The Queen desired me to follow her; several of her women went with me.

---

1. The princess did not take this precious trinket when she quitted the Queen's *entresol*. Into what hands did it fall? It would adorn the richest treasury. The exalted piety of Madame Elisabeth gave to all she said and did a noble character, descriptive of that of her soul. On the day on which this worthy descendant of Saint Louis was sacrificed, the executioner, in tying her hands behind her back, raised up one of the ends of her handkerchief in front. Madame Elisabeth, with calmness, and with a voice which seemed not to come from the earth, said to him, "In the name of modesty, cover my bosom." I learned this trait of heroism from Madame de Serilly, who was condemned the same day as the princess, but who obtained a respite at the moment of the execution, Madame de Montmorin, her relation, declaring that her cousin was pregnant.

At four o'clock the Queen came out of the King's chamber and told us she had no longer any hope; that M. Mandat, who had gone to the Hôtel de Ville to receive further orders, had just been assassinated, and that the people were at that time carrying his head about the streets. Day came. The King, the Queen, Madame Elisabeth, Madame, and the Dauphin went down to pass through the ranks of the sections of the National Guard; the cry of *"Vive le Roi!"* was heard from a few places. I was at a window on the garden side; I saw some of the gunners quit their posts, go up to the King, and thrust their fists in his face, insulting him by most brutal language. Messieurs de Salvert and de Bridges drove them off in a spirited manner. The King was as pale as a corpse. The royal family came in again. The Queen told me that all was lost; that the King had shown no energy; and that this sort of review had done more harm than good.

I was in the billiard-room with my companions; we placed ourselves upon some high benches. I then saw M. d'Hervilly with a drawn sword in his hand, ordering the usher to open the door to the French *noblesse*. Two hundred persons entered the room nearest to that in which the family were; others drew up in two lines in the preceding rooms. I saw a few people belonging to the Court, many others whose features were unknown to me, and a few who figured technically without right among what was called the *noblesse*, but whose self-devotion ennobled them at once. They were all so badly armed that even in that situation the indomitable French liveliness indulged in jests. M. de Saint-Souplet, one of the King's equerries, and a page, carried on their shoulders instead of muskets the tongs belonging to the King's antechamber, which they had broken and divided between them. Another page, who had a pocket-pistol in his hand, stuck the end of it against the back of the person who stood before him, and who begged he would be good enough to rest it elsewhere. A sword and a pair of pistols were the only arms of those who had had the precaution to provide themselves with arms at all. Meanwhile, the numerous bands from the faubourgs, armed with pikes and cutlasses, filled the Carrousel and the streets adjacent to the Tuileries. The sanguinary Marseillais were at their head, with cannon pointed against the Château. In this emergency the King's Council sent M. Dejoly, the Minister of Justice, to the Assembly to request they would send the King a deputation which might serve as a safeguard to the executive power. His ruin was resolved on; they passed to the order of the day. At eight o'clock the department repaired to the Château. The *procureur-syndic*, seeing that the guard within was ready to join the assailants, went into the King's closet and requested to speak to him in private. The King received him in his chamber; the Queen was with him. There M. Rœderer told him that the King, all his family, and the people about them would inevitably perish unless his Majesty immediately determined to go to the National Assembly. The Queen at first opposed this advice, but the *procureur-syndic* told her that she rendered herself responsible for the deaths of the King, her children, and all who were in the palace. She no longer objected. The King then consented to go to the Assembly. As he set out, he said to the minister and persons who surrounded him, "Come, gentlemen, there is nothing more to be done here." The Queen said to me as she left the King's chamber, "Wait in my apartments; I will come to you, or I will send for you to go I know not whither." She took with her only the Princesse de Lamballe and Madame de Tourzel. The Princesse de Tarente and

Madame de la Roche-Aymon were inconsolable at being left at the Tuileries; they, and all who belonged to the chamber, went down into the Queen's apartments.

We saw the royal family pass between two lines formed by the Swiss grenadiers and those of the battalions of the Petits-Pères and the Filles Saint Thomas. They were so pressed upon by the crowd that during that short passage the Queen was robbed of her watch and purse. A man of great height and horrible appearance, one of such as were to be seen at the head of all the insurrections, drew near the Dauphin, whom the Queen was leading by the hand, and took him up in his arms. The Queen uttered a scream of terror, and was ready to faint. The man said to her, "Don't be frightened, I will do him no harm;" and he gave him back to her at the entrance of the chamber.

I leave to history all the details of that too memorable day, confining myself to recalling a few of the frightful scenes acted in the interior of the Tuileries after the King had quitted the palace.

The assailants did not know that the King and his family had betaken themselves to the Assembly; and those who defended the palace from the side of the courts were equally ignorant of it. It is supposed that if they had been aware of the fact the siege would never have taken place.

The Marseillais began by driving from their posts several Swiss, who yielded without resistance; a few of the assailants fired upon them; some of the Swiss officers, seeing their men fall, and perhaps thinking the King was still at the Tuileries, gave the word to a whole battalion to fire. The aggressors were thrown into disorder, and the Carrousel was cleared in a moment; but they soon returned, spurred on by rage and revenge. The Swiss were but eight hundred strong; they fell back into the interior of the Château; some of the doors were battered in by the guns, others broken through with hatchets; the populace rushed from all quarters into the interior of the palace; almost all the Swiss were massacred; the nobles, flying through the gallery which leads to the Louvre, were either stabbed or shot, and the bodies thrown out of the windows.

M. Pallas and M. de Marchais, ushers of the King's chamber, were killed in defending the door of the council chamber; many others of the King's servants fell victims to their fidelity. I mention these two persons in particular because, with their hats pulled over their brows and their swords in their hands, they exclaimed, as they defended themselves with unavailing courage, "We will not survive!—this is our post; our duty is to die at it." M. Diet behaved in the same manner at the door of the Queen's bedchamber; he experienced the same fate. The Princesse de Tarente had fortunately opened the door of the apartments; otherwise, the dreadful band seeing several women collected in the Queen's *salon* would have fancied she was among us, and would have immediately massacred us had we resisted them. We were, indeed, all about to perish, when a man with a long beard came up, exclaiming, in the name of Pétion, "Spare the women; don't dishonour the nation!" A particular circumstance placed me in greater danger than the others. In my confusion I imagined, a moment before the assailants entered the Queen's apartments, that my sister was not among the group of women collected there; and I went up into an *entresol*; where I supposed she had taken refuge, to induce her to come down, fancying it safer that we should not be separated. I did not find her in the room in question; I saw there only our two *femmes de chambre* and one of the Queen's two *heyducs*, a man of great height and military aspect. I saw that he was pale, and sitting on a bed. I cried out to him, "Fly! the footmen and our people are already safe." "I cannot," said the man to me; "I am dying of fear." As he spoke I heard a number of men rushing hastily tip the staircase; they threw themselves upon him, and I saw him assassinated.

I ran towards the staircase, followed by our women. The murderers left the *heyduc* to come to me. The women threw themselves at their feet, and held their sabres. The narrowness of the staircase impeded the assassins; but I had already felt a horrid hand thrust into my back to seize me by my clothes, when some one called out from the bottom of the staircase, "What are you doing above there? We don't kill women." I was on my knees; my executioner quitted his hold of me, and said, "Get up, you jade; the nation pardons you."

The brutality of these words did not prevent my suddenly experiencing an indescribable feeling which partook almost equally of the love of life and the idea that I was going to see my son, and all that was dear to me, again. A moment before I had thought less of death than of the pain which the steel, suspended over my head, would occasion me. Death is seldom seen so close without striking his blow. I heard every syllable uttered by the assassins, just as if I had been calm.

Five or six men seized me and my companions, and, having made us get up on benches placed before the windows, ordered us to call out, "The nation for ever!"

I passed over several corpses; I recognised that of the old Vicomte de Broves, to whom the Queen had sent me at the beginning of the night to desire him and another old man in her name to go home. These brave men desired I would tell her Majesty that they had but too strictly obeyed the King's orders in all circumstances under which they ought to have exposed their own lives in order to preserve his; and that for this once they would not obey, though they would cherish the recollection of the Queen's goodness.

Near the *grille*, on the side next the bridge, the men who conducted me asked whither I wished to go. Upon my inquiring, in my turn, whether they were at liberty to take me wherever I might wish to go one of them, a Marseillais, asked me, giving me at the same time a push with the butt end of his musket, whether I still doubted the power of the people? I answered "No," and I mentioned the number of my brother-in-law's house. I saw my sister ascending the steps of the parapet of the bridge, surrounded by members of the National Guard. I called to her, and she turned round. "Would you have her go with you?" said my guardian to me. I told him I did wish it. They called the people who were leading my sister to prison; she joined me.

Madame de la Roche-Aymon and her daughter, Mademoiselle Pauline de Tourzel, Madame de Ginestoux, lady to the Princesse de Lamballe, the other women of the Queen, and the old Comte d'Affry, were led off together to the Abbaye.

Our progress from the Tuileries to my sister's house was most distressing. We saw several Swiss pursued and killed, and musket-shots were crossing each other in all directions. We passed under the walls of the Louvre; they were firing from the parapet into the windows of the gallery, to hit the *knights of the dagger*; for thus did the populace designate those faithful subjects who had assembled at the Tuileries to defend the King.

The brigands broke some vessels of water in the Queen's first antechamber; the mixture of blood and water stained the skirts of our white gowns. The *poissardes* screamed after us in the streets that we were attached to the *Austrian.* Our protectors then showed some consideration for us, and made us go up a gateway to pull off our gowns; but our petticoats being too short, and making us look like persons in disguise, other *poissardes* began to bawl out that we were young Swiss dressed up like women. We then saw a tribe of female cannibals enter the street, carrying the head of poor Mandat. Our guards made us hastily enter a little public-house, called for wine, and desired us to drink with them. They assured the landlady that we were their sisters, and good patriots. Happily the Marseillais had quitted us to return to the Tuileries. One of the men who remained with us said to me in a low voice: "I am a gauze-worker in the faubourg. I was forced to march; I am not for all this; I have not killed anybody, and have rescued you. You ran a great risk when we met the mad women who are carrying Mandat's head. These horrible women said yesterday at midnight, upon the site of the Bastille, that they must have their revenge for the 6th of October, at Versailles, and that they had sworn to kill the Queen and all the women attached to her; the danger of the action saved you all."

As I crossed the Carrousel, I saw my house in flames; but as soon as the first moment of affright was over, I thought no more of my personal misfortunes. My ideas turned solely upon the dreadful situation of the Queen.

On reaching my sister's we found all our family in despair, believing they should never see us again. I could not remain in her house; some of the mob, collected round the door, exclaimed that Marie Antoinette's confidante was in the house, and that they must have her head. I disguised myself, and was concealed in the house of M. Morel, secretary for the lotteries. On the morrow I was inquired for there, in the name of the Queen. A deputy, whose sentiments were known to her, took upon himself to find me out.

I borrowed clothes, and went with my sister to the Feuillans. We got there at the same time with M. Thierry de Ville-d'Avray, the King's first *valet de chambre*. We were taken into an office, where we wrote down our names and places of abode, and we received tickets for admission into the rooms belonging to Camus, the keeper of the Archives, where the King was with his family.

As we entered the first room, a person who was there said to me, "Ah! you are a brave woman; but where is that Thierry,[1] that man loaded with his master's bounties?" "He is here," said I; "he is following me. I perceive that even scenes of death do not banish jealousy from among you."

Having belonged to the Court from my earliest youth, I was known to many persons whom I did not know. As I traversed a corridor above the cloisters which led to the cells inhabited by the unfortunate Louis XVI and his family, several of the grenadiers called me by name. One of them said to me, "Well, the poor King is lost! The Comte d'Artois would have managed it better." "Not at all," said another.

The royal family occupied a small suite of apartments consisting of four cells, formerly belonging to the ancient monastery of the Feuillans. In the first were the men who

---

1. M. Thierry, who never ceased to give his sovereign proofs of the most respectful and unalterable attachment, was one of the victims of the 2nd of September.

had accompanied the King: the Prince de Poix, the Baron d'Aubier, M. de Saint Pardou, equerry to Madame Elisabeth, MM. de Goguelat, de Chamilly, and de Huë. In the second we found the King; he was having his hair dressed; he took two locks of it, and gave one to my sister and one to me. We offered to kiss his hand; he opposed it, and embraced us without saying anything. In the third was the Queen, in bed, and in indescribable affliction. We found her accompanied only by a stout woman, who appeared tolerably civil; she was the keeper of the apartments. She waited upon the Queen, who as yet had none of her own people about her. Her Majesty stretched out her arms to us, saying, "Come, unfortunate women; come, and see one still more unhappy than yourselves, since she has been the cause of all your misfortunes. We are ruined," continued she; "we have arrived at that point to which they have been leading us for three years, through all possible outrages; we shall fall in this dreadful revolution, and many others will perish after us. All have contributed to our downfall; the reformers have urged it like mad people, and others through ambition, for the wildest Jacobin seeks wealth and office, and the mob is eager for plunder. There is not one real patriot among all this infamous horde. The emigrant party have their intrigues and schemes; foreigners seek to profit by the dissensions of France; every one has a share in our misfortunes."

The Dauphin came in with Madame and the Marquise de Tourzel. On seeing them the Queen said to me, "Poor children! how heartrending it is, instead of handing down to them so fine an inheritance, to say it ends with us!" She afterwards conversed with me about the Tuileries and the persons who had fallen; she condescended also to mention the burning of my house. I looked upon that loss as a mischance which ought not to dwell upon her mind, and I told her so. She spoke of the Princesse de Tarente, whom she greatly loved and valued, of Madame de la Roche-Aymon and her daughter, of the other persons whom she had left at the palace, and of the Duchesse de Luynes, who was to have passed the night at the Tuileries. Respecting her she said, "Hers was one of the first heads turned by the rage for that mischievous philosophy; but her heart brought her back, and I again found a friend in her."[1] I asked the Queen what the ambassadors from foreign powers had done under existing circumstances. She told me that they could do nothing; and that the wife of the English ambassador had just given her a proof of the personal interest she took in her welfare by sending her linen for her son.

I informed her that, in the pillaging of my house, all my accounts with her had been thrown into the Carrousel, and that every sheet of my month's expenditure was signed by her, sometimes leaving four or five inches of blank paper above her signature, a circumstance which rendered me very uneasy, from an apprehension that an improper use might be made of those signatures. She desired me to demand admission to the committee of general safety, and to make this declaration there. I repaired thither instantly and found a deputy, with whose name I have never become acquainted. After hearing me he said that he would not receive my deposition; that Marie Antoinette was

---

1. During the Reign of Terror, I withdrew to the Château de Coubertin, near that of de Dampierre. The Duchesse de Luynes frequently came to request I would repeat to her what the Queen had said about her at the Feuillans; we went together, and she would say, as she went away, "I have often need to request you to repeat those words of the Queen."

THE PRIVATE LIFE OF MARIE ANTOINETTE

now nothing more than any other Frenchwoman; and that if any of those detached papers bearing her signature should be misapplied, she would have, at a future period, a right to lodge a complaint, and to support her declaration by the facts which I had just related. The Queen then regretted having sent me, and feared that she had, by her very caution, pointed out a method of fabricating forgeries which might be dangerous to her; then again she exclaimed, "My apprehensions are as absurd as the step I made you take. They need nothing more for our ruin; all has been told."

She gave us details of what had taken place subsequently to the King's arrival at the Assembly. They are all well known, and I have no occasion to record them; I will merely mention that she told us, though with much delicacy, that she was not a little hurt at the King's conduct since he had quitted the Tuileries; that his habit of laying no restraint upon his great appetite had prompted him to eat as if he had been at his palace; that those who did not know him as she did, did not feel the piety and the magnanimity of his resignation, all which produced so bad an effect that deputies who were devoted to him had warned him of it; but no change could be effected.

I still see in imagination, and shall always see, that narrow cell at the Feuillans, hung with green paper, that wretched couch whence the dethroned Queen stretched out her arms to us, saying that our misfortunes, of which she was the cause, increased her own. There, for the last time, I saw the tears, I heard the sobs of her whom high birth, natural endowments, and, above all, goodness of heart, had seemed to destine to adorn any throne, and be the happiness of any people! It is impossible for those who lived with Louis XVI and Marie Antoinette not to be fully convinced, while doing full justice to the King's virtues, that if the Queen had been from the moment of her arrival in France the object of the care and affection of a prince of decision and authority, she would have only added to the glory of his reign.

What affecting things I have heard the Queen say in the affliction caused her by the belief of part of the Court and the whole of the people that she did not love France! How did that opinion shock those who knew her heart and her sentiments! Twice did I see her on the point of going from her apartments in the Tuileries into the gardens, to address the immense throng constantly assembled there to insult her. "Yes," exclaimed she, as she paced her chamber with hurried steps, "I will say to them: Frenchmen, they have had the cruelty to persuade you that I do not love France!—I! the mother of a Dauphin who will reign over this noble country!—I! whom Providence has seated upon the most powerful throne of Europe! Of all the daughters of Maria Theresa am I not that one whom fortune has most highly favoured? And ought I not to feel all these advantages? What should I find at Vienna? Nothing but sepulchres! What should I lose in France ? Everything which can confer glory!"

I protest I only repeat her own words; the soundness of her judgment soon pointed out to her the dangers of such a proceeding. "I should descend from the throne," said she, "merely, perhaps, to excite a momentary sympathy, which the factious would soon render more injurious than beneficial to me."

Yes, not only did Marie Antoinette love France, but few women took greater pride in the courage of Frenchmen. I could adduce a multitude of proofs of this; I will relate two traits which demonstrate the noblest enthusiasm: The Queen was telling me that, at the coronation of the Emperor Francis II, that Prince, bespeaking the admiration of a French general officer, who was then an emigrant, for the fine appearance of his troops, said to him, "There are the men to beat your *sans culottes!*" "That remains to be seen, Sire," instantly replied the officer. The Queen added, "I don't know the name of that brave Frenchman, but I will learn it; the King ought to be in possession of it." As she was reading the public papers a few days before the 10th of August, she observed that mention was made of the courage of a young man who died in defending the flag he carried, and shouting, "*Vive la Nation!*" "Ah! the fine lad!" said the Queen; "what a happiness it would have been for us if such men had never left off crying, '*Vive le Roi!*'"

In all that I have hitherto said of this most unfortunate of women and of queens, those who did not live with her, those who knew her but partially, and especially the majority of foreigners, prejudiced by infamous libels, may imagine I have thought it my duty to sacrifice truth on the altar of gratitude. Fortunately I can invoke unexceptionable witnesses; they will declare whether what I assert that I have seen and heard appears to them either untrue or improbable.

XXIII

THE Queen having been robbed of her purse as she was passing from the Tuileries to the Feuillans, requested my sister to lend her twenty-five louis.[1]

I spent part of the day at the Feuillans, and her Majesty told me she would ask Pétion to let me be with her in the place which the Assembly should decree for her prison. I then returned home to prepare everything that might be necessary for me to accompany her.

On the same day (11th August), at nine in the evening, I returned to the Feuillans. I found there were orders at all the gates forbidding my being admitted. I claimed a right to enter by virtue of the first permission which had been given to me; I was again refused. I was told that the Queen had as many

---

1. On being interrogated, the Queen declared that these five-and-twenty louis had been lent to her by my sister; this formed a pretence for arresting her and myself, and led to the death of that virtuous mother of a family.

people as were requisite about her. My sister was with her, as well as one of my companions, who came out of the prisons of the Abbaye on the 11th. I renewed my solicitations on the 12th; my tears and entreaties moved neither the keepers of the gates, nor even a deputy, to whom I addressed myself.

I soon heard of the removal of Louis XVI and his family to the Temple. I went to Pétion accompanied by M. Valadon, for whom I had procured a place in the post-office, and who was devoted to me. He determined to go up to Pétion alone; he told him that those who requested to be confined could not be suspected of evil designs, and that no political opinion could afford a ground of objection to these solicitations. Seeing that the well-meaning man did not succeed, I thought to do more in person; but Pétion persisted in his refusal and threatened to send me to La Force. Thinking to give me a kind of consolation, he added I might be certain that all those who were then with Louis XVI and his family would not stay with them long. And in fact, two or three days afterwards the Princesse de Lamballe, Madame de Tourzel, her daughter, the Queen's first woman, the first woman of the Dauphin and of Madame, M. de Chamilly, and M. de Huë were carried off during the night and transferred to La Force. After the departure of the King and Queen for the Temple, my sister was detained a prisoner in the apartments their Majesties had quitted for twenty-four hours.

From this time I was reduced to the misery of having no further intelligence of my august and unfortunate mistress but through the medium of the newspapers or the National Guard, who did duty at the Temple.

The King and Queen said nothing to me at the Feuillans about the portfolio which had been deposited with me;

no doubt they expected to see me again. The minister Roland and the deputies composing the provisional government were very intent on a search for papers belonging to their Majesties. They had the whole of the Tuileries ransacked. The infamous Robespierre bethought himself of M. Campan, the Queen's private secretary, and said that his death was feigned; that he was living unknown in some obscure part of France, and was doubtless the depositary of all the important papers. In a great portfolio belonging to the King there had been found a solitary letter from the Comte d'Artois, which, by its date, and the subjects of which it treated, indicated the existence of a continued correspondence. (This letter appeared among the documents used on the trial of Louis XVI.) A former preceptor of my son's had studied with Robespierre; the latter, meeting him in the street, and knowing the connection which had subsisted between him and the family of M. Campan, required him to say, upon his honour, whether he was certain of the death of the latter. The man replied that M. Campan had died at La Briche in 1791, and that he had seen him interred in the cemetery of Epinay. "Well, then," resumed Robespierre, "bring me the certificate of his burial at twelve to-morrow; it is a document for which I have pressing occasion." Upon hearing the deputy's demand I instantly sent for a certificate of M. Campan's burial, and Robespierre received it at nine o'clock the next morning. But I considered that, in thinking of my father-in-law, they were coming very near me, the real depositary of these important papers. I passed days and nights in considering what I could do for the best under such circumstances.

I was thus situated when the order to inform against those who had been denounced as suspected on the 10th of

August led to domiciliary visits. My servants were told that the people of the quarter in which I lived were talking much of the search that would be made in my house, and came to apprise me of it. I heard that fifty armed men would make themselves masters of M. Auguié's house, where I then was. I had just received this intelligence when M. Gougenot, the King's *maître d'hôtel* and receiver-general of the taxes, a man much attached to his sovereign, came into my room wrapped in a riding-cloak, under which, with great difficulty, he carried the King's portfolio, which I had entrusted to him. He threw it down at my feet, and said to me, "There is your deposit; I did not receive it from our unfortunate King's own hands; in delivering it to you I have executed my trust." After saying this he was about to withdraw. I stopped him, praying him to consult with me what I ought to do in such a trying emergency. He would not listen to my entreaties, or even hear me describe the course I intended to pursue. I told him my abode was about to be surrounded; I imparted to him what the Queen had said to me about the contents of the portfolio. To all this he answered, "There it is; decide for yourself; I will have no hand in it." Upon that I remained a few seconds thinking, and my conduct was founded upon the following reasons. I spoke aloud, although to myself; I walked about the room with agitated steps; M. Gougenot was thunderstruck. "Yes," said I, "when we can no longer communicate with our King and receive his orders, however attached we may be to him, we can only serve him according to the best of our own judgment. The Queen said to me, 'This portfolio contains scarcely anything but documents of a most dangerous description in the event of a trial taking place, if it should fall into the hands of revolutionary persons.' She mentioned, too, a single document which would, under the same circumstances, be useful. It is my duty to interpret her words, and consider them as orders. She meant to say, 'You will save such a paper, you will destroy the rest if they are likely to be taken from you.' If it were not so, was there any occasion for her to enter into any detail as to what the portfolio contained? The order to keep it was sufficient. Probably it contains, moreover, the letters of that part of the family which has emigrated; there is nothing which may have been foreseen or decided upon that can be useful now; and there can be no political thread which has not been cut by the events of the 10th of August and the imprisonment of the King. My house is about to be surrounded; I cannot conceal anything of such bulk; I might, then, through want of foresight, give up that which would cause the condemnation of the King. Let us open the portfolio, save the document alluded to, and destroy the rest." I took a knife and cut open one side of the portfolio. I saw a great number of envelopes endorsed by the King's own hand. M. Gougenot found there the former seals of the King,[1] such as they were before the Assembly had changed the inscription. At this moment we heard a great noise; he agreed to tie up the portfolio, take it again under his cloak, and go to a safe place to execute what I had taken upon me to determine. He made me swear, by all I held most sacred, that I would affirm, under every possible emergency, that the course I was pursuing had not been dictated to me by anybody; and that whatever might be the result, I would take all the credit or all the blame upon myself.

---

1. No doubt it was in order to have the original seals ready at a moment's notice, in case of a counter-revolution, that the Queen desired me not to quit the Tuileries. M. Gougenot threw the seals into the river, one from off the Pont-Neuf, and the other from near the Pont-Royal.

I lifted up my hand and took the oath he required; he went out. Half an hour afterwards a great number of armed men came to my house; they placed sentinels at all the outlets; they broke open *secrétaires* and closets of which they had not the keys; they searched the flowerpots and boxes; they examined the cellars; and the commandant repeatedly said, "Look particularly for papers." In the afternoon M. Gougenot returned. He had still the seals of France about him, and he brought me a statement of all that he had burnt.

The portfolio contained twenty letters from Monsieur, eighteen or nineteen from the Comte d'Artois, seventeen from Madame Adélaïde, eighteen from Madame Victoire, a great many letters from Comte Alexandre de Lameth, and many from M. de Malesherbes, with documents annexed to them. There were also some from M. de Montmorin and other ex-ministers or ambassadors. Each correspondence had its title written in the King's own hand upon the blank paper which contained it. The most voluminous was that from Mirabeau. It was tied up with a scheme for an escape, which he thought necessary. M. Gougenot, who had skimmed over these letters with more attention than the rest, told me they were of so interesting a nature that the King had no doubt kept them as documents exceedingly valuable for a history of his reign, and that the correspondence with the Princes, which was entirely relative to what was, going forward abroad, in concert with the King, would have been fatal to him if it had been seized. After he had finished he placed in my hands the *procès-verbal*, signed by all the ministers, to which the King attached so much importance, because he had given his opinion against the declaration of war; a copy of the letter written by the King to the

Princes, his brothers, inviting them to return to France; an account of the diamonds which the Queen had sent to Brussels (these two documents were in my handwriting); and a receipt for four hundred thousand francs, under the hand of a celebrated banker. This sum was part of the eight hundred thousand francs which the Queen had gradually saved during her reign, out of her pension of three hundred thousand francs per annum, and out of the one hundred thousand francs given by way of present on the birth of the Dauphin. This receipt, written on a very small piece of paper, was in the cover of an almanac. I agreed with M. Gougenot, who was obliged by his office to reside in Paris, that he should retain the *procès-verbal* of the Council and the receipt for the four hundred thousand francs, and that we should wait either for orders or for the means of transmitting these documents to the King or Queen; and I set out for Versailles.

The strictness of the precautions taken to guard the illustrious prisoners was daily increased. The idea that I could not inform the King of the course I had adopted of burning his papers, and the fear that I should not be able to transmit to him that which he had pointed out as necessary, tormented me to such a degree that it is wonderful my health endured the strain.

The dreadful trial drew near. Official advocates were granted to the King; the heroic virtue of M. de Malesherbes induced him to brave the most imminent dangers, either to save his master or to perish with him. I hoped also to be able to find some means of informing his Majesty of what I had thought it right to do. I sent a man, on whom I could rely, to Paris, to request M. Gougenot to come to me at Versailles: he came immediately. We agreed that he should see M. de Malesherbes without availing himself of any intermediate person for that purpose.

M. Gougenot awaited his return from the Temple at the door of his hôtel, and made a sign that he wished to speak to him. A moment afterwards a servant came to introduce him into the magistrates' room. He imparted to M. de Malesherbes what I had thought it right to do with respect to the King's papers, and placed in his hands the *procès-verbal* of the Council, which his Majesty had preserved in order to serve, if occasion required it, for a ground of his defence. However, that paper is not mentioned in either of the speeches of his advocates; probably it was determined not to make use of it.

I stop at that terrible period which is marked by the assassination of a King whose virtues are well known; but I cannot refrain from relating what he deigned to say in my favour to M. de Malesherbes: "Let Madame Campan know that she did what I should myself have ordered her to do; I thank her for it; she is one of those whom I regret I have it not in my power to recompense for their fidelity to my person, and for their good services." I did not hear of this until the morning after he had suffered, and I think I should have sunk under my despair if this honourable testimony had not given me some consolation.

Publisher's note

Here Madame Campan's journal ends, shortly after the death of her sister. In January 1793, the King was executed. Ten months later, on October 16th, Marie Antoinette was also put to death, one of the thousands upon thousands taken by the guillotine during The Reign of Terror. At the time of her death Marie Antoinette was 37 years old.

About the Author

Jeanne-Louise-Henriette Campan, was born in Paris in 1752. Though her family was of modest means she was well schooled. At the age of fifteen she could speak English and Italian, and was appointed reader to the three daughters of Louis XV. Campan was appointed first lady of the bedchamber by Marie Antoinette; and she continued to be her faithful attendant till she was forcibly separated from the Queen at the sacking of the Tuileries on the 20th of June 1792. Madame Campan survived the Terror, but was penniless. In order to support herself she established a school at St Germain. Eventually Campan was appointed superintendent of the academy founded by Napoleon at Écouen for the education of the daughters and sisters of members of the Legion of Honor. She held the post until it was abolished at the restoration of the Bourbons. Campan retired to Mantes, where she spent the rest of her life among friends.

HISTORICAL MEMOIRS FROM 1500 BOOKS

The Private Life of Marie Antoinette by Madame Campan – An intimate account of the intrigue and drama of the royal court from the Queen's trusted Lady-in-Waiting. (September 2006)

A Minstrel In France by Harry Lauder – A world famous performer's life is forever changed by the loss of his beloved son in World War I. With a piano lashed to his jeep Lauder tours the battlefront in France paying tribute to the troops. (October 2006)

A Year With A Whaler by Walter Noble Burns – The stories of the able-bodied seamen, the great mammals, and the ever changing sea are the central figures in this narrative of a carefree boy shipping out and a wise man returning. (November 2006)

Thirty Years A Detective by Allan Pinkerton – From the founder of the Pinkerton agency an insider's look at criminals, their mindsets, and their most famous schemes (December 2006)

A New Voyage Round the World by William Dampier – A fascinating travelogue, a scientific journey, and a buccaneering adventure from Dampier – gentleman sailor and pirate. (January 2007)

The Arctic Prairies by Ernest Thompson Seton – Two naturalists travel two thousand miles of river by canoe in search of caribou. A true adventure from an early environmentalist. (February 2007)

The Life and Times of Frederick Reynolds by Himself – A noted 18th century dramatist's account of life behind the theater curtain from staging a play to managing the celebrities to making a living. (March 2007)

To Cuba and Back by Richard Henry Dana – The best-selling author's account of his 1859 trip to the tropical island where colonial expansionism and slavery meet head on. (March 2007)

Excerpt from

A MINSTREL IN
FRANCE

by

HARRY LAUDER

to be published by 1500 Books
in October 2006

At the foot of the ridge I saw men fighting for the first time – actually fighting, seeking to hurt an enemy. It was a Canadian battery we saw, and it was firing, steadily and methodically, at the Huns. Up to now I had seen only the vast industrial side of war, its business and its labor. Now I was, for the first time, in touch with actual fighting. I saw the guns belching death and destruction, destined for men miles away. It was high angle fire, of course, directed by observers in the air.

But even that seemed part of the sheer, factory-like industry of war. There was no passion, no coming to grips in hot blood, here. Orders were given by the battery commander and the other officers as the foreman in a machine shop might give them. And the busy artillery-men worked like laborers, too, clearing their guns after a salvo, loading them, bringing up fresh supplies of ammu-nition. It was all methodical, all a matter of routine.

"Good artillery work is like that," said Captain Godfrey, when I spoke to him about it. "It's a science. It's all a matter of the higher mathematics. Everything is worked out to half a dozen places of decimals. We've eliminated chance and guesswork just as far as possible from modern artillery actions."

But there was something about it all that was disappointing, at first sight. It let you down a bit. Only the guns themselves kept up the tradition. Only they were acting as they should, and showing a proper passion and excitement. I could hear them growling ominously, like dogs locked in their kennel when they would be loose and about, and hunting. And then they would spit, angrily. They inflamed my imagination, did those guns; they satisfied me and my old-fashioned conception of war and fighting, more than anything else that I had seen had done. And it seemed to me that after they had spit out their deadly charge they wiped their muzzles with red tongues of flame, satisfied beyond all words or measure with what they had done.

We were rising now, as we walked, and getting a better view of the country that lay beyond. And so I came to understand a little better the value of a height even so low and insignificant as Vimy Ridge in that flat country. While the Germans held it they could overlook all our positions, and all the advantage of natural placing had been to them. Now, thanks to the Canadians, it was our turn, and we were looking down.

Weel, I was under fire. There was no doubt about it. There was a droning over us now, like the noise bees make, or many flies in a small room on a hot summer's day. That was the drone of the German shells. There was a little freshening of the artillery activity on both sides, Captain Godfrey said, as if in my honor. When one side increased its fire the other always answered – played copy cat. There was no telling, ye ken, when such an increase of fire might not be the first sign of an attack. And neither side took more chances than it must.

I had known, before I left Britain, that I would come under fire. And I had wondered what it would be like: I had expected to be afraid, nervous. Brave men had told me, one after another, that every man is afraid when he first comes under fire. And so I had wondered how I would be, and I had expected to be badly scared and extremely nervous. Now I could hear that constant droning of shells, and, in the distance, I could see, very often, powdery squirts of smoke and dirt along the ground, where our shells were striking, so that I knew I had the Hun lines in sight.

And I can truthfully say that, that day, at least, I felt no great fear or nervousness. Later I did, as I shall tell you, but that day one overpowering emotion mastered every other. It was a desire for vengeance! You were the Huns – the men who had killed my boy. They were almost within my reach. And as I looked at them there in their lines a savage desire possessed me, almost overwhelmed me, indeed, that made me want to rush to those guns and turn them to my own mad purpose of vengeance.

It was all I could do, I tell you, to restrain myself – to check that wild, almost ungovernable impulse to rush to the guns and grapple with them myself – myself fire them at the men who had killed my boy. I wanted to fight! I wanted to fight with my two hands – to tear and rend, and have the consciousness that I flash back, like a telegraph message from my satiated hands to my eager brain that was spurring me on.

But that was not to be. I knew it, and I grew calmer, presently. The roughness of the going helped me to do that, for it took all a man's wits and faculties to grope his way along the path we were following now. Indeed, it was no path at all that led us to the Pimple – the topmost point of Vimy Ridge, which changed hands half a dozen times in the few minutes of bloody fighting that had gone on here during the great attack.

The ground was absolutely riddled with shell holes here. There must have been a mine of metal underneath us. What path there was zigzagged around. It had been worn to such smoothness as it possessed since the battle, and it evaded the worst craters by going around them. My madness was passed now, and a great sadness had taken its place. For here, where I was walking, men had stumbled up with bullets and shells raining about them. At every step I trod ground that must have been the last resting-place of some Canadian soldier, who had died that I might climb this ridge in a safety so immeasurably greater than his had been.

If it was hard for us to make this climb, if we stumbled as we walked, what had it been for them? Our breath came hard and fast – how had it been with them? Yet they had done it! They had stormed the ridge the Huns had proudly called impregnable. They had taken, in a swift rush, that nothing could stay, a position the

Kaiser's generals had assured him would never be lost – could never be reached by mortal troops.

The Pimple, for which we were heading now, was an observation post at that time. There there was a detachment of soldiers, for it was an important post, covering much of the Hun territory beyond. A major of infantry was in command; his headquarters were a large hole in the ground, dug for him by a German shell – fired by German gunners who had no thought further from their minds than to do a favor for a British officer. And he was sitting calmly in front of his headquarters, smoking a pipe, when we reached the crest and came to the Pimple.

He was a very calm man, that major, given, I should say, to the greatest repression. I think nothing would have moved him from that phlegmatic calm of his! He watched us coming, climbing and making hard going of it. If he was amused he gave no sign, as he puffed at his pipe. I, for one, was puffing, too – I was panting like a grampus. I had thought myself in good condition, but I found out at Vimy Ridge that I was soft and flabby.

Not a sign did that major give until we reached him. And then, as we stood looking at him, and beyond him at the panorama of the trenches, he took his pipe from his mouth.

"Welcome to Vimy Ridge!" he said, in the manner of a host greeting a party bidden for the weekend. I was determined that that major should not outdo me. I had precious little wind left to breathe with, much less to talk, but I called for the last of it.

"Thank you, major," I said. "May I join you in a smoke?"

"Of course you can!" he said, unsmiling.

"That is, if you've brought your pipe with you." "Aye, I've my pipe," I told him. "I may forget to pay my debt, but I'll never forget my pipe." And no more I will.

So I sat down beside him, and drew out my pipe, and made a long business of filling it, and pushing the tobacco down just so, since that gave me a chance to get my wind. And when I was ready to light up I felt better, and I was breathing right, so that I could talk as I pleased without fighting for breath.

My friend the major proved an entertaining chap, and a talkative one, too, for all his seeming brusqueness. He pointed out the spots that had been made famous in the battle, and explained to me what it was the Canadians had done. And I saw and understood better than ever before what a great feat that had been, and how heavily it had counted. He lent me his binoculars, too, and with them I swept the whole valley toward Lens, where the great French coal mines are, and where the Germans have been under steady fire so long, and have been hanging on by their eyelashes.

It was not the place I should choose, ordinarily, to do a bit of sight-seeing. The German shells were still humming through the air above us, though not quite so often as they had. But there were enough of them, and they seemed to me close enough for me to feel the wind they raised as they passed. I thought for sure one of them would come along, presently, and clip my ears right off. And sometimes I felt myself ducking my head

— as if that would do me any good! But I did not think about it; I would feel myself doing it, without having intended to do anything of the sort. I was a bit nervous, I suppose, but no one could be really scared or alarmed in the unplumbable depths of calm in which that British major was plunged!

It was a grand view I had of the valley, but it was not the sort of thing I had expected to see. I knew there were thousands of men there, and I think I had expected to see men really fighting. But there was nothing of the sort. Not a man could I see in all the valley. They were under cover, of course. When I stopped to think about it, that was what I should have expected, of course. If I could have seen our laddies there below, why, the Huns could have seen them too. And that would never have done.

I could hear our guns, too, now, very well. They were giving voice all around me, but never a gun could I see, for all my peering and searching around. Even the battery we had passed below was out of sight now. And it was a weird thing, and an uncanny thing to think of all that riot of sound around, and not a sight to be had of the batteries that were making it!

Hogge came up while I was talking to the major. "Hello!" he said. "What have you done to your knee, Lauder?" I looked down and saw a trickle of blood running down, below my knee. It was bare, of course, because I wore my kilt.

"Oh, that's nothing," I said.

I knew at once what it was. I remembered that, as I stumbled up the hill, I had tripped over a bit of barbed wire and scratched my leg. And so I explained. "And I fell into a shell-hole, too," I said. "A wee one, as they go around here." But I laughed. "Still, I'll be able to say I was wounded on Vimy Ridge."

I glanced at the major as I said that, and was half sorry I had made the poor jest. And I saw him smile, in one corner of his mouth, as I said I had been "wounded." It was the corner furthest from me, but I saw it. And it was a dry smile, a withered smile. I could guess his thought.

"Wounded!" he must have said to himself, scornfully. And he must have remembered the real wounds the Canadians had received on that hillside. Aye, I could guess his thought. And I shared it, although I did not tell him so. But I think he understood.

He was still sitting there, puffing away at his old pipe, as quiet and calm and imperturbable as ever, when Captain Godfrey gathered us together to go on. He gazed out over the valley.

He was a man to be remembered for a long time, that major. I can see him now, in my mind's eye, sitting there, brooding, staring out toward Lens and the German lines. And I think that if I were choosing a figure for some great sculptor to immortalize, to typify and represent the superb, the majestic imperturbability of the British Empire in time of stress and storm, his would be the one. I could think of no finer figure than his for such a statue. You would see him, if the sculptor followed my thought, sitting in front of his shell-hole on Vimy Ridge, calm, dispassionate, devoted to his duty and the day's work, quietly giving the directions that guided the British guns in their work of blasting the Hun out of the refuge he had chosen when the Canadians had driven him from the spot where the major sat.

We hope you enjoyed Madame Campan's THE PRIVATE LIFE OF MARIE ANTOINETTE. This edition was redesigned from a 1910 English language translation. The original French language book was published in 1823. For additional information and other interesting historical memoirs from 1500 Books, visit our web site at www.1500Books.net.